ALTERITIES

ALTERITIES

Criticism, History, Representation

THOMAS DOCHERTY

CLARENDON PRESS · OXFORD
1996

Oxford University Press, Walton Street, Oxford OX2 6DP
Oxford New York
Athens Auckland Bangkok Bombay
Calcutta Cape Town Dar es Salaam Delhi
Florence Hong Kong Istanbul Karachi
Kuala Lumpur Madras Madrid Melbourne
Mexico City Nairobi Paris Singapore
Taipei Tokyo Toronto
and associated companies in
Berlin Ibadan

Oxford is a trade mark of Oxford University Press

Published in the United States
by Oxford University Press Inc., New York

British Library Cataloguing in Publication Data
Data available

Library of Congress Cataloging in Publication Data
Docherty, Thomas.
Alterities / Thomas Docherty.
Includes bibliographical references and index.
1. Criticism. 2. Critical theory. I. Title.
PN98.S6D62 1996
801'.95—dc20 95-41326

ISBN 0-19-818358-5 (pbk.)
ISBN 0-19-818357-7

1 3 5 7 9 10 8 6 4 2

Typeset by Pure Tech India Limited, Pondicherry.
Printed in Great Britain
on acid-free paper by
Biddles Ltd,
Guildford and King's Lynn

For Hamish

Preface

THE argument of this book is that criticism is a matter of *attitude.* In particular, the critical attitude favoured in the following arguments is one which acknowledges the *difficulty* of criticism, a difficulty deriving from an intrinsic resistance to criticism within aesthetic practice. Consequently, I contend that it is necessary to adopt an ascetic stance or attitude towards a substantial *alterity* in the aesthetic which, I claim, is the founding condition of the very possibility of criticism itself. This is to make a claim not for the *autonomy* of art, but for its *heteronomy vis-à- vis* the Subject. Explicitly, I indicate the ways in which the dominant mode of criticism in our times is but a cover for a psychopolitical anxiety which has been addressed and countered by the production of a philosophy of *identity*: the main task of such criticism is to console the Subject (either a psychoanalytic Subject or a historical and political agent) in the face of her or his anxiety that the world and its aesthetic practices may be evading our conscious control or apprehension. This book prefers to accept the threatening possibility that the world may not be 'there' *for* a Subject of consciousness, with the consequence that a new, pessimistic, and stoical attitude may be required in the critical engagement with an art whose condition is that it is of a fundamentally *different* order of being from that which is already known to and by consciousness.

The arguments are necessary at this time for reasons which are largely institutional. The enormous success of 'theory' in recent decades has brought about a critical—and pedagogical—situation which is, in my own view, indefensible. Let it be clear from the outset that the problem is not the engagement with theory itself; only the anti-intellectual would hold that we should not make such an engagement. Rather, the academic institution within which this engagement is made and validated is one which has clearly reined in the critical possibilities available through the confrontation with theory. The extraordinarily compressed time within which a history of literature or of cultures is to be 'learnt' leads to precisely the kinds of anxiety I describe as 'psychopolitical': the student must of necessity look for ways of saving time in the (business-like and quasi-industrial, 'modern') efficiency with which she or he carves a route through a daunting amount of work; the teacher finds it increasingly necessary to offer critical methodologies rather than to discuss specific critical engagements, as if it might be left to 'our servants' to negotiate such menial tasks as actually having specific things to argue about specific texts. The hoped-for 'democratizing' impetus of theory has, in the face of institutional and ideological pressures, produced yet another 'aristocratic' attitude, one which is all the more dangerous because its inherent anti-democratic tendency is occluded, even from its practitioners. In short, the result is not only that the entire critical practice is conditioned by a philosophy of identity in which consolation lies in 'unmasking' an ostensibly recalcitrant subtextual force, but also that such 'unmasking' is made at the cost of ignoring or circumventing the specific difficulties and resistances of art themselves and is made for the purpose of self-assurance. 'Progress', the condition of modernization, is based upon the assumption that the truth discovered in unmasking must be that which is available here and now: axiomatically, truth here is not 'what is better in the way of belief', but rather simply is 'what we think here, now', in contradistinction to the 'error' that we now call the past. That is to say, criticism has become too simplistic, too prematurely utopian, in the sense that it fails to acknowledge the difficulty of art and in that it assumes an *availability*, here and now, that is to say *immediately*, of art. In what follows, I hope to restore and rehabilitate an attitude of a specific *humility*. The critic's task is to locate (and, if necessary, to produce) difficulty; and, in what follows, I argue that such difficulty arises from a *heteronomy* which is the condition of art or of the aesthetic itself.

Northrop Frye used to argue that if he did not 'like' a literary work, all that this meant was that he had not yet found an adequate way of reading it. The view taken here is different from this. It is precisely at those moments when I believe that I have found an adequate way of reading that I become worried at my own critical *inadequacies*, for I hold the view that such a 'literacy' is a pretence, a way of avoiding that which is art. The critic who seeks alterity and heteronomy is the critic who resists the *intellectual* (as well as the commercial) commodification of art.

Many people have influenced and shaped the thinking in the following pages, as will be clear from my footnote documentation. I wish also to acknowledge here the assistance I have been given while writing this book from colleagues with whom I have discussed its arguments. Sometimes, these conversations were with audiences who kindly responded to my addresses in the Universities of Konstanz, Cambridge, Paris (Nanterre), Sunderland, Dublin. Some of the material has appeared in different forms in Edmund J. Smyth (ed.), *Postmodernism and Contemporary Fiction* ('The Ethics of Alterity'); Nicola Miller and Maurice Biriotti (eds.), *What is an Author?* ('Agency and Understanding'); Antony Easthope and John O. Thompson (eds.), *Contemporary Poetry Meets Modern Theory* ('Ana-'); Neil Corcoran (ed.), *The Chosen Ground* ('Initiations, Tempers, Seductions'). I thank the editors and publishers for permission to use the reworked materials here. Others whom I also wish to thank for their various kind assistances are Seamus Deane, Valentine Cunningham, Christopher Butler, Steven Connor, Christopher Norris, and colleagues and students in University College Dublin and in Trinity College Dublin. Jason Freeman and his colleagues in Oxford University Press encouraged me in this work. None of the foregoing would be capable of the errors which, despite their better advice, remain in my text, and which I claim as my own. As ever, Bridie May Sullivan sustained me during the writing; without her, this book would not have been possible.

Contents

Introduction: Criticism between Terror and Love

1. THE SUBJECT OF TERROR

Modern criticism is conditioned by terror. It begins from an anxiety about its object (be that a text or any artefact whose source is independent of—other than—the critic); and its response to such a fear of Otherness, of the object-as-such, is the production of a subject of consciousness characterized firstly by a presumed understanding and consequent appropriation of objects, and subsequently by mastery over or control of its ostensibly recalcitrant Others. All the increasingly baroque complexities of modern criticism—from rhetorical analysis through discussions of taste and sensibility and onwards to formalist, psychoanalytic, Marxist, feminist, hermeneutic criticisms ending eventually in deconstruction—are but instances and examples of the various and sometimes increasingly desperate tactics deployed by criticism in order to validate its subjects at the cost of the radical otherness of its object, the text or the world. In short, modern criticism is based on the premiss that the object—and alterity as such—is but a scandal perpetrated in the interests of the subject; it is based on a philosophy of Identity which is inimical to a real engagement with alterity, and thus it is inimical to precisely that historical materialism which is frequently ostensibly its founding condition.

The arguments of this book strive to restore a historical materialism to criticism, but argue that the only way of doing so is through an adequate attention to alterity as such, threatening though this may be to the subject of consciousness. The arguments trace a postmodern mood whose condition is profoundly *ethical* to the extent that it finds, running alongside the discourse of a tacit terror, a corollary and critical discourse of *pity*.[1] Its concern is for a criticism marked by the demand for

[1] The postmodern turn to the ethical is not entirely at odds, of course, with the demands of the materialist and the political. Yet as I argue in this study and also in

justice; and eventually it will be seen that such a criticism might best be described in terms of a philosophy of love.[2] For many, this restoration of an ostensibly metaphysical concept to criticism will be outrageous. Yet I wish to stress from the outset that, as an articulation of the ethical relation to alterity, such 'love' is but a rehabilitation of what Benjamin thought of as the 'aura' of the work of art: its historical and material locatedness whose very substance resists the consciousness of subjectivity, resists appropriation through technology.[3] Baudrillard's extraordinarily serious attention to the object as such, together with its power over the subject, is but one manifestation of the play of historical and material forces characterized by the terms of *seduction*. The return to a specific 'metaphysical' attitude in criticism is indicative of the fact that we are proceeding beyond what Badiou describes as 'the age of the poets', beyond the 'linguistic turn' in philosophy and criticism;[4] and the consequence is a slightly humbler mood for a criticism which no longer pretends that the world can be seen as text, that political

my *After Theory* (London: Routledge, 1990; 2nd edn.; Hemel Hempstead: Harvester-Wheatsheaf, forthcoming), I consider Marxism to be limited by a damaging structural Optimism evident in its subscription to theory as such. In *After Theory* I argued for a link between a new Pessimism and an attention to singularity. Alasdair MacIntyre, in *After Virtue* (2nd edn.; London: Duckworth, 1985) takes issue, from a different angle, with Marxism, but finds it equally optimistic (though the lower case, distinguishing this from Leibnizian philosophy, is important). It does not follow for MacIntyre that, in giving up on Marxism, one is condemned to a 'generalized social pessimism' (p. 262); rather, he claims that in attempting to form new localized communities based in the moral traditions, one can find a specific hope. I agree on the necessity of the ethical turn; I do not accept that optimism is simply an issue to be discussed in terms of the relative degree of positive hope one might have for the future.

[2] This 'love' in relation to philosophy, the aesthetic and the political, is not new, having been addressed by Plato, Denis de Rougemont, and a host of philosophers in between. Yet it has become more insistent in theoretical criticism recently. See, for examples, Roland Barthes, *Fragments d'un discours amoureux* (Paris: Seuil, 1976), Georges Bataille, *Eroticism* (1957; trans. Mary Dalwood; London: Marion Boyars, 1987); Elisabeth Badinter, *L'Amour en plus* (Paris: Flammarion, 1988); Alain Badiou, *Conditions* (Paris: Seuil, 1992), and *Manifeste pour la philosophie* (Paris: Seuil, 1989); Julia Kristeva, *Histoires d'amour* (Paris: Denoël, 1983); Alain Finkielkraut, *La Sagesse de l'amour* (Paris: Gallimard, 1984); Jean Baudrillard, *De la séduction* (Paris: Denoël, 1979); Jacques Derrida, 'Envois', in *La Carte postale* (Paris: Flammarion, 1980).

[3] See, of course, Walter Benjamin, 'The Work of Art in the Age of Mechanical Reproduction', in *Illuminations*, ed. Hannah Arendt (trans. Harry Zohn; Glasgow: Fontana, 1973).

[4] Badiou, *Manifeste*, 49 ff.

issues are merely matters of discourse, that poetry, even 'the poetry of the future', might be 'capable of saving us'.[5]

One foundation of modern 'terrorist' criticism can be found in the thinking of Descartes, whose radically 'skeptic disposition' is a precursor of much in contemporary cultural criticism.[6] The *Discours de la méthode* makes it clear that the trajectory to be followed in his philosophy is dangerous, and not to be recommended to everyone. One reason for this, of course, is not just the initial immaterialization of the objective world but also the metaphorical 'suicide' involved in the doubting of the subject's own existence. This terroristic extremism is, of course, merely a tactic in the Cartesian strategy in which the world's *meaning*, if not its very being, is to be finally referred to the self-present subject of consciousness who now acts as a stable centre for the elaboration of a stringent and ascetic truth. The terror of the death of the subject is but an exercise in *katharsis*, instrumental in the re-emergence of the subject purged of its ideological blindness, gifted with insight.[7]

When Kant develops this scepticism into a question of the difference between, on the one hand, a knowledge of the object as it appears to consciousness and, on the other, a knowledge of the object itself, Hegel responds in general terms that:

> This conceit which understands how to belittle every truth, in order to turn back into itself and gloat over its own understanding, which knows how to dissolve every thought and always find the same barren Ego instead of any content—this is a satisfaction which we must leave to itself, for it flees from the universal, and seeks only to be for itself.[8]

[5] The allusion to 'the poetry of the future' is, of course, to Marx in *The Eighteenth Brumaire of Louis Bonaparte* (Peking: Foreign Languages Press, 1978), 13. It was I. A. Richards who, following Arnold, made the claim that poetry might be capable of saving us. See his *Science and Poetry* (London: Kegan Paul, Trench, Trubner & Co., 1935), 90.

[6] The phrase 'skeptic disposition' is borrowed here from Eugene Goodheart, *The Skeptic Disposition in Contemporary Criticism* (Princeton, NJ: Princeton University Press, 1984).

[7] See Dalia Judowitz, *Subjectivity and Representation in Descartes* (Cambridge: Cambridge University Press, 1988); and, on the *Discours* as fiction, see Hugh Kenner, *Samuel Beckett* (London: John Calder, 1962), 81, and cf. Jacques Barzun, *Classic, Romantic and Modern* (London: Secker & Warburg, 1962), 87–8.

[8] G. W. F. Hegel, *The Phenomenology of Spirit* (trans. A. V. Miller; Oxford: Oxford University Press, 1977), 52, § 80.

(It is worth indicating, in passing, that Hegel hereby undermines the projects of grand theory, which we can identify as that form of theory aiming at the production of metanarratives, of totality. Too often, the theoretical discourse has lost sight of a referentially grounded truth in the interests of sustaining its own internal logic and rigorous coherence.) Yet Hegel must himself also begin not from the production of a stable subject, but rather from the deictic, 'thisness', as a specifically Hegelian *universal*. Asking for the meaning of 'now' or 'here': that is, asking, unlike Descartes, for the meaning of the mere *location* of the subject of consciousness, Hegel indicates the fact that the meaning of 'now' is fundamentally based upon a kind of *différance*. The 'now' that is 'night', for instance, is countered by the 'now' some hours later, a 'now' that is 'day':

> The Now that is Night is *preserved*, i.e. it is treated as what it professes to be, as something that *is*; but it proves itself to be, on the contrary, something that is *not*. The Now does indeed preserve itself, but as something that is *not* Night; equally, it preserves itself in face of the Day that it now is, as something that also is not Day, in other words, as a *negative* in general . . . A simple thing of this kind which *is* through negation, which is neither This nor That, a *not-This*, and is with equal indifference This as well as That—such a thing we call a *universal*.[9]

For Hegel, the frightening otherness of the object—its resistance to consciousness—becomes instrumental in generating the subject's efforts in coming to knowledge. Once more, a terroristic struggle is in question, however; for when one subject faces another, the former realizes that there is a threat to its subjecthood, in that, for the Other, it is but an object. Hence the terrifying struggle, reminiscent of Descartes but yet more violent as two individuals face each other, presenting themselves as 'I':

> This presentation is a twofold action: action on the part of the other, and action on its own part. In so far as it is the action of the *other*, each seeks the death of the other. But in doing so, the second kind of action, action on its own part, is also involved; for the former involves the staking of its own life. Thus the relation of the two self-conscious individuals is such that they prove themselves and each other

[9] Ibid. 60, § 96.

> through a life- and-death struggle. They must engage in this struggle, for they must raise their certainty of being *for themselves* to truth . . . And it is only through staking one's life that freedom is won . . . This trial by death, however, does away with the truth which was supposed to issue from it.[10]

The Romantic—and tragic—struggle emerging from this master–slave dialectic produces not only Marxism, but also a more recent critical phenomenon in the reader-response criticism once advocated by Fish in which the object is identified precisely through its autodestruction: the subject of reading triumphs over its object, the text, by watching it consume itself.[11] The finest realization of such struggles, however, lies in that form of deconstruction in which the critic asserts her or his own subjectivity in the face of the aporetic structure of a text which unweaves itself even as its weft is being formulated or woven. When de Man reads Proust, he is careful to stress that 'the deconstruction is not something we have added to the text but it constituted the text in the first place':[12] de Man's manœuvres simply reveal a deconstruction that was always already there as the founding principle of the text's (im)possibility in the first place.

If Hegel repeats the gesture of Descartes in the attenuated form in which he begins from the deictic *location* of the subject, then one might say that this itself is open to the further development in the twentieth-century literary form that seems least afraid of objects: the *nouveau roman* in the hands of Robbe-Grillet or Perec. Robbe-Grillet begins one of the major examples of the *nouveau roman*, his text of *Dans le labyrinthe*, with what looks almost like a parody of the *Phenomenology of Spirit*: 'Je suis seul ici, maintenant, bien à l'abri.'[13] This text is one which enables Barthes to formulate the thesis of the 'death of the author' precisely at the moment when Robbe-Grillet himself is asserting that, in his fiction, there is nothing but subjectivity, even if

[10] Ibid. 113–14, § 187–8.

[11] See Stanley Fish, *Self-Consuming Artifacts* (Berkeley and Los Angeles: University of California Press, 1972). Fish's move into the adoption of a full neo-pragmatist position follows more or less fully logically from the particular mode of reader-response criticism he once advocated.

[12] Paul de Man, *Allegories of Reading* (New Haven: Yale University Press, 1979), 17.

[13] Alain Robbe-Grillet, *Dans le labyrinthe* (Paris: Minuit, 1959), 9.

that subject is peculiarly vacuous, the so-called 'je-néant', a subject whose identity is based entirely upon his descriptions of objects.[14] While for Robbe-Grillet this is an issue of aesthetic, formal, and metaphysical interest, for Perec, of course, in *Les Choses*, it is used to raise questions of political and social interest for a culture organized around the commodity and its consumption.

In short, the terror upon which modern criticism lays its foundations in a trajectory from the prioritization of the subject in Descartes to the priority of the object in Baudrillard is one characterized by a specific terror of alterity. The fear is that the subject—even consciousness itself—might not be entirely autonomous and self-generating, that it might be in some way dependent upon its Others, dependent upon objects. The result is a history of criticism based not only upon the construction of Identity, but also based upon various strategies by which the Other is to be tamed or reined in. Hence that 'imperialism of consciousness' foreseen in Hegel's master–slave dialectic, a power-knowledge which begins, in class terms, by proposing a specific class-based aesthetic agenda as normative and neutral, and which culminates in explicit forms of colonialism. As Marc Guillaume writes, there is a difference—not often enough attended to—between otherness and alterity:

> dans tout autre, il y a l'autrui—ce qui n'est pas moi, ce qui est différent de moi, mais que je peux comprendre, voire assimiler—et il y a aussi une altérité radicale, inassimilable, incompréhensible et même impensable. Et la pensée occidentale ne cesse de prendre l'autre pour autrui, de *réduire* l'autre à autrui.[15]

Citing Michel de Certeau, Guillaume goes on to claim that 'L'Autre est l'absent de l'histoire'. My claim is that modern criticism is that which deliberately absents the Other from

[14] On the death of the author, see Roland Barthes, *Image–Music–Text* (ed. and trans. Stephen Heath; Glasgow: Fontana, 1977); on Robbe-Grillet's assertions of subjectivity, see Alain Robbe-Grillet, 'Notes sur la localisation et les déplacements du point de vue dans la description romanesque', *La Revue des lettres modernes*, 5/36–8 (Summer, 1958), 128–30 (or 256–8; this issue of *La Revue* has double pagination). The term 'je-néant' comes from Bruce Morrissette, *The Novels of Robbe-Grillet* (Ithaca, NY: Cornell University Press, 1975), 114.

[15] Marc Guillaume and Jean Baudrillard, *Figures de l'altérité* (Paris: Descartes & Cie, 1994), 10.

history in an effort to legitimize the critic as an *autonomous* subject of consciousness. The much-vaunted autonomy central to Habermasian constructions of enlightenment is based upon the absenting of alterity, occasionally by strategies which focus, paradoxically, upon the object itself, including a range of cultural practices from close textual analysis, through existential awareness of *autrui* in the production of rationally ordered discursive societies, to brash consumerism. The task for the critic who wishes to restore the materiality of a world outside of consciousness to criticism is to find a means of addressing *l'autre* without reducing it to *autrui*: it is to find a means of thinking alterity, of constructing a critical philosophy which will eschew the solace of identity—always predictable—in the interests of an alterity for which the subject is precisely unprepared.

2. OBJECTS OF RESISTANCE

As Benjamin made clear when he considered the work of art in the age of mechanical reproduction, the relation between the subject of consciousness and the historical object is not merely one of space: this relation is also conditioned by temporality. The limitations of modern criticism derive largely from the fact that, in the haste to comprehend (rather than merely apprehend) and to domesticate the object for consciousness, such a temporality must be denied in the object. This is for the simple reason that the object must be seen as an inherently *stable* entity if it is to be appropriated by consciousness, commodified by discourse, represented in art, reified by heritage or 'culture'. It is the subject who is considered, in these terms, as the only appropriate site for temporality, specifically in the notion of its *formation* or of the time required for *Bildung* or the cultural education in which the subject gains an increase in cultural capital and is thus privileged by the change we call culture. To consider culture in this way necessitates the denial of temporality to the artefacts of culture: it is as if they exist only for the present moment in which the subject identifies itself, as if they exist to allow me to say 'I': thus their 'aura'—or, as I would prefer it, their very historical materiality—is lost.

The most common way of evacuating history from the object is through the construction of a historical narrative whose purpose is to explain the present instance of the subject: an 'it happened that' whose purpose and function is to explain the 'here, now'. That is to say, the past is seen as other than the subject only to the extent that it exists *for* the subject; but insofar as it can be appropriated by the subject, it is not usually seen as other than itself, as conditioned by an intrinsic *differing*. Such a criticism, which attends to the past in order to reveal its commensurability with the present, the 'here, now' of the subject, is conditioned by a philosophical Optimism as well as being profoundly monotheological. Serres points out that such a notion of time depends upon the idea of a series of epistemological breaks marked under the sign of 'progress'. So, for instance, between ancient mythology and contemporary science there is the intervention of a break which characterizes the present moment by a truth whose character is precisely that it supersedes the past. Such a thesis, argues Serres, 'm'a toujours paru de l'ordre de la religion: entre un archaïsme perdu et l'ère nouvelle, il y a un événement, la naissance d'un nouveau temps'.[16] This notion of progress is one which prefers self-legitimation to the legitimation of propositions about the world: we advance through the gradual elimination of past errors, and 'Ouf! nous sommes enfin entrés dans le vrai.'[17] This, says Serres, is the temporal equivalent of that pre-Copernican spatial strategy of placing the earth and humanity at the centre of the universe in order to satisfy our narcissism (a narcissism, one might add, in which the other is seen as an attenuated reflection or form of the self). Through the notion of progress,

> nous ne cessons d'être au sommet, à la pointe, à l'extrême perfection du développement. Du coup, nous avons toujours raison, pour la simple, banale et naïve raison que nous vivons au moment présent . . . Ce schéma nous permet d'avoir, en permanence . . . non seulement raison mais la meilleure des raisons possibles.[18]

To legitimize one's truth-claims precisely upon the fact that they are spoken 'here, now', upon the fact that they derive from

[16] Michel Serres, *Éclaircissements: Entretiens avec Bruno Latour* (1992; Paris: Flammarion, 1994), 76.
[17] Ibid. 76. [18] Ibid. 76–7.

a present 'I', is anathema to a genuinely *critical* attitude to truth. For truth to be truth, it must be transpositional: that is, not merely dependent upon the position of its speaking subject, especially when that subject is more concerned with the formation of its own identity than with truths about the world outside of its identity. A criticism exerted in the interests of demonstrating the integrity of the critic's or judge's self is precisely a criticism which lacks justice, preferring to satisfy instead the prejudices inscribed in the critic's theoretical self-image.[19]

In worldly terms, perhaps the most thoroughgoing examination of the theoretical issues involved here is to be found in the writing of Homi Bhabha. Bhabha consistently complicates the issues of post-colonialism by taking into account the temporal relation between colonizer and colonized and the historical intra-relations constitutive of the identity of the colonized. That is to say, he sees colonialism not just as a geo-political issue, but also as a chrono-political matter. A proper attention to the question of the nation, for instance, demands that we find

> that the space of the modern nation-people is never simply horizontal. Their metaphoric movement requires a kind of 'doubleness' in writing; a temporality of representation that moves between cultural formations and social processes without a centred logic. And such cultural movements disperse the homogeneous, visual time of the horizontal society.[20]

What is in question here is a problem posed as a consequence of deconstruction, specifically deconstruction as it was exercised in the hands of de Man. In a consideration of 'The Rhetoric of Temporality', de Man had famously proposed that the 'doubleness' (duplicity, undecidability, diplomacy) constitutive of irony 'demonstrates the impossibility of our being

[19] This, I believe, is the flaw which threatens the argumentation in the recent work of Christopher Norris. The demand for a specific 'integrity' is, in fact, a demand for a (covert) introduction of the will into reason, precisely the flaw which, according to Lyotard, necessitates a reconsideration of the enlightenment project. See Christopher Norris, *The Truth about Postmodernism* (Oxford: Blackwell, 1993), and *Truth and the Ethics of Criticism* (Manchester: Manchester University Press, 1994); see also Jean-François Lyotard, 'Svelte Appendix to the Postmodern Question' (trans. Thomas Docherty), in Richard Kearney (ed.), *Across the Frontiers* (Dublin: Wolfhound Press, 1988), 265.

[20] Homi K. Bhabha, *The Location of Culture* (London: Routledge, 1994), 141.

historical'.[21] De Man consistently reduced the history that is ontology to the epistemological issues inscribed in the writing of the self, in 'autobiography'; but such autobiography was, for reasons it is too simple to caricature, itself a problem of language and not of reference.[22] Such a state of affairs is, of course, intolerable for a materialist historical criticism. And for Bhabha, the question addressed in 'Dissemination' from which I quote above is not one simply specific to the issue of the legacies of colonialism; rather, it has ramifications reaching down to the very issue of our becoming historical. This is most apparent in a consideration of Jameson, in whose thought Bhabha perceives a limitation occasioned by the drive to reduce the temporal to the spatial, the important corollary of which strategy for my own argument is that it stabilizes the critical object, *locates* it in relation to a self-legitimizing subject, the Optimistic subject satirized above by Serres. In the examination of that famous and by now (for Jameson at least) almost paradigmatic site of the postmodern, the Bonaventure hotel, Bhabha finds that 'what is manifestly new about this version of international space and its social (in)visibility is its temporal measure . . . The non-synchronous temporality of global and national cultures opens up a cultural space—a third space—where the negotiation of incommensurable differences creates a tension peculiar to borderline existences.'[23] Later, Bhabha indicates the properly Benjaminian origin of this position when he writes that 'This space of the translation of cultural difference *at the interstices* is infused with that Benjaminian temporality of the present which makes graphic a moment of transition, not merely the continuum of history'.[24]

This is clearly important for its political implications. If it is the case that the subordinated culture in a colonialist relation is

[21] Paul de Man, *Blindness and Insight* (2nd edn.; London: Methuen, 1983), 211.

[22] See de Man (ibid., p. xii) for the by now (with hindsight) somewhat eerily echoing phrases: 'I am not given to retrospective self-examination and mercifully forget what I have written with the same alacrity I forget bad movies—although, as with bad movies, certain scenes or phrases return to embarrass and haunt me like a guilty conscience.' It is too easy, of course, to tarnish deconstruction with the political embarrassment associated with de Man's writings made at the time when he was more influenced by phenomenology than by anything proposed by Derrida.

[23] Bhabha, *The Location of Culture*, 218.

[24] Ibid. 224.

conditioned by an inner temporality as much as—if not more than—by its spatial locatedness, then the discourse of the political itself has to be modified. Further, such a discourse can be modified through the introduction of an attention to the materiality of the object-culture, a materiality whose condition is precisely temporal, *historical*. For a thinker such as Virilio, temporality was always the very condition of the political in the first place. Virilio takes the view that the formation of the city, the site of the *polis* or of polity in modernity, is not simply an effect of geography. Rather, the ramparts and boundaries which demarcate the inside of the city (and thus which demarcate political enfranchisement or even official civic existence) are built upon a relation of *speed*: those 'inside' have the advantage over those outside precisely by dint of being more 'advanced', which means that they have managed to retard their Others in the interests of their own political and civic existence or identity.[25] To acknowledge the implication of this is to acknowledge also that the political itself—the site for a materialist criticism—is not in itself stable, but is rather conditioned by mutability. Writ large for criticism, this means that a *political* criticism must not take its object for granted: in a specific sense, the object is *not there* in the first place, for its condition is that it is marked by an interior historicity which subjects it to constant modification, constant shifting. The proper 'object' of the critic who is aware of the materiality of history is, paradoxically, an object conditioned not by its appearance relative to a covert essence, but rather an object conditioned precisely by its temporal disappearance or 'immaterialization'. In so far as the internal historical differences constitutive of the object cannot properly be 'stabilized' without commodification, reification, or representation, it follows that the object of criticism is marked by 'singularity': if the object not only differs from us but also from itself, then we can at best speak of the series of singular instantiations of the object, its specific conditions (always changing) across its own history. It is a simplification of the relation between the critical subject and her or his objects to pretend that the object exists only in our own history, for thus

[25] See e.g. Paul Virilio, *Vitesse et politique* (Paris: Galilée, 1977), *L'Horizon négatif* (Paris: Galilée, 1984), *L'Espace critique* (Paris: Christian Bourgois, 1984), *L'Inertie polaire* (Paris: Christian Bourgois, 1990).

we accept entirely—and indeed we endorse—the loss of aura, a loss which is rather a loss of the singular historical specificity of the object as such. Such an attention to singularity, of course, questions the theoretical project itself: singularity is itself a critique of theory, though not necessarily implying a rejection of the philosophy upon which theory as a discourse based upon taxonomical generality has been built.

The importance of a historical criticism is matched only by the necessity of a materialist criticism, with an attendant focus on what we might call the 'thinginess' of the world. I argue later in this book for Duns Scotus as a proto-postmodernist precisely because of his attention to the singularity of the object, its *haecceitas*. The modern, in its theoretical drive, not only stabilizes the object of criticism but reduces it to an aspect of the singularity of the critical subject. Henceforth, culture is identified with *products* and their ownership, with the resultant triumph of an 'absolute bourgeois'.[26] To change such a state of affairs requires more than just a change of ownership of the aesthetic object. Not only must a materialist criticism be aware of the thing, its object, in all its material (historical) otherness, it must also find a different relation to the object. The result is a revaluation of the relation between the critical subject and its objects as such; but this is also, of course, a revival of the issue of *ethics*. The properly ethical, I argue in the pages following, is impossible under the sign of capital, and requires a specifically postmodern philosophy of love.

3. ETHICS AND EVENTS

This is not a problem of recent date. One important early examination of the issues involved here lies in that much maligned 'unfinished' text by Shakespeare or someone else, *Timon of Athens*. This play is important for my purposes because it demonstrates, long before Derrida and Lyotard, the impossibility of an ethics that would find its adequate description in Mauss or Levinas. The play is more or less contemporaneous

[26] See T. J. Clark, *The Absolute Bourgeois: Artists and Politics in France 1848–1851* (2nd edn.; London: Thames & Hudson, 1982).

with the more explicitly 'political' tragedies: *King Lear*, *Coriolanus*, *Macbeth*, and is consistent with their interests in the emergence of a specific conception of the state as one founded upon particular forms of legitimized violence. But these texts also clearly feel the pressures of the emergence of a new form of *economic* determinations of the political, consistent with an emergent capitalism which thinks all human relations in terms of investments and returns, calculations and predictions.

Timon's reputation for quite extraordinary generosity is based upon the misconception that he is wealthy. At first, only Flavius, his steward, knows that he has nothing to give in fact, and that, consequently, every promise of a *gift* becomes an IOU, a *debt*. Timon's claim is that his wealth and his love are 'freely given': that is, that his love is given without expectation of or desire for a return in kind. The problem is that the play demonstrates that such an ethic is simply impossible: the given is always inserted into an economy of exchange, the purpose of which is not only to establish human relation but also—and for the purposes of this study, much more importantly—to manipulate time. When the 'debts' are called in, what Timon finds is precisely a foreclosing of time, a situation in which 'the future comes apace'.[27]

Capital, or in this case the wealth which Timon believes to be his, is fundamentally a means of controlling the otherwise *unpredictable* nature of the future. In that it is based upon the promise, specifically the promise of a future return for a present investment, the capitalist relation establishes a tight link between two moments in time such that the future is made to appear to be dependent upon, consequential upon, the 'here, now' precisely as the 'here, now' is in fact demonstrating its intrinsic conditioning by the future. Lyotard is clear on this in 'Time Today', when he points out that the system of exchange is one in which the first phase of the exchange (the 'giving') takes place if and only if the second phase (the 'return') is guaranteed. And so, 'In this manner, the future conditions the present, Exchange requires that what is future be as if it were present. Guarantees, insurance policies, security are means of

[27] Shakespeare, *Timon of Athens*, II. ii.

neutralizing the case as occasional, or, as we say, to forestall eventualities [*pré-venir l'ad-venir*].'[28]

The second phase of the exchange, the future, must thus be seen to be totally 'accountable' from and for the present (first phase) which has programmed it; and the system of exchange itself depends upon (its wish for) such predictability and control in which the vagaries of an otherwise unaccountable future might be forestalled. As Lyotard has it, capital can now be seen for what it is, 'time stocked in view of forestalling what comes about'.[29]

When Derrida ponders a similar issue a little later, he indicates the necessary link between the notion of giving and that of the temporal condition of narrative, such that 'to give' implies and necessitates a narrative whose condition is delay, deferral, temporizing irresolution:

> The gift is not a gift, the gift only gives to the extent it *gives time*. The difference between a gift and every other operation of pure and simple exchange is that the gift gives time . . . The thing must not be restituted *immediately and right away*. There must be time, it must last, there must be waiting.[30]

When Shakespeare makes *Timon of Athens*, he is exploring—indeed, producing for critical examination—precisely the same issues; and what he finds is that, given the condition of Timon's society, the 'free giving' upon which Timon's character—his *ethos*—rests, is fundamentally impossible. The given is always inserted, whether Timon wishes it or not, into an economy of exchange whose purpose is the control of time or, more precisely, the control and forestalling of unpredictability. The emergence of the laws of exchange constitutive of a normative capitalism is one which precludes the possibility of a specific *ethics*; for the ethics of a purely 'free' or, better, *autonomous*

[28] Jean-François Lyotard, *The Inhuman* (trans. Geoffrey Bennington and Rachel Bowlby; Cambridge: Polity Press, 1991), 66.

[29] Ibid.

[30] Jacques Derrida, *Given Time 1. Counterfeit Money* (trans. Peggy Kamuf; Chicago: University of Chicago Press, 1992), 41. It is worth adding here that while, for Derrida if not Lyotard, the pressing issue is whether it is possible 'to give', Shakespeare's text adds the further complication in which it is asked whether it is possible to give when others cannot receive: is it possible 'to take' is as vital a question, and one which undermines the anarchic notion that theft (or even a theft which is a 'counter-theft' made against the 'owners') is some kind of critique of capital.

giving is one which produces unpredictability itself. The condition of autonomy so highly valued in enlightenment is an unpredictability; yet such 'unpreparedness' or unpredictability is in fact anathema to enlightenment science and philosophy itself, one main purpose of which is to base the free agency of the subject (a subject emancipated from the powers of myth) upon her or his theoretical and therefore predictive knowledge.

The stress upon prediction is a response to the fact of human death, as an event in the future which cannot have meaning unless and until it is inserted into a narrative.[31] Yet Timon's suicide fundamentally becomes his one desperate 'ethical' act, an act demonstrative of autonomy in that it is fundamentally absurd, literally an act which cannot be 'accounted' for in the text's logic, structure, or economy. Timon is a precursor of Camus, for whom 'Il n'y a qu'un problème philosophique vraiment sérieux: c'est le suicide'.[32] *Timon* is such a dark play because it denies the possibility of love, of the freely given ethical relation to the Other. The result is that Timon, in a kind of protest against a social law which recognizes only the priority of the individuated self, and finding himself unable to deny himself in his preferred but unrecognized orientation towards alterity, is reduced to an act of self-harm or autodestruction in an attempt to demonstrate that he does not centre his world's meanings upon the priority of himself and his own identity.

Such an impossibility of ethics under the sign of an emergent capitalism becomes all the more vexed in the history of culture from the late Renaissance onwards. Yet the argument of this book is one which strives to locate the ethical demand for justice and which finds it, in criticism, in a postmodern attitude towards alterity. Such a mood faces the risks inherent in the unpredictable; but, by so doing, refuses to reduce the materiality of history to the merest level of the significant narrative: it attends, so to speak, to the thing or to the event and not merely to the superficial instantiations of culture, the symbols of the event.

[31] See Jean Baudrillard, *L'Échange symbolique et la mort* (Paris: Gallimard, 1976).

[32] Albert Camus, *Le Mythe de Sisyphe* (Paris: Gallimard, 1942), 15.

PART ONE

1. *The Modern Thing: Metaphor and the Event of Representation*

When thinkers such as Matthew Arnold or I. A. Richards argued for the therapeutic powers of poetry in society, what they suggested was that poetry enabled a specific 'form of attention'.[1] Poetry was capable of saving us because it was seen as the repository of governing ideas and ideals; there was a quality of thinking in poetry, a quality of abstract conceptual thought often emotively communicated and therefore rhetorically persuasive, which could help a humanity that was considered to be increasingly devoid of monotheological certitudes, increasingly 'enlightened', independent, and autonomous. Unable to represent ourselves in a consensually agreed religious narrative, we were to turn to the secular modes of metaphor, finding in a local experience a more general truth according to which we could live our lives in both a socially and a personally ameliorated condition. The unenlightened religious sphere of the social was to be replaced by a metaphorical thinking in which I see myself in the other subjects of history among whom I am condemned to live; and poetry was to enable such a meeting between free subjects.

In the resulting relation between the aesthetic and the political, between art and social living, something—some *thing*—gets lost. While focusing on our forms of attention, the cultural criticism of modern poetry occludes the fact that much of the writing was actually about real things, objects in the world; and, in the rush to establish ameliorated social and interpersonal relations, the things, the material objects on which modernist poetry specifically focused its form of attention, were lost. When criticism considers the corpse in Baudelaire, the domestic pins, needles, windows of Dickinson, the red wheelbarrow of Williams, typically it eschews visualization of the

[1] The phrase (though not the meaning of it) is taken from Frank Kermode, *Forms of Attention* (New York: Oxford University Press, 1967).

things themselves, preferring to prioritize instead their supposed semantic and metaphorically given significance.

I shall argue a specific relation between the modern and the postmodern with respect to the literary 'thing'. Literary modernism was—ostensibly at least—always concerned with the activity of 'seeing things'. Conrad's 'Preface' to *The Nigger of the 'Narcissus'* proposed, in what operated almost as a modernist manifesto, that the task of the artist was 'by the power of the written word to make you hear, to make you feel . . . before all, to make you *see*'. Yet, though he stresses in the 'Preface' the importance of the visible universe, Conrad also indicates that the artist must 'descend within himself', thus turning precisely away from the visible world. What interested Conrad—and modernism as a movement—was the reality of the external world mediated by a specific presiding consciousness or subject which defined itself against its alterior world.[2] In Joycean 'epiphanies', in Proustian 'souvenirs involontaires', in Eliotic 'objective correlatives', in the poetry of Imagism, we have an art dominated by a visual or sensuous demand; but what is to be seen and felt is something constitutive not of the objective world of things but rather something constitutive of the inner subjective life of consciousness faced with its contemporary reality.

The advice of Virginia Woolf in her attack on Wells, Bennett, and Galsworthy, that we must 'look within' if we are to find reality, is consistent with this drive to constitute an image of the subject under the duress of duration, or in time. Pound defined the image as 'that which presents an intellectual and emotional complex in an instant of time'.[3] Imagism was a proto-*chosisme*, certainly; but Robbe-Grillet would later evacuate from the perception of things precisely the anthropomorphic interests of a human consciousness (at least in theory).[4] In literary modernism, consequently, we have the insistent appearance of the recursive text, the self-referential or self-conscious text, the text charting the development of the writer who writes precisely the

[2] Joseph Conrad, 'Preface' to *The Nigger of the 'Narcissus'* (1897; repr. Harmondsworth: Penguin, 1979), 13, 11. Cf. Michael H. Levenson, *A Genealogy of Modernism* (Cambridge: Cambridge University Press, 1984; repr. 1986), 1–2.

[3] See Levenson, *Genealogy*, 127–8, on the development in Pound of a different attitude which calls the status of the 'thing' as such into question.

[4] See Alain Robbe-Grillet, *Pour un nouveau roman* (Paris: Minuit, 1963).

text we are now engaged in reading. This no doubt has a romantic source in Wordsworth's *Prelude*; but in modernism it enlists Gide's *Les Faux-monnayeurs*, Proust's *A la recherche du temps perdu*, Joyce's *A Portrait of the Artist as a Young Man*, and continues all the way down to Greene's *The End of the Affair* and beyond. The modernist text is a 'text of surveillance' in which the subject of surveillance and its object come to be identical with each other, permitting the definition of the identity of the subject through a metaphorical overcoming of its Others.

Politically, of course, a nightmare of near-total social surveillance is usually considered more appropriate to a postmodern culture, to the kinds of dystopian worlds proposed in Zamyatin's *We*, Orwell's *1984*, Huxley's *Brave New World*. It is a post-war culture that has gained the requisite technological expertise to make a complete and computerized surveillance of the subject possible. Jameson, of course, argues that it is not the modern but rather the postmodern which is 'essentially a visual culture'.[5] How, then, can we disentangle the kinds of 'seeing' and the kinds of 'thing' at stake between the modern and the postmodern?

Heidegger pondered some of the multivalent senses of the word 'thing' (considering it primarily as a word, of course) in his etymological manœuvres.[6] For present purposes, I will retain two such senses, both adverted to by Heidegger. The first is a 'thing' in the sense of an ancient gathering, a community, or (as I shall henceforth refer to it) a consensus. The second is the 'thing' in the more contemporary (and customary) sense of a material object existing in ontologically real conditions. My argument goes that in modernism we have 'things' only in the ancient sense; and that the form appropriate to this in literature is one dominated by the humanist anthropology of metaphor. By contrast, in the postmodern there is a more humble attempt to start 'seeing things' in the sense of attending to objects. Such a postmodernism denies the possibility of metaphor, thereby making the event of representation itself extremely complex.

[5] See Fredric Jameson, *Postmodernism or, the Cultural Logic of Late Capitalism* (London: Verso, 1991), *passim*.

[6] Martin Heidegger, 'The Thing', in Heidegger, *Poetry, Language, Thought* (trans. Albert Hofstadter; New York: Harper & Row, 1975).

Part of Heidegger's meditations on the 'thing' focused attention on a medieval gathering. It might be useful here to cast the argument in terms appropriate to the medieval formation, if only to ensure that the meaning of the term 'postmodern' as here understood is determined not by chronology but by mood. One might suggest, thus, that when Aquinas follows an Aristotelian logic in arguing for the harmony of faith and reason, thereby establishing a metaphorical link between faith and reason, he is being modern; when Duns Scotus, on the other hand, prefers to consider the *haecceitas* of things in themselves, he is being postmodern.

These propositions form part of a larger argument in this book. Walter Benjamin warned of the dangers inherent in the aestheticization of politics. It is my contention that, in its predilection for the geometrical abstraction of metaphor, in its drive towards the constitution of cultural 'form' and the establishment of a cultural identity at the expense of the material and recalcitrant object, modernism becomes precisely the proper name for such an aestheticization of politics. Postmodernism's attention to the objectal 'thing' addresses exactly the kinds of anxiety expressed by Benjamin, but still inadequately addressed by radical cultural criticism.[7]

I shall argue here for a renewed attention to the status of the thing in poetry; and I shall further argue that such a renewed attention is consonant with a postmodern critical attitude. The poetry of Seamus Heaney (precisely as an ostensibly unlikely example) will be taken as a paradigmatic instance of a larger and more general state of affairs. In his poetry, Heaney has always been concerned with 'things', with the small, ostensibly mundane objects of everyday life. Such objects, however, are usually the kernel of a narrative. When, in 'Granite Chip', Heaney sees a stone taken from the tower in which Joyce briefly lived, it becomes an excuse for a meditation uniting Hamlet, Scotland, Saul Bellow, and the Bible; when he sees an old smoothing iron, it provokes reminiscences and stories about his mother (in 'Old Smoothing Iron'). Looking at things, Heaney sees beyond them, revealing a buried life or a concealed history

[7] Benjamin's anxieties are expressed in 'The Work of Art in the Age of Mechanical Reproduction', in *Illuminations*, ed. Hannah Arendt (trans. Harry Zohn; Glasgow: Fontana, 1973).

which lies under the apparent solidity of the object itself. The title of a recent collection, *Seeing Things*, promises—paradoxically—something less visionary in that it suggests that Heaney will look at the object in neo-Arnoldian fashion, 'as in itself it really is'. Such a tension, between, on the one hand, a neo-romantic visionary poetry (*seeing*, a seeing beyond things in metaphorical vein), and, on the other, a humbler *chosiste* writing (seeing *things* themselves), is a tension which is pertinent to the fraught relations between a modernist literary attitude and a postmodern mood in criticism.

1. THE MODERN THING

There are 'no ideas but in things', wrote William Carlos Williams. 'Not Ideas about the Thing but the Thing Itself', proclaimed Wallace Stevens. An 'idea', however, is already a representation: *eidos, eidolon,* an image. In these poets of modernism we have a problem of representation, a problem concerning the proper relation between 'things' and the 'ideas' of such things. Writing of the history of imagery, W. J. T. Mitchell argues that 'an image cannot be seen *as such* without a paradoxical trick of consciousness, an ability to see something as "there" and "not there" at the same time'.[8]

The perception of an image *as* an image involves us in a specific *deception* or irony with respect to the status of the real. We must have an ironic attitude, believing that something's absence is really its presence and vice versa. Let us call this the 'ironic of representation'. When de Man considers irony, writing in 'The Rhetoric of Temporality' about Baudelaire's 'De l'essence du rire', he argues that irony is 'a problem that exists within the self', a problem which demonstrates 'the impossibility of our being historical'. Baudelaire offers the 'comic' example of a man falling in the street. De Man argues that, if this man is philosophical, we actually have two selves involved in the fall: there is the empirical self which is about to be hurt by stumbling into a material object; and there is also what de Man calls the 'linguistic self', a self which knows that the

[8] W. J. T. Mitchell, *Iconology* (Chicago: University of Chicago Press, 1986), 17.

empirical man is falling but which is unable to do anything about this predicament in the empirical or historical world. The man in the case had been living in error, argues de Man, for he had presumed a commensurability between the material world and his consciousness. The fall corrects this error, but in correcting it condemns the man to live forever in the epistemological paucity of the realm of pure *self*-knowledge only, a realm in which the linguistic self—the subject of consciousness—can never coincide with itself and must therefore live in irony. De Man thus drives a wedge between the realm of material history, on the one hand, and the merest inner temporality of the linguistic self, on the other. The consciousness of the ironic subject may thus have a temporal existence, but its 'interior' temporality is completely divorced from the external temporalities of history. External history is thus collapsed or reduced into the aesthetic form of the ironic and self-ironizing structure of the linguistic self.[9]

Clément Rosset points out that in all theory of comedy, such as we find it in Kant, Hegel, Schopenhauer, Freud, and Bergson (and now, we may add, in Baudelaire deconstructed by de Man), the comic depends on noting a discrepancy between the real and its representation: laughter arises when we become aware that our idea of the real is found to be inadequate to the fact of the reality itself. But, says Rosset, this would imply that comedy would evaporate when there is no such discrepancy; and this, clearly, is patently false. The real itself is absurd whenever it lacks a *Grund*, a *principe de raison*:

> Il n'est rien dont l'existence ne soit fondée par une raison, dit ce principe; si l'on renonce à ce principe—ainsi que le recommande notre théorie qui, assimilant réel et singulier, prive la réalité de tout fondement extérieur à elle—la conséquence s'ensuit d'elle-même: toute réalité est assurément 'singulière', dans les deux sens du terme, et toute existence est bouffonne.[10]

This argument is part of Rosset's general theory of 'idiocy'. This theory of the *idiotes* suggests that something is real precisely to

[9] Paul de Man, 'The Rhetoric of Temporality', in *Blindness and Insight* (2nd edn.; London: Methuen, 1983). For a fuller analysis of this essay in relation to the question of the disintegration of the link between consciousness and history, see my *After Theory* (London: Routledge, 1990), 100 ff.

[10] Clément Rosset, *L'Objet singulier* (new expanded edn.; Paris: Minuit, 1979), 36.

the extent that it is singular and thus unamenable to representation of itself; for any representation, amounting to a duplication, would thereby call into question the ontological singularity of the real as itself. If the real cannot 'speak for itself' idiotically (idiomatically or singularly) then it is not real at all. For Rosset (as also perhaps for Wordsworth's 'Idiot Boy'), reality is characterized by the ontological fullness of self-presence. For Rosset, representation amounts to what Derrida would consider a 'dangerous supplement' to such ontological fullness; for, if an object's representation of itself can constitute an authentic part of its essence, then the object prior to its representation cannot have been ontologically full in the first place, requiring rather a representation in order to reveal its fullness.

Following from Rosset, we might suggest that the 'death of tragedy' proposed by Steiner as an event in the late seventeenth century has not, in fact, yet taken place. All modern theory of representation is not comic enough, in the sense that it is not 'idiotic' enough, not yet able to attend to the singular specificity of the materiality of the historical object, to its Scotist *haecceitas*. The ironic of representation, whose most accomplished and sophisticated form comes in the deconstructive practices of de Man and Derrida, is a condition of a modern thinking whose only consequence can be a tragic Idealism.[11] De Man 'scapegoats' the historical world, substituting for it the merest interiority of temporality, such as we have it in Bergsonian *durée*.

Such an interiority of temporality is the founding condition of the great secularizing modern form, the narrative of the *Bildungsroman*. Elizabethan–Jacobean tragedy, specifically in the figure of Hamlet, and neo-classical tragedy, paradigmatically in the figure of Phèdre, are the precursors of the great modernist *Bildungsroman* form. The *Bildungsroman* is ostensibly dominated entirely by time, by the temporal growth and development of its heroes, Wilhelm Meister, Julien Sorel, Elizabeth Bennet, and so on, all of whom have had to learn from the great temporizer, Hamlet, or from the woman who would tamper

[11] See George Steiner, *The Death of Tragedy* (London: Faber & Faber, 1961). Cf. my comments on tragedy in *On Modern Authority* (Brighton: Harvester, 1987); cf. also Clément Rosset, *La Philosophie tragique* (Paris: Quadrige/PUF, 1960; repr. 1991), and Christine Buci-Glucksmann, *Tragique de l'ombre* (Paris: Galilée, 1990).

with time and destiny, Phèdre. But, as Franco Moretti points out, the hero of the *Bildungsroman* must use her or his time to discover the 'proper' ways in which she or he can be inserted into the surrounding social sphere. Borrowing the term from Dilthey, Moretti argues that this form is dominated by the drive towards *Zusammenhang*: 'Zusammenhang . . . tells us that a life is meaningful if the *internal* interconnections of individual temporality . . . imply at the same time an opening up to the *outside*, an ever wider and thicker network of external relationships with "human things".'[12] Plot-as-time, as the gradual unfolding and development of relations, is made to match plot-as-space, as pattern or form. Plot as potential history is made to coalesce with the rituals or with the aesthetic form of a society's ideology, whose norms the hero has had to learn to internalize. This formal aesthetic space of the social formation is what we would now recognize as ideology or consensus. As consensus, it is precisely a 'thing' in the ancient sense of a gathering together. The modernist text, of which the *Bildungsroman* is a paradigmatic example in fiction and of which deconstruction is the most sophisticated form in theory, is thus contaminated by the antiquarianism of consensus, which it inflects in the form of ideology (and most often, of course, in the more specific form of the ideology of a bourgeois liberalism).

If we understand the 'thing' in its other sense, as the material historical object, then the 'modern thing' in literature or criticism simply does not exist as such. Modernism knows only the thing as consensus. Derrida is aware of the problem here. In 'Force et signification' he attacks structuralism for its failure to attend to force, arguing that structuralism wrenches force into form by the processes of a geometrical thinking whose roots he finds in Descartes. To that extent, structuralism is like the *Bildungsroman*, wrenching the potentially dissonant force of the outsider into the form of the socialized rituals of an aesthetically or formally self-regulating or autonomous polity.

Yet Derrida is complicit with the object of his attack, for he confuses the merest interiority of temporality with an objective material history. Lyotard makes the stronger attack, in *Discours, figure*. There, Lyotard argues that the entire structuralist

[12] Franco Moretti, *The Way of the World* (trans. Albert Sbragia; London: Verso, 1987), 18.

project (and I am arguing that this applies to the entire *theoretical* project) depends upon two interrelated propositions, neither of which is tenable. The viability of semiotic theoretical analysis depends firstly upon the *premature* translation of 'things' into 'signs': in short, structuralism collapses the ontology of material history ('things') into the epistemology of a material whose essence is that it is more or less immediately available to understanding ('signs'). Secondly, it requires the prioritization of 'reading' over 'seeing', with the result that the sensuousness of vision as such is to be flattened into the geometric abstraction of 'text'. Structuralists concern themselves with 'reading signs' instead of 'seeing things'.[13]

Modernism, whose literary form is narrative and whose philosophical form is 'theory', is now easily defined. Cultural modernism is characterized by the tendency to translate things into signs, ontology into epistemology, *prematurely*. It collapses the materiality of history into the immediacy of a consciousness which is validated by consensus and thus by a philosophy of Identity in which the 'I' finds itself mirrored and legitimized in the 'you' of 'society' or 'culture'. Modernism is thus precisely the name for the ideology which so worried Benjamin, the ideology whose articulation depends precisely upon the aestheticization of the political, upon the discovery of a form for force. It follows from this that the appropriate form of modernist thinking is the metaphorical representation. Representation in the algebraic form 'X = Y' is crucial to any thought which prioritizes the abstract or conceptual over the sensuous. Such representation, whose proper domain is that of the de Manic or Idealist 'linguistic self', is purely and merely aesthetic, unable to assume the status of the historical 'event', much less that of the political event.

2. THE EVENT OF REPRESENTATION

In his early poetry, Seamus Heaney adopts a thoroughly metaphorical—'modern'—mode. His presiding metaphors link writing to digging, poetry to archaeology, himself to Virgil

[13] Jacques Derrida, 'Force et signification', in *L'Écriture et la différence* (Paris: Seuil, 1967); Jean-François Lyotard, *Discours, figure* (Paris: Klincksieck, 1971).

(in the *Georgics* or *Eclogues*), himself to Hamlet, Ireland to Jutland, iron-age sacrificial rites to tribal atrocities in contemporary Northern Ireland, the earth to the mother, and so on. The consensual 'thing' whose norms he strives to validate, whose ideology he believes will grant him recognition, is the consensus of the mythic nation, a post-colonial Ireland healed of its historical wounds. Like Yeats or Synge searching for a language adequate to the rebirth of a nation, like Dante whose vernacular established a cultural identity for another fractured nation in a medieval moment, like Lowell whose biography perversely 'represents' a particular America, Heaney wants to be the poet who is a 'representation' of Ireland. He finds such representational form in metaphor which, as Rosset's work shows, denies precisely the singularity of the identity of either Heaney or Ireland.

This is a poetry of a literal 'con-fusion', mixing the voice of the poet with the identity of a nation. For clear, if usually unstated, political reasons, Heaney needs precisely the ancient forms of consensus: the 'thing' of Ireland is fractured into enough singular factions unable to agree because of tribalisms. But in doing this, he fails to see history—fails, that is, to see the materiality of his objects—and he adopts instead the visionary stance of the seer who looks beyond the mere phenomenal appearances of things in the Orphic hope of finding a constituency, a consensus for his poetry. He is not a poet in search of a voice; he is a voice in search of a community which will speak him, a voice in search of a subjectivity. However, there is a seeming departure from this in the later poetry, and especially in the volume *Seeing Things*, where Heaney's writing enters a new and difficult phase, looking for the event of representation.

Heaney is clearly interested in 'things', in objects still. This time, it is as if he will limit himself to the description of material objects, to seeing appearances in a *chosiste* fashion. Accordingly, we have a great deal of description which attempts mimetic adequacy through a wrenching of language into awkward and unexpected forms, in a manner extremely reminiscent of the Scotist-influenced poet of *haecceitas*, Hopkins. The following examples read almost as if they were parodies of Hopkins; yet they have none of the intent of parody. Are they then pastiche, in the Jamesonian sense of a parody without content or critical point? They are not that either. Rather, they read as if Heaney, simply like Hopkins (but without the religious paraphernalia) wishes to offer us things-in-themselves. Consider lines such as:

> Then
> roll-over, turmoil, whiplash!
>
> ('A Haul')

> Blessed be down-to-earth! Blessed be highs!
> Blessed be the detachment of dumb love
> In that broad-backed, low-set man
>
> ('Man and Boy')

> The deep, still, seeable-down-into water
>
> ('Seeing Things')

> Riveted steel, turned timber, burnish, grain,
> Smoothness, straightness, roundness
> Sweat-cured, sharpened, balanced, tested, fitted,
> The springiness, the clip and dart of it
>
> ('The Pitchfork')

> *In the name of the Father and of the Son* AND . . .
>
> ('The Biretta')

> Willed down, waited for, in place at last and for good.
> Trunk-hasped, cart-heavy, painted an ignorant brown.
> And pew-strait, bin-deep, standing four-square as an ark.
>
> . . . .
>
> . . . cargoed with
> Its own dumb, tongue-and-groove worthiness
> And un-get-roundable weight . . .
>
> ('The Settle Bed')

Nouns turning to adjectives and adjectives turning to nouns characterize this writing. It is as if, especially in those phrases which combine noun and adjective together ('cart-heavy', 'bin-deep'), Heaney is finding some kind of neo-classical essential epithet, and is trying to suggest an essence of the things in themselves of which he writes. He is also keen in this collection to offer many examples of single nouns or adjectives existing in sentences without any governing verb, as if we could see things better when they are not in motion, not motivated by a verb.

His resulting preponderance of anacoluthon in *Seeing Things* seems to derive from a desire to see things still and in themselves, and not, as the modernists or futurists might have had it, *forme in mutazione*.[14] Thus we have passages such as the following:

> Bare flags. Pump-water. Winter-evening cold.
>
> ('Scrabble')

> Matutinal. Mother-of-pearl
> Summer come early. Slashed carmines
> And washed milky-blues.
>
> ('A Pillowed Head')

> An all-night drubbing overflow on boards
> On the veranda.
>
> ('The Sounds of Rain')

> Shifting brilliancies. Then winter light
> In a doorway, and on the stone doorstep
> A beggar shivering in silhouette.
>
> ('Lightenings, i')

> Overhang of grass and seedling birch
> On the quarry face.
>
> ('Lightenings, ii')

> Whitewashed suntraps. Hedges hot as chimneys.
> Chairs on all fours. A plate-rack braced and laden.
> The fossil poetry of hob and slate.
>
> ('Settings, xiii')

In what sense is this not simply a recurrence of Imagism? In Imagist poetry, there is the implication of a point of view from which the objects make sense, and from which they can be inserted into a meaningful and necessary narrative. Imagist poems exist for and by the subject of consciousness, a subject which identifies itself against an exterior world of difference. That modern subject is also assured of a position of mastery because, though it distinguished itself from its own Others in the exterior world, it none the less finds similarities, metaphors,

[14] 'Forme in mutazione' is the title of a sculpture by Giorgio Zaccaro. All quotations here are from Seamus Heaney, *Seeing Things* (London: Faber, 1992).

among the objects of that exterior world, and, by yoking such differences together, determines its own position as a subject not only of consciousness but also—in so far as it is in a position of subjective mastery over the external world of perception—as a subject of history, an agent.

In verse such as this, however, Heaney approaches a bare *chosisme* beyond Imagism, as if he is gradually ridding himself of metaphor in a post-humanist voiding of subjectivity which will allow him not 'to see life steadily and to see it whole', but rather to bear witness to it in its singular objectal fragmentation. It is almost as if Baudrillard had written some of this, in the striving to construct the world from the point of view of the objects rather than from that of a subject of consciousness.[15]

Hence, we might say, the clearly expressed desire to hold on to things, as in the following examples where the consciousness tries to find a more than arbitrary link between word and object, between consciousness and history:

> The first real grip I ever got on things
> ('Wheels Within Wheels')
>
> . . . Secure
> The bastion of sensation. Do not waver
> Into language. Do not waver in it.
> ('Lightenings, ii')
>
> It exhilarated me
> . . . .
> A whole new quickened sense of what *rifle* meant
> ('Settings, xxi')
>
> Where does spirit live? Inside or outside
> Things remembered, made things, things unmade?
> ('Settings, xxii')
>
> Be literal a moment.
> ('Crossings, xxxiii')

In many of the poems in *Seeing Things*, the habitual metaphorical structure of Heaney's thinking seems to come under some pressure. He begins to try to see things stripped of their

[15] For the theoretical underpinning of this statement, see Jean Baudrillard, *Les Stratégies fatales* (Paris: Grasset, 1983).

Yeatsian 'Coat'. But it is precisely at this point that something new and extremely interesting happens. The point at which the poet sees a thing turns out to be exactly the moment when it becomes unamenable to representation, and Heaney is forced to evoke it only by acknowledging its disappearance, its invisibility. This, of course, is the ghostly side of the coin in the cliché of the title: if one is charged with 'seeing things', typically it implies that the things in question are not really there.

Consider, for example, the central section of the title poem in *Seeing Things*, in which the poet describes the carving on a cathedral façade:

> . . . Lines
> Hard and thin and sinuous represent
> The flowing river. Down between the lines
> Little antic fish are all go. Nothing else,
> And yet in that utter visibility
> The stone's alive with what's invisible . . .

Heaney is less interested in what is represented or figured by the lines of the carving, and is more intent on the spaces 'Down between the lines'. What lacks in this poem is the obvious lack: in that 'Nothing else' at the end of the line, who could fail to hear the silent verb, in the echo of Donne's 'Nothing else is' from 'The Sun Rising'? The 'is', or *being*, is precisely what is absent at so many stages in these poems, as in all the examples cited earlier when Heaney simply lists nouns or adjectives. Being as such gives way to beings, existants, 'things' in all their objecthood. Yet the reality of such beings depends paradoxically precisely on their singularity, and hence their unrepresentability or their invisibility:

> The first real grip I ever got on things
> Was when I learned the art of pedalling
> (By hand) a bike turned upside down
> Its back wheel preternaturally fast.
> I loved the disappearance of the spokes,
> The way the space between hub and rim
> Hummed with transparency.
>
> ('Wheels Within Wheels')

The real is that which always exceeds the capacity of representation to propose it, as Heaney makes clear in this poem,

'Wheels Within Wheels', where 'enough was not enough. Who ever saw | The limit in the given anyhow?' One has to proceed beyond representation to get at the real; and it turns out to be no more nor less visible than an airy nothing, as in 'Seeing Things' part 2:

> All afternoon, heat wavered on the steps
> And the air we stood up to our eyes in wavered
> Like the zig-zag hieroglyph for life itself.

The poem 'A Basket of Chestnuts' considers the portrait of Heaney painted by Edward Maguire in 1973, a portrait which adorned the cover of the first edition of *North*. But what interests the poet now is what is invisible in the representation:

> A basketful of chestnuts shines between us.
> One that he did not paint when he painted me—
>
> Although it was what he thought he'd maybe use
> As a decoy or a coffer for the light
> He captured in the toecaps of my shoes.
> But it wasn't in the picture and is not.

It is precisely because 'it wasn't in the picture and is not' that, paradoxically, the basketful of chestnuts 'is'. For it is because it is unamenable to representation, to being painted or even described, that it remains singular, bearing all the reality of a 'thing' whose 'actual weight' becomes real precisely as it is lightened in the opening lines of the poem.

3. THE INVISIBLE MAN

In these poems, then, Heaney discovers that the attempt to see the reality of things turns the act of representation into an event, in which not only is an abstract Being replaced by beings, but also the subject of consciousness finds its position somewhat humiliated precisely by the reality of those Others or objects against which the subject defines itself in a demonstration of mastery or control. The modern mode of representation is predicated upon a phenomenological opposition between appearance and reality. But, in the postmodern mood, the proper opposition is that between appearance and disappearance, which, as Virilio has indicated, is itself the dominant political dialectic or opposition in contemporary cultures.[16]

In the present context of the poems in *Seeing Things*, poems organized around and haunted throughout by the ghostly absence (the being there precisely because absent) of Heaney's father, Heaney is finding a way of dealing with the reality of death. Wittgenstein famously declared the non-eventual status of death: 'Death is not an event in life. It is not lived through.' But Heaney takes the logic of this to prove the reality of a Heideggerian being-towards-death, and to prove the reality of death itself. The poems here operate in the mode of the classical apostrophe, like Hardy's poems of 1912–13 or like Dunn's *Elegies*. The collection opens with a translation from Virgil, in which Heaney casts himself as Aeneas requesting 'one look, one face-to-face meeting with my dear father'; and it closes with a companion translation from Dante, himself a follower of Virgil, in which the poet is denied access by Charon to the far side of death, denied the sight of his father. It is as if Heaney's father's very disappearance is what guarantees his continued existence, his 'being' as a dead father, the material and historical continuity of him not as a living person but as a ghost, as precisely the (paradoxically invisible) reality of the object of Heaney's sight. The idiosyncratic singularity, the ontological reality, of Heaney's father lies precisely in his many and varied disappearances. No longer seeing consensus, which operates at the level of phenomenological appearance or ideology, Heaney can see things, with all the madness, all the counter-rationalities, that this implies.

We might suggest, in concluding this kind of reading, that the singularity of reality, its 'idiocy', so to speak, has some major consequences for our critical practice. A choice has become available. We can continue to look for consensus as critics. That way lies the ideology called modernism, in which we read intertextually, taxonomically, formally, theoretically; and in this we become complicit with the aestheticization of the political. Alternatively, we propose the end of this kind of theory;

[16] Paul Virilio, *L'Horizon négatif* (Paris: Galilée, 1984), *L'Espace critique* (Paris: Christian Bourgois, 1984), *Vitesse et politique* (Paris: Galilée, 1977), *War and Cinema* (trans. Patrick Camiller; London: Verso, 1989).

we acknowledge the singularity and specificity of the text and of the textual event; we attend to the historical event of representation in all its difficulty or even impossibility. This way lies postmodernism; and this way also, despite what I shall later outline as a deep Pessimism, lies political hope for those interested in emancipation from consensus-based notions of truth, from ideology.

2. *The Ethics of Alterity: Postmodern Character*

. . . I do beguile
The thing I am by seeming otherwise
(*Othello*, II. i)

It is by now a commonplace that postmodern fiction calls into question most of the formal elements of narrative that an earlier mode took for granted. The notion of 'character' is no exception: like the political dissidents of some totalitarian regimes, 'characters' have begun to disappear. But 'disappearance' itself has become a crucial component of postmodern characterization, and is not merely the result of an 'assault upon character', such as Maddox saw it in Joyce.[1] In all former understandings of the process of characterization in narrative, one simple and *phenomenological* dichotomy prevails: appearance versus reality. Reading character has always been a process whereby the reader learns to probe and bring to light the usually occluded murky depths of individual essences. She or he reads the visible presentation of character as a mere 'index of implications'; and the process of reading involves the revelation of those implications, the 'depths' or idiosyncracies of particularized individuated characters. It is thus that 'character', as an element distinguishable from the narrative in which it is formally embedded, is produced. Further, much criticism has taken a moralistic stance with regard to such produced characters, judging the characters and their actions as if they did indeed exist independently of the fiction in which they are implicated. This has resulted in a criticism which, while moralizing and limited to considerations of 'personal' existence, is none the less

[1] See James H. Maddox, Jr., *Joyce's 'Ulysses' and the Assault upon Character* (New Brunswick: Rutgers University Press, 1978); Thomas Docherty, *Reading (Absent) Character* (Oxford: Oxford University Press, 1983); Paul Virilio, *Esthétique de la disparition* (Paris: Galilée, 1989).

profoundly *unethical*, if we think of ethics in any serious philosophical fashion.[2]

Under the influence of existentialist philosophy, the notion of an essential reality in postmodern narrative has consistently been called into question. The result, in characterological terms, is twofold: first, the paradigm of 'appearance versus reality' is replaced by a post-phenomenological dialectic of 'appearance versus disappearance'; secondly, character never actually 'is', but is always rather *about-to-be*, its identity endlessly deferred. This elusiveness of character, it is often suggested, makes postmodern narrative in some sense 'unreadable'; and many readers do find it tedious in its disappointment of their characterological expectations and in its consequent disappointment of easy and simple moralizing. Lennard J. Davis explores this view; but his response is not to suggest, as have critics like Bayley, Harvey, or Swinden, that the novel or narrative is somehow inherently bound up with an interest in character or in 'human being' as an axiomatic given.[3] On the contrary, Davis argues, like Zeraffa, that the paradigmatic shift in postmodern characterization and the consequent 'unreadability' of narratives demonstrate that 'the very idea of character in the novel is itself ideological', by which he means to suggest that character, and any interest in these 'essential individuals', is historically and culturally specific, the product of a particular ideological moment and mood.[4]

[2] The question here is whether moral criticism should be simply a question of 'evaluations' of characters, based upon some pre-judicial set of moral preferences, or whether criticism might more seriously take ethics into account with the consequence that subjectivity—the subject position from which evaluations are made—is itself called into question. In a word, the difference is between a neo-Leavisite moral criticism which is making its return in the thinking of critics such as Wayne C. Booth, in, for example, *The Company We Keep* (Berkeley and Los Angeles: University of California Press, 1988), on the one hand, and, on the other, a criticism informed by the thought of, for example, Levinas or the Lyotard of Lyotard and Jean-Loup Thébaud, *Just Gaming* (trans. Wlad Godzich; Manchester: Manchester University Press, 1985). The thesis of this book takes this entire orientation in a different direction, culminating in an argument about the centrality of love in postmodern criticism.

[3] See Lennard J. Davis, *Resisting Novels* (London: Methuen, 1987); John Bayley, *The Characters of Love* (London: Constable, 1960); W. J. Harvey, *Character and the Novel* (London: Chatto & Windus, 1965); Patrick Swinden, *Unofficial Selves* (London: Macmillan, 1973).

[4] Davis, *Resisting Novels*, 107; cf. Michel Zeraffa, *Personne et personnage* (Paris: Klincksieck, 1969).

Two views on the history of narrative are in contention here. The first offers a historicist 'argument of periodicity' which charts various changes in the development of narrative forms. This argument goes that, once upon a time, there were novels with plots, ethnographic settings, and recognizable individuals known as characters; this was at a moment when the individual was becoming interesting in and for herself or himself for religious and political reasons (a dominance of individualistic Protestantism and a nascent capitalism, tying individuals to a destiny or to a wage). Then the Industrial Revolution took place and characters entered into a strife-ridden relation with their environment, being characters only to the extent that they circumvented the dehumanizing effects of the mechanics of plot and the determinacy of ethnographic setting.[5] At a yet later moment, characters became archetypal models, as authors 'looked within' to describe the life of the human psyche in itself and in general.[6] Finally, in the postmodern period, characters disappear altogether and narratives become boring. This is a neat history, but wrong in its theoretical orientation, for it assumes that there was indeed a time when individuals did exist as some kind of essence which was not always already an ideological construction.

A more radical view, as Jameson suggests, is

> what one might call the poststructuralist position . . . not only is the bourgeois individual subject a thing of the past, it is also a myth; it *never* really existed in the first place; there have never been autonomous subjects of that type. Rather, this construct is merely a philosophical and cultural mystification which sought to persuade people that they 'had' individual subjects and possessed this unique personal identity.[7]

In a West, at least, which is witnessing a resurgence of a particular earlier moment of capitalist development and its concomitant 'values', there is an obvious ideological reason for stimulating this nostalgic desire for an earlier historical

[5] See Hippolyte Taine, *History of English Literature*, 4 vols. (Edinburgh: Edinburgh University Press, 1873–1908).

[6] See Virginia Woolf, 'Modern Fiction', in *The Common Reader* (2nd ser.; London: Hogarth Press, 1929), 189.

[7] Frederic Jameson, 'Postmodernism and Consumer Society', in Hal Foster (ed.), *Postmodern Culture* (London: Pluto Press, 1983), 115.

moment when 'we were all individuals', and for an earlier mode of narrative which seemingly charted and celebrated that individuality. But this latter and more radical view allows us to suggest that postmodern narrative and the types of characterization it produces simply 'lay bare' the techniques and problems of character which have in fact *always* existed in narrative. Postmodern narrative, in its demystifying revelation of the technical elements of fictional characterization, allows for a radical rereading of the history of narrative, calling into question the supposed certainties of the individuated essences of characters in an earlier fiction dominated by the 'appearance-versus-reality' paradigm. Further, such a rereading will allow for the production of a more serious consideration of the ethical demand in reading character. The result, I argue, is an ethical first philosophy determined by a specific attitude of the subject to alterity.

In the present argument, I shall firstly outline a historical trajectory of the development of narratives with specific regard to the theory of character and characterization since the eighteenth century. In this first part of the chapter, it will become clear that the primacy afforded to character in the novel has been a constant means of evading the temporality of character, the existence of character in and through time. This is so even in cases where criticism has been able to write of the 'development' of characters in a specific text, for 'development' has never been considered as any substantial or essential change; on the contrary, it is seen as a full 'coming to being' or *anagnorisis* of the latent potential of personality (reality) which was always there but which had simply been occluded under spurious or disguising appearance. This evasion of temporality has itself been instrumental in allowing criticism's evasion of history, in which criticism has 'bracketed off' characters from novels, and novels from their historical situation and ideological moment. The first part of the argument, then, returns historicity to the dimension of character and of the process of reading character, a return which postmodern characterization makes all the more urgent.

Secondly, I shall examine the 'economy of identity' which has been crucial to prior understandings of character in narrative. This 'economy of identity' will be seen to be fully ideological, and called into question by the appearance in the *nouveau roman* and since of a contrary 'economy of *alterity*', whereby the supposed 'identity' of character is based, paradoxically, upon difference or, more precisely, upon Derridean *différance*, thus opening up a temporal dimension of character.

A third section will further this work in terms of the 'ethics of reading'. The fully temporal and heterogeneous mode of character which is prioritized in postmodern narrative affects the identity of the reading subject, decentring her or his consciousness in the act of reading character. Such a 'marginalization' of the reader, giving her or him the status of a Kristevan 'subject-in-process', has the peculiar effect of characterizing the paradigmatic reader of postmodern narrative as predominantly—if ideologically—feminized. It is thus that the chapter will properly focus the ethics of alterity, or of a kind of 'Desdemonism' in postmodern narrative, the beguiling or seduction of the self of the reader as subject, as a replacement of 'the thing I am' with a 'seeming otherwise'. This, prefigured in the scepticisms of Shakespeare's *Othello*, marks a significant change in the way we think the notion of character in postmodern narrative. In the past, or especially in Marxisant studies or theories which aim to address the historicity or ideology of fictions, critics have been invited to consider the mode of *pro*duction of a text and its characters. Following Baudrillard, and because of the specific demands of postmodern characterization, I suggest that this priority be replaced by the *se*duction of characterization.[8] It is axiomatic to my argument that, in postmodern narrative, character as such is never produced (it 'disappears'); rather, we have the seduction of the process of characterization, a scenario of seduction which radically involves the confusion of the ontological status of character with that of reader and author. If character is always 'seeming otherwise' in postmodern narrative, and if this is reflected in the reader or reading subject-in-process, this reader can never be fully present to her or his own consciousness but is always proleptically deferring the satisfactions of identity, always craving 'the poetry of the

[8] For the theory behind this, see Jean Baudrillard, *De la séduction* (Paris: Denoël, 1979).

future' towards which she or he is seduced.[9] In the earlier reading of character, there is established a basically phenomenological situation, in which character and reader 'posit' and 'position' each other for the understanding of character to take place. This 'character-as-position' is replaced in my argument here by a more fully *ethical* reading, restoring to the *ethos* its more proper sense of *dis*position.[10] The ethics of alterity disposes a reading subject-in-process towards a historical futurity in which she or he constantly defers the production of identity or of an empirically determined self-present selfhood. It is this disappearance of a transcendent self which is the most valuable effect of postmodern characterization and of an ethics of alterity in which a consciousness can properly engage with its Other in the form of history.

1. THE EVASION OF HISTORY: CHARACTER, EMPIRE, IDENTITY

Prose narrative consolidates in a specific form known as the 'novel' in the eighteenth century, an age in which an emerging dominant intellectual formation characterized 'its' culture as one of the triumph of specific forms of Reason and of Enlightenment, and in which an ideology of liberalism—which was simultaneously bourgeois and critical—stressed the importance of individualism (though not of specific individuals) in the social formation. Conventionally, the novel is thought to respond to this by recognizing the importance of the individual, and hence by focusing on named and individuated characters. But these characters are also the site of the dramatization of 'enlightenment'; and, as such, they become the models of a particular manifestation of what the age and its emergent ideology considers as 'reasonable'. The novel, typically, organizes itself around a plot in which an individual character stands at a tangent to her or his society (and is thus 'interesting' to the extent that she or he is extraordinary), and proceeds to the

[9] The allusion here is to Karl Marx, *The Eighteenth Brumaire of Louis Bonaparte* (Peking: Foreign Languages Press, 1978), 13.

[10] This is a further development of my argument in *Reading (Absent) Character* (Oxford: Oxford University Press, 1983), ch. 1.

reconciliation of society and individual in a movement which identifies or brings into harmony the interests of both and which reveals those interests to be reasonable and now also self-evident, because brought to light.

While operating as a critique of a social formation, the novel orients the reader through the *point de repère* of a recognizable character; and, given the double necessities of both having this character stand out and having it act as an alias for the reader, it in turn usually becomes the main centre of interest. The character, as our way into the hypothesized world of the fiction, becomes its main message too. It would clearly be fallacious to suggest that 'character' did not appear in writing prior to this historical moment; however, it was only during the Enlightenment that character came to have this central, determining, and organizing dominance as the model for 'individuality' in a social formation, as a recognizable and exemplary 'type'.

This age is also, crucially, the age which saw the invention of a specific category of primary relevance to character in the novel, for it was during this century that the concept of 'human nature' as something transcendent of particular historical context was invented. Foucault has argued that 'man is only a recent invention, a figure not yet two centuries old, a new wrinkle in our knowledge [who] will disappear again as soon as that knowledge has discovered a new form'.[11] The delineaments of this new form are now being traced in postmodern modes of knowledge, narrative, and characterization.

The construction of 'human nature' in the eighteenth century went hand in hand with the supervention of antiquity: it represented the 'ancients' winning the 'battle of the books' and the battle of competing philosophies against the 'moderns', and was thus also a major defeat for an emergent 'modernity'.[12] The ancient tradition, in the form of a continuity hypothesized from antiquity, suggested that the present, eighteenth-century state of affairs and state of understanding had always been the case. To this extent, it was supposed to be *natural*, non-secular,

[11] Michel Foucault, *The Order of Things* (London: Tavistock Publications, 1970), p. xxiii.

[12] For an illuminating rethinking of this opposition between antiquity and modernity, see Stanley Rosen, *The Ancients and the Moderns* (New Haven: Yale University Press, 1989).

non-historical. The concept of Enlightenment, that very metaphor of bringing into the light, enacts the trope which is axiomatic to the novel and its characters, for it claims simply to render visible a latent nature that was always there. The corollary of this, of course, is that there *is* an essential nature which is located in the human being which makes her or him able to be in conformity with the wider 'natural' environment, or social formation. 'Man', according to this argument, is always and everywhere the same, at the most fundamental of levels; 'man' has simply to be brought always from his darkness into enlightenment, where his fundamentally identical characteristics will become self-evident, visible. If we transpose these metaphors of light and dark, we arrive at a 'white mythology': 'the white man takes his own mythology, Indo-European mythology, his own *logos*, that is, the *mythos* of his idiom, for the universal form of that he must still wish to call Reason.'[13] If humanity is always and everywhere the same, traditional and non-secular rather than geographically and historically culture-specific, a justification is provided for the excesses of imperialism: in principle, the oppressed is being 'enlightened', granted a social position and existence in the world of the colonialist, who of course assumes his own 'enlightenment', an enlightenment supposedly guaranteed by a rationalist epistemology and a traditionalist antiquarianism. Further, the coining of 'human nature' also allows for the construction of a cultural form whose task it is to dramatize the bringing to light of this mysterious truth of human being. In prose narrative, character accordingly becomes understood as an allegorical type: not only 'individual' but also, as in the tradition of bourgeois democracy, 'representative'.[14]

It is here, of course, that many critics have identified a radical potential in the form of the novel, for it seems to be inherent in the novel form that a certain democratic importance is afforded the individual within a dominant social formation.[15]

[13] Jacques Derrida, *Margins: of Philosophy* (trans. Alan Bass; Brighton: Harvester, 1982), 213.

[14] See Ian Watt, *The Rise of the Novel* (Harmondsworth: Penguin, 1957); Gabriel Josipovici, *The World and the Book* (London: Macmillan, 1971).

[15] See e.g. Alan Swingewood, *The Novel and Revolution* (London: Macmillan, 1975); George Orwell, *Inside the Whale* (Harmondsworth: Penguin, 1962); Raymond Williams, *The English Novel from Dickens to Lawrence* (London: Chatto & Windus,

But another way of looking at this suggests that the novel thus understood, as a bourgeois liberal-democratic form, is a primary locus of bourgeois values and of the regularization, legitimation, even normativization of certain bourgeois codes, together with the assimilation of other, contrary codes and practices which remain silenced or which are shown to be 'unreasonable' by the novel and its characters. In this case, the novel would be valued by a bourgeois society precisely because it works as a 'strategy of containment', containing and limiting its critical impetus precisely in the instant when it appears to be exercising it to the utmost.

Thus, the notion of character as locus of the revelation of an essential human nature provides a form which, while seeming to grant some measure of independence and a democratic equality to the individual, actually serves to proffer a normative legitimate role for the individual in a specific social formation: in short, the novel's characters enact certain practices as socially *normative*. For example, Defoe's Robinson Crusoe can 'express' his innermost self in his construction of life on his island; but no matter how this is done in detail, the text works to legitimize the practices of the same economic individualism which bolsters the imperialist and colonialist expansion of trade routes. *Moll Flanders*, similarly, may perform a critique of the social codes which lead to its central character's criminality; but the text and Moll herself simply reiterate the legitimization of the notion of private property in the mercantile and sexual realms. To take a later example, Jane Austen's novels, while certainly granting a huge central importance to individual women characters as the main centre of attention and interest, simply operate to legitimize the bourgeois marriage and family which marginalized women in the first place.

If the novel operates culturally as a conservative art-form, then it does so primarily because of the way in which its characters have been theorized and understood, as representative examples of human nature. Reading character in this way involves a simple *anagnorisis*: characterization enacts a scene of recognition in which the reader discovers, essentially, the

1973); Terry Eagleton, *Criticism and Ideology* (London: New Left Books, 1976); Zeraffa, *Personne et personnage*.

'truth' of herself or himself reflected in the character; or, as we say, the reader 'identifies' with the character.[16] The reader 'discovers' a nature or essence of character which was always already known by that reader, for she or he shares in its 'human nature'. Thus, such a theoretical notion of the 'truth of identity', in the revelation of an essential human nature through characters in narrative, circumvents cultural specificity and historical and other differences: since human nature is, by definition, always and everywhere the same, and since 'most great novels exist to reveal and explore character',[17] then an eighteenth-century fiction seems to exist to reveal and explore fundamentally the same thing as a late twentieth-century fiction.

Prior theoretical understanding of character as a locus of an essential identity has worked to legitimize a particular non-secular understanding of human being, of what it is to be a human in a social formation. With an eighteenth-century Optimism, this understanding assumes that, in the relations between individuals and the social formation which they construct and which simultaneously constructs them, 'whatever is, is RIGHT',[18] or at least that to change the order of things would be 'unreasonable', 'unenlightened', or simply criminally 'illegitimate'. But, in fact, if character is anything in narrative, it is a locus of temporal difference. While it could be argued that portraiture or photography is, in its essentials, an art of simultaneity, its product to be perceived 'at once' and in space, it is certainly the case that narrative is sequential, that its constituent elements, including characterization, come as a piecemeal process and in a fragmentary mode. Postmodern narrative makes this abundantly clear, for it insists on offering the merest fragments of character, without ever allowing for a fully coherent construction of an identifiable whole; it is, as it were, like a series of torn photographs, a photo-montage; and frequently, in its narcissistic self-consciousness, it offers fragmentary portraits of the artist or writer.[19] Postmodern narrative stresses the 'difference' from which an 'identity' is always

[16] Davis, *Resisting Novels*, 124 ff.

[17] Harvey, *Character and the Novel*, 23.

[18] Alexander Pope, 'Essay on Man', in *Poems*, ed. John Butt (London: Methuen, 1975), 515.

[19] See Linda Hutcheon, *Narcissistic Narrative* (Waterloo: Wilfrid Laurier University Press, 1980).

recuperated, salvaged, or forged in those prior theorizations of the process of characterization. That earlier notion is concerned with establishing and identifying a finished *product*, the character as named, identifiable individual susceptible, as a product, to the modes of capitalist exploitation; this postmodern mode establishes the differences which are revealed as the 'characterization' progresses as *process*, without ever managing to establish a final product, and thus—'weakly'—resisting such capitalist appropriation and containment.[20]

Some modernist narratives take this 'heterogeneity' of character, the notion of character as process, into account. While a writer such as Lawrence thought that he was mining a seam of essential reality in character, Woolf was examining, often in a wilfully incoherent mode, the ambiguities offered by characters who never actually acted but were rather always 'between the acts'. She was interested in characterization as a process whereby the supposed essence of character always escaped, where characters were always somehow elusive, never fully 'there', like the ghostly Mrs Ramsay in *To the Lighthouse* or the 'character', such as it is, of Percival in *The Waves*. Woolf's novels are largely about the process whereby the relations between characters always escape reification; they are thus often largely about the *failure* to write a 'character' as the bearer or some essential truth of human nature; and consequently an interest in character is replaced by an examination of the mobile and fluid interrelations among shadowy half-articulated, even half-represented, figures. Similar arguments could be advanced concerning, for instance, Mann's delineation of the relations between Aschenbach and Tadzio in *Death in Venice*; another important example would be Proust's *A la recherche du temps perdu*, in which, despite the autobiographical impetus, the text tells us little of the 'essence' of Marcel, replacing that by a series of shifting relations with Swann, Albertine, Saint-Loup, and so on. In the later example, the reader reaches, at the 'close' of the novel, a hypothetical understanding of Marcel; but, since the novel ends at the point where Marcel becomes a writer and can now write the text which we thought had just been read, the

[20] This 'weak' resistance here is modelled on what Gianni Vattimo and Pier Aldo Rovatti have usefully described as 'il pensiero debole'. See their co-edited volume, *Il pensiero debole* (Milan: Feltrinelli, 1983).

reading exercise has, logically, to be repeated, but at a different level of understanding. Hence, it follows that the 'identity' which the reader proposes for Marcel at the close of the novel is to undergo a differential epistemological shift in a reiteration of the reading of the character.

Even in these modernist experiments, however, it is to be stressed that character is still organized around the basic notion of *anagnorisis* or re-cognizability: the individual characters can, at some level, be 'known', cognized, and recognized. Theorists of character have always made a distinction between characters in novels and persons in a 'life' which is supposed to be constitutively different from textual semiotics. This distinction, fundamentally, hinges on the opposition between ontology and epistemology. As Davis puts it, in a formulation which echoes Bayley:

> Personality is what living beings have. Our personalities may not be coherent; they may not be readily understood by us; they may be misinterpreted or not even accessible to others; but they are what we refer to when we refer to ourselves. 'Character' on the other hand is what people in novels have. They are characters with characteristics.[21]

Personality is purposeless and complex; character is purposeful and simple, a small set of traits definable through essential epithets which are not only essentially *knowable* but also recognizable precisely because they are *iterable* in the life of the personality. Personalities are deemed to have a degree of existential contingency which is lacking in characters who merely enact functions in organized plots and delimited locations. Where personality is an ontological category, character is an epistemological one. Importantly, however, in prior theorizations of character there has been an implication that in this literary instance epistemology is determinant of ontology: character gives us models on which to formulate personality: 'Madame Bovary, c'est moi.'

If character has been most frequently construed as the medium through which we can gain access to the world of the social formation being elaborated in the text, then it is important that the character be epistemologically comprehensible. If

[21] Davis, *Resisting Novels*, 111.

this medium becomes as seemingly contingent as personalities in the different ontological level of 'real life' or history, if it becomes inconsistent or fundamentally shadowy, 'disapparent' or unknowable, unrecognizable, then there enters a confusion between categories. What has been assumed by the reader to be an epistemological category begins to operate in the manner of an ontological one: the 'fictionality' of the text and its characters is called into question and there arises a confusion about the relative ontological status of characters, on the one hand, and of readers or authors, on the other. It is precisely such a confusion that we see most frequently entertained and even celebrated in postmodern narrative.

The confusion can take either of two orientations. On the one hand, it can operate in a conservative mode, whereby 'characters' are 'raised' to the level of personalities, without the text ever casting any doubts upon that ontological category itself. This would be the case, for instance, in a text such as *Daniel Martin* by John Fowles, where Fowles introduces what Hamon calls *personnages-référentiels*[22]—that is, proper personal names from the realm of history—and where these names or *personnages* are introduced at the same level as the other 'fictive' characters in the text, sometimes even described as interacting with the characters. In *Daniel Martin*, the critic Kenneth Tynan appears as a 'character', with the result of confusing or eradicating the ontological distinction between such a 'personality' and the 'characters' of Daniel or Jenny in that text. A similar working of the same manœuvre is to be found in cases where a character, introduced in one text, reappears, perhaps in a minor role, in another. This happens, for example, in the novels of Alison Lurie, where 'Leonard Zimmern' figures in a central role in *The War between the Tates* and reappears in a more peripheral role in *Foreign Affairs*. This 'character', figuring in texts eleven years apart, appears to transcend the limitations of a role in one plot, and the illusion is thus created that what seemed to operate at the epistemological level of character now begins to operate as if it were at the ontological level of personality.

On the other hand, the confusion of character and personality can have a more radical dimension, in which the result is the

[22] Philippe Hamon, 'Pour un statut sémiologique du personnage', *Littérature*, 4 (1972), repr. in Roland Barthes *et al.*, *Poétique du récit* (Paris: Seuil, 1977).

calling into question of the ontological status of author and reader, the problematizing of the notion of the subject of consciousness as a historical entity. In this case, personality becomes transfigured as nothing more or less than a nexus of semiotic signification: persons in history become equated with characters as the effects of textuality, and become signifiers devoid of a signified. This view is elaborated by Federman when he argues that

> the people of fiction, the fictitious beings, will also no longer be well-made characters who carry with them a fixed identity, a stable set of social and psychological attributes—a name, a situation, a profession, a condition, etc. The creatures of the new fiction will be as changeable, as illusory, as nameless, as unnamable, as fraudulent, as unpredictable as the discourse that makes them up. This does not mean, however, that they will be mere puppets. On the contrary their being will be more genuine, more complex, more true-to-life in fact, because they will not appear to be simply what they are; they will be what they are: word-beings . . . That creature will be, in a sense, present to his own making, present to his own absence.[23]

To be present to one's own absence in this way is to witness the dialectic of appearance and disappearance. When characters become as contingent as personalities in this way, the result is that they 'participate in the fiction only as a grammatical being',[24] and become aware of their purely linguistic or textual status, precisely to the extent that they are incoherent, self-contradictory, fragmentary, and contingent as personality. The category of personality, then, is radically questioned, and the validity of its claims to a stable ontological status is doubted. The most obvious examples of this would be texts such as Sorrentino's *Mulligan Stew*, the 'magic realism' of Marquez's *Autumn of the Patriarch*, or Ronald Sukenick's *98.6*, where 'Ron' operates firstly as a seemingly coherent medium on the fiction, and then proceeds to become inconsistent, incoherent, and the merest empty signifier whose 'meaning' constantly varies in a thoroughly contingent manner. In cases such as these, what was taken as an ontological category produces an epistemological problem.

[23] Raymond Federman (ed.), *Surfiction: Fiction Now . . . and Tomorrow* (Chicago: Swallow Press, 1975), 12–13.

[24] Ibid.

The problem raised by this category confusion in postmodern characterization can be properly articulated in Heideggerian terms as a question of 'fundamental ontology and the search for the human place'. That mode of understanding character (the 'pre-modernist' mode, so to speak) is almost entirely epistemological. It renders 'other people' fundamentally knowable, offering the reader the illusion of having a stable position from which her or his own identity is guaranteed through its distinction from a basically knowable and recognizable 'otherness' or alterity. The epistemological steadiness or predictability of 'character' in this older mode grants the reader a position of security in her or his own identity, an identity which is of a different—prior—ontological status from that of the character and which transcends that lower or dependent status. In short, it offers the illusion of a control over the characters, whereby the reader can place or locate them in the plot not only in relation to each other but also in relation to the reader's own position, a position which, in transcending the hypothetical world of the characters, offers the illusion of omniscience and its corollary, omnipotence. This situation is precisely akin to a mode of imperialist control of the Other in general in which, by pretending to 'know' the Other fully and comprehensibly, a self can assure itself of its own truths and originary status. To this extent, 'reasonable' characters in the paradigmatic plot of enlightenment share that eighteenth-century predilection for the imperialist or colonialist control not only of other places (the 'human place' of the Other), but also of other 'positions';[25] in novelistic terms, this translates into control of other 'points of view', other discourses, or, in short, of other characters. It is this imperialism of reading character which the more radical problematization of the ontological status of the reader, such as we have it in postmodern characterization, begins to challenge. It does so by problematizing the 'human place', by converting the stability of 'position' into the mutable displacements of 'disposition', or, to put this in poststructuralist terms, by displacing the reader and deconstructing the relation which obtains between reader and character.

[25] See Davis, *Resisting Novels*, 52 ff.

Robbe-Grillet is well known for his iconoclastic attacks on the conventions of the novel, and certainly the conventional 'character' in his work begins to disappear. Yet he also vigorously asserts the primacy of subjectivity in his *chosiste*, 'thingy' novels. These two positions, attacking character and instating human subjectivity in his texts, can perhaps be reconciled when we consider the influence of cinema on his writing. He remarks that:

> Sous l'influence, ou non, de telles exigences du récit cinématographique, le roman à son tour semble prendre conscience des mêmes problèmes. D'où est vu cet objet? Sous quel angle? A quelle distance? Avec quel éclairage? Le regard s'y arrête-t-il longtemps, ou passe-t-il sans insister? Se déplace-t-il, ou bien reste-t-il fixe? Le romancier perpétuellement omniscient et omniprésent est ainsi récusé. Ce n'est plus Dieu qui décrit le monde, c'est l'homme, *un* homme. Même si ce n'est pas un personnage, c'est en tout cas *un œil d'homme*. Le roman contemporain, dont on répète volontiers qu'il veut exclure l'homme de l'univers, lui donne donc en réalité la première place, celle de l'observateur.[26]

The attack on character turns out to be an attack on the particular kind of imperialist epistemology which promises the possibility of full enlightenment, the hypothetical omniscience of the 'pre-modern' reader. In cinema, the point of view is strictly limited and localized, and when Robbe-Grillet avails of cinematic technique in his writing, he can claim to be attacking the epistemological status and tenets on which conventional character rests, and to be replacing them with something making a greater claim on ontological presence.

The assignation of a place to the reader, like that for an audience in cinema, is crucial in this approach. It would be apposite to suggest that this is merely an articulation of what happens in much modernist fiction, such as that of James, Conrad, or Ford, in which the reader is deliberately denied immediate access to the omniscient perspective she or he frequently is assumed to have in that mythic 'classic realist text', the Victorian or realist novel. But it is vital to note that, even in those modernist texts which are narrated from one or more

[26] Alain Robbe-Grillet, 'Notes sur la localisation et les déplacements du point de vue dans la description romanesque', *La Revue des lettres modernes*, 5/36–8 (Summer 1958), 128–30 (and 256–8: this issue of *La Revue* has double pagination).

local points of view or by incompetent narrators, the entire text can finally be harnessed in the brace of full epistemological satisfaction. *Nostromo*, for instance, offers only confusion in its opening juxtaposition of a number of points of view and temporal perspectives, but that initial fragmentation is proleptically instrumental in the establishing of a more encompassing position or place from which all the contradictions can be reconciled, allowing thereby the recuperation of the text as an entire and self-present whole, available to a consciousness proposed and constructed as being equally self-present. Such a *provisional* series of displacements in modernist fiction could be compared with the multiple openings of Flann O'Brien's *At Swim-Two-Birds*, the fundamental shift of position in Butor's *La Modification*, or the series of mutually exclusive and contradictory points of view which operate throughout Robbe-Grillet's *Dans le labyrinthe*, such as the opening description of the weather 'outside'. While the trajectory in the modernist experiment with point of view remains firmly within that 'imperialist' epistemological project, moving from mystification to enlightenment, in the postmodern experiment that orientation is reversed.

A novel which sits precisely on the borderline traced here between modernist and postmodern characterization is Robbe-Grillet's *La Jalousie*. The central 'character' of this text, usually referred to in criticism after Morrissette as *le mari jaloux*,[27] remains unnamed and is not described throughout the entire text. In most fiction, proper names operate as 'pegs on which to hang descriptions':[28] they promise coherence and identity, organizing varied points of view into recognizable locations. But in texts which eschew such use of the proper name, as in Sarraute's *Portrait d'un inconnu*, Wurlitzer's *Flats*, or, here, Robbe-Grillet's *La Jalousie*, a different set of problems arises. In *La Jalousie*, the reader is able to hang a number of descriptions around 'A . . .' and 'Franck', but remains unable to localize the character traits which accrue to what Morrissette calls the *je-néant*, the narratorial figure who remains anonymous. But it is

[27] Bruce Morrissette, *Les Romans de Robbe-Grillet* (Paris: Minuit, 1963).

[28] The phrase comes from John Searle, *Speech Acts* (Cambridge: Cambridge University Press, 1970); but cf. Jacques Derrida, *Limited Inc. a b c* (Baltimore: Johns Hopkins University Press, 1977), and Docherty, *Reading (Absent) Character*.

precisely this narratorial figure who operates as the reader's point of access to the world of the text, including its descriptions of the other 'characters'. The result is that it is the reader who comes to inhabit this position, the position behind the blinds, from which the world and the text of *La Jalousie* are generated, and from which 'jealousy' originates. This text does not work to produce a character suffering from the character-trait of jealousy as his distinguishing mark; on the contrary, it seduces the reader into occupying the position defined by the trait, now thus a personality-trait rather than a mere character-trait, since it is located in the reader whose ontological place is in history.

This is a fully *phenomenological* performance, offering the reader a perceptual space in and through which she or he, as the subject of the experience of *La Jalousie*, mediates the sense of the world of things or objects described within the text. The reader comes to 'inhabit' the place from which the text is generated. The logic of this is that the desired effect is not so much to give the reader an account or epistemological *understanding* of a jealous character; on the contrary, it is to produce a jealous *experience*, an experience whose historical or existential reality is not to be doubted, even if it remains not epistemologically understood or accessible. The text operates in the more radical mode of questioning the ontological validity of the reader's status, rendering the position of the reader as an effect of textuality; to this extent it is postmodern in its seduction of the reader, making the reader the primary 'character' of the text's enactment. However, as a still *phenomenological* performance, it also allows for the stabilization of the subject-position of the reader: in other words, it grants the reader an *identity*, classifiable as the 'Subject of Jealousy', and this identity is not modified by any *temporal* displacement or difference in the position of the reading subject. The text sets up *spatial* relations between reader and character, but still is not fully open to history, even though the 'character' in the text operates at the level of the historical personality of the reader, by eliding as much as possible the space, distance, or difference between the reader and the text's 'je'. Access to an ontological mode is gained; but this is an ontology without history, a being without time, to put it in Heideggerian terms.

This type of novel hovers on the edge of the postmodern, but allows for the full confusion explored by existentialist thought in, for example, the character of Antoine Roquentin in Sartre's *La Nausée*, who ponders a famous dilemma:

Voici ce que j'ai pensé: pour que l'événement le plus banal devienne une aventure, il faut et il suffit qu'on se mette à le *raconter*. C'est ce qui dupe les gens; un homme, c'est un conteur d'histoires, il vit entouré de ses histoires et des histoires d'autrui, il voit tout ce qui lui arrive à travers elles; et il cherche à vivre sa vie comme s'il la racontait.
Mais il faut choisir: vivre ou raconter.[29]

When Sartre ponders this, the very terms of the debate postulate the notion of a true or authentic 'real' Self which lies covered under a fictive one; and such are the terms of the debate between ontology and epistemology, between personality and character. This debate remains profoundly humanist, proposing a dichotomy of surface (appearance) and depth (reality) which has dominated the understanding of characterization at all moments prior to the postmodern. But, under the influence of cinematic characterization and its immediacy of presentation of characters, albeit from strictly delineated positions, there is no longer any depth to character. 'Character' in these terms does indeed disappear, for everything is always already on display, is 'obscene' as Baudrillard would have it, since surface is all that there is. Beckett's Unnamable is precisely this kind of fictive character:

perhaps that's what I feel, an outside and an inside and me in the middle, perhaps that's what I am, the thing that divides the world in two, on the one side the outside, on the other the inside, that can be as thin as foil, I'm neither one side nor the other, I'm in the middle, I'm the partition, I've two surfaces and no thickness, perhaps that's what I feel, myself vibrating, I'm the tympanum, on the one hand the mind, on the other the world, I don't belong to either . . .[30]

This *ghostly* 'medium' is, as we have already seen in the case of Heaney, the typical postmodern figure. The spatial metaphor of surface and depth is replaced, after the influence of cinema,

[29] Jean-Paul Sartre, *La Nausée* (1938; repr. Paris: Folio, 1977), 61–2.
[30] Samuel Beckett, *Molloy; Malone Dies; The Unnamable* (London: John Calder, 1979), 352. For the 'obscene' in Baudrillard, see Jean Baudrillard, *L'Autre par lui-même* (Paris: Galilée, 1987).

by temporal sequence and development: a figure in one scene or 'shot' can be thoroughly transfigured by the next, thus countering the notion of a transcendent self lying 'behind' the surface 'apparitions' and 'disappearances'. In fact, according to Eisenstein, it is precisely such a *discontinuity* between shots that is of the essence of cinematic montage; and, in postmodern narrative, such a discontinuity is taken on as a challenge to the notion of a 'real' identity or self-sameness which underpins various mystifying or disguised 'appearances'.[31] In the first instance, what is challenged thereby is the conventional figuring of the real world as a seamless, continuous, monologically sense-making unitary whole; but, as we shall see later in this book, in the end it is even the very status of the 'real' itself as an originary concept from which representations are derived which is challenged in some postmodern alterior thinking. In postmodern narrative, 'character', such as it is, is there immediately and in all its 'obscenity': the medium that is character is itself unmediated, and it is this that distinguishes such characterization from all previous modes.

In narratological terms, character is nothing other than the potential for story, for the releasing of temporality and sequence, or, in short, for narrative itself. This is outlined by Todorov in his argument that character be understood as *homme-récit*:

> Le personnage n'est pas toujours, comme le prétend James, la détermination de l'action; et tout récit ne consiste pas en une 'description de caractères'. Mais qu'est-ce alors que le personnage? *Les Mille et une nuits* nous donnent une réponse très nette que reprend et confirme le *Manuscrit trouvé à Saragosse*; le personnage, c'est une histoire virtuelle qui est l'histoire de sa vie. Tout nouveau personnage signifie une nouvelle intrigue. Nous sommes dans le royaume des hommes-récits.[32]

Vivre, then, is *raconter*; or, as Foucault would have it, social formations and the very concept of identity are formed through the interplay of discourses. But the postmodern turning of this involves the multiplication of identities (often under the sign of

[31] See Sergei Eisenstein, *The Film Sense* (trans. and ed. Jay Leyda; London: Faber, 1986).

[32] Tzvetan Todorov, *Poétique de la prose* (Paris: Seuil, 1971), 81–2.

the one proper name) and the consequent fragmentation of the phenomenological subject-position which is afforded the reader in a text such as *La Jalousie* and its modernist precursors. Instead of offering the reading subject a specific or identifiable single ontological space, a 'clearing' in which a supposedly non-temporal identity can be established, postmodern narrative not only renders the reader of the status of textual discourse, making her or him the merest effect of the interplay of linguistic discourses, it also 'dis-positions' the reader, produces a *number* of conflicting positions from which the narrative is to be read.

The most basic manner in which this attack on the singularity of the human's 'place' is carried out is through the elaboration of a multiplicity of conflicting narratives or *hommes-récits*. In Robbe-Grillet's *Dans le labyrinthe*, for instance, each mention of the 'character' of the soldier operates as the release for another narrative beginning, often a narrative which contradicts the one which was in sequence before it. If the reader is using this character in a mode similar to the *je-néant* in *La Jalousie*, then the effect is to replace the elaboration of a particular, specifiable place for the reading subject with a non-specific, non-identifiable sequence of changing or altered positions or dispositions. This is the situation described by Borges in his story 'The Garden of Forking Paths'. Here, Stephen Albert ponders Ts'ui Pen's labyrinthine manuscripts. He imagines the way in which Ts'ui Pen might have realized the task of writing an infinite, unending book, and can come up with nothing better than the circular text (such as Proust's *A la recherche du temps perdu*, Gide's *Les Faux-monnayeurs*, Joyce's *Finnegans Wake*, and so on), until he lingers on a particular sentence in the manuscript:

> I lingered, naturally, on the sentence: *I leave to the various futures (not to all) my garden of forking paths*. Almost instantly, I understood: 'the garden of forking paths' was the chaotic novel; the phrase 'the various futures (not to all)' suggested to me the forking in time, not in space. A broad rereading of the work confirmed the theory. In all fictional works, each time a man is confronted with several alternatives, he chooses one and eliminates the others; in the fiction of Ts'ui Pen, he chooses simultaneously—all of them. *He creates*, in this way, diverse futures, diverse times which themselves also proliferate and fork.

> Here, then, is the explanation of the novel's contradictions. Fang, let us say, has a secret; a stranger calls at his door; Fang resolves to kill him. Naturally, there are several possible outcomes: Fang can kill the intruder, the intruder can kill Fang, they both can escape, they both can die, and so forth. In the work of Ts'ui Pen, all possible outcomes occur; each one is the point of departure for other forkings.[33]

Some postmodern narratives are like this hypothetical fiction. While modernist and earlier modes of narrative and characterization offer the reader a set of spatial relations (a plot) in and through which she or he finds a specific identity or place from which to know the fiction and to recognize its characters, postmodern narrative offers a proliferation of such positions, denying priority to any of them. This is the case in the heavily overplotted fictions of Pynchon, where the introduction—or eruption—of a character's name is the signal for another plot or for a further disorienting turn in an already complex baroque intrigue, as in Pynchon's own self- parody, 'The Courier's Tragedy', in the midst of *The Crying of Lot 49*.

The temporal disposition or dislocation of the reading subject described here is itself dramatized as the material of Calvino's *Se una notte d'inverno un viaggiatore*, in which, owing to a series of errors at the binder's, various hypothesized 'novels' are interleaved with each other in a framework of steady self-alteration. The position or disposition (*ethos*) of 'the Reader' is itself the subject of the narrative here, for he has constantly to shift his position and expectations, as he shifts from one text to another. The Reader then becomes multiple, as Calvino introduces 'other' readers of the various novels and provides dialogue and debate among them all. This multiplication of 'the Reader' (and the confusion of the *character* of the Reader with 'real' readers of the text) is an analogue of what happens to characterization in postmodern narrative generally. All that Calvino has done is to take the initial sentence of a hypothetical text, split it up into its various component phrases, and then to propose each such fragmenary phrase as the beginning of a new narrative, a narrative which is released by the phrase and

[33] Jorge Luis Borges, *Labyrinths*, ed. Donald A. Yates and James E. Irby (various trans.; Harmondsworth: Penguin, 1978), 51.

by its introduction if not of a character then at least of a position from which the text is understood and read. The phrases are then simply linked in sequence. This fragmentation of a narrative, its multiplication (through what we will call, after Lyotard, 'phrasing' and 'linking' of phrases[34]) into a series of seemingly unrelated and disconcertingly different narratives, generates at the same time a multiplicity of positions for the reading subject; but each such position is now strictly different—altered—from those that go before and after. 'The Reader', as a supposedly single, essential identity, disappears, and is replaced by a series of 'dispositions' (moods, ethical stances), shifts of position from which the text can be understood. The reader, then, is, as it were, released into the temporality of narrative, shifting position at every instant of reading Calvino's text. As Jip 'n' Zab suggest at the start of Brooke-Rose's *Xorandor*, 'One, it's important to be two'; and in this novel the 'character' of Xor7 (itself a pun on 'Exocet') also becomes multiple, hovering uncertainly between computer and Lady Macbeth, whose lines it picks up and plays back.[35]

While 'pre-modern' characterization (which also includes modernist modes) is concerned with the production of identity, postmodern narrative fractures such a homogeneity in both the 'characters' and the reading subject. Postmodern narrative seeks to circumvent the phenomenological elaboration of a definable spatial relation obtaining between a transcendent ontological reading subject and an equally fixed and non-historical object of that reader's perception, the 'character'. Earlier modes of characterization are related to the imperialist and colonialist impetus of modernity's appropriation of space, and the grounds on which a position of intentional authority is afforded an imperial self through its 'knowledge' of and understanding of an oppressed characterological or epistemological Other. Postmodern characterization disturbs this position by the interjection of a temporal component in the process of reading character, replacing the notion of 'position' with

[34] See Jean-François Lyotard, *The Differend* (trans. Georges van den Abbeele; Manchester: Manchester University Press, 1988).

[35] Christine Brooke-Rose, *Xorandor* (London: Paladin, 1986), 7 and *passim*.

that of the poststructuralist displacement or 'disposition'. In short, postmodern characterization seeks to return the dimension of history which earlier modes of characterization, or of the theoretical understanding of character as 'identity', deny.

That denial of history in earlier theorizations of character is accompanied by a denial of politics. The bias of the novel, since its moment of inception, towards biography is obvious. The central characters of such fiction are interesting for criticism precisely to the extent that they are the locus of *anagnorisis*, some moment of recognition or of turning and troping of the character. This is what passes for the supposedly temporal development of character in earlier modes of reading character. Such *anagnorisis* does not offer any fundamental change or 'disposition' in the reading of character; but even if it did (as previous theory suggests), then it has the vital corollary of identifying change in the novel as something that always happens at the level of the individual rather than in the wider socio-political formation itself. Davis writes:

> Ideologically speaking . . . character gives readers faith that personality is, first, understandable, and second, capable of rational change. As part of the general ideology of middle-class individualism, the idea that the subject might be formed from social forces and that change might have to come about through social change is by and large absent from novels. Change is always seen as effected by the individual. In a novel like *Hard Times* only personal moral changes will bring about the amelioration of family conditions. The family problems of Louisa and Tom will bring about the change in their father that will help solve the problems of the working class in Manchester. Likewise, Elizabeth Bennet's marriage to Darcy or Pamela's to Mr B. will somehow improve upper-class values a bit.[36]

This reduction of politics to morality is entirely in keeping with a liberalism which operates on the suppression of history (replacing history with eternal, immanent 'truths' of human nature) and the elimination of politics (replaced with 'values'). Postmodern characterization offers a challenge to this, with implications that go far beyond the realm of merely aesthetic predilections.

[36] Davis, *Resisting Novels*, 119.

2. A DIFFERENT ECONOMY

Postmodern characterization, then, advances an attack on the notion of identity, or of an essential Selfhood which is not traduced by a temporal dimension which threatens that Self with heterogeneity. In short, it leads to the elaboration of 'characters' (if they can still be called such, given their confusing ontological status) whose existence (rather than essence) is characterized by *difference* (rather than identity). Postmodern figures are always differing, not just from other characters, but also from their putative 'selves'. Whereas previously characters were considered as entities 'present-to-themselves' or, to put this in existentialist terms, finally reduced to the status of an essential selfhood and thus reified as *en-soi*, exchangeable as commodities, postmodern characters always dramatize their own 'absence' from themselves.

Postmodern characters typically fall into incoherence: character-traits are not repeated, but contradicted; proper names are used, if at all, inconsistently; signposts implying specific gender are confused; a seemingly animate character mutates into an inanimate object; and so on. At every stage in the representation of character, the finality of the character, a determinate identity for the character, is deferred as the proliferation of information about the character leads into irrationality, incoherence, or self-contradiction. There is never a final point at which the character can be reduced to the status of an epistemologically accessible essential quality or list of qualities or 'properties'. What is at stake in this is the entire notion of 'representation'. As in most art-forms and cultural practices, the postmodern impetus is almost synonymous with the questioning of representation.

Following in the wake of an existentialist philosophical tradition, many postmodern characterizations seem to argue that there is always a discrepancy between the character who acts and the character who watches herself or himself acting. There is, as it were, a temporal distance between agency and self-consciousness regarding that agency, a fine example of which is Barth's fiction, 'Menelaiad'. This text enacts the continual deferral of coincidence between the narrating subject and the subject narrated, even though these are ostensibly identical, namable as 'Menelaus'. As a result, 'Menelaus', paradoxically, is 'identified', or better characterized, as that which is always differing from himself. There is a series of confusions about the ontological presence of the character, such that at any moment in the text when it seems that 'Menelaus' *is* somewhat, immediately a difference is produced, and an alternative or new narrative is released.

The voice of Menelaus (for that is all there is in this tale) begins to relate the story of his life to Telemachus, Peisistratus, and a hypothesized listener (actually, of course, the ear of the reader). During the tale, he tells of meeting Helen, who demanded the tale of his life; within this tale, now on a different level and in a different temporal frame, he met Proteus, who asked for the tale of his life, and so on. There are, then, a number of *hommes-récits* identified under the sign of Menelaus; but this fiction begins to unravel or untangle that supposed self-identical sign or identity, to release all the different figures, masquerading under the identical proper name which supposedly offers them a non-temporal, non-historical identity, and produces a multi-layered narrative. In characterological terms, the result is that the consciousness that identifies itself as 'Menelaus' is always out of step or non-identical with the voice of Menelaus and with the actions which Menelaus supposedly performed. The very telling of the tale of his life, an act which is supposed to proffer and guarantee identity, in fact produces this radical *décalage* or self-difference as the constituent of the being of 'Menelaus'. Menelaus is thus never fully present-to-himself; every time he identifies himself, he has to do so by adverting to a different Menelaus, one who exists in a different temporal and narrative frame and one who exists, therefore, at a different ontological level from the narrating consciousness. Worse than this, within one of the tales Menelaus indicates his fully temporal predicament. He changes places and times on every occasion at which he tries to fix or identify himself, as is fully seen in his encounter with Proteus:

' " 'My problem was, I'd leisure to think. My time was mortal, Proteus's im-; what if he merely treed it a season or two till I let go? What was it anyhow I held? If Proteus once was Old Man of the Sea and now Proteus was a tree, then Proteus was neither, only Proteus; what I held were dreams. But if a real Old Man of the Sea had really been succeeded by real water and the rest, then the dream was Proteus. And Menelaus! For I changed too as the long day passed: changed my mind, replaced myself, grew older. How hold on until the "old" (which is to say the young) Menelaus rebecame himself? . . . ' " . . .'[37]

Menelaus is, if anything, the character as Heideggerian *Dasein*; the 'being' of Menelaus, such as it is, is endlessly deferred, endlessly seeming otherwise and reiterating itself in an altered figuration. Its identity is characterized by this potentially endless differing from itself, the perpetual deferring of an essential selfhood: 'the thing I am' is replaced—or, indeed, *constituted*—by a 'seeming otherwise'. The character is constantly disappearing from its own surface, constantly escaping the parameters which the text implies for its figuration: in short, the character is constantly 'being there', constantly evading the fixity of a definite or identifiable and single 'place' for itself. To this extent, it becomes the merest series of instantiations of subjectivity, rather than a characterological entity: it has no place, but a series of dispositions (moods, ethics), as the parameters of its figuration shift and metamorphose in temporal sequence.

There is a difficulty with the very notion of 'representation' of a character whose condition is that it is never present to itself in the first place but is always 'ec-statically' escaping the constraints of self-presence.[38] Yet it is precisely here that the politics of a 'different economy' or an economy of difference can enter into a consideration of postmodern characterization.

Previous theories of characterization are all, as I have stressed, dependent upon the paradigmatic dichotomy of appearance and reality; and their narratives are always 'apocalyptic' in the sense that they move from mystification to enlightenment and revelation as to the 'truth' of the character and its identity. The narrative trajectory is from the heterogeneity of different appearance to a presumed homogeneity of a real identity. It follows from this that what we can call the 'economy of identity' is based upon a supposed equality between the self of a character, on the one hand, and that character's narrative of

[37] John Barth, *Lost in the Funhouse* (New York: Doubleday, 1968), 142.
[38] For this notion of 'ecstasy', see Docherty, *Reading (Absent) Character*.

the self, on the other: this is the *homme* as *récit* in Todorov's terms. The character is adequately 're-presented' in the narrative; the self-presence of an identity reiterated in its mimetic relaying in the tale. Further, this equation is commutable. For it is not simply the case that characters in fiction are the mimetic echoes or representations of selves in history; on the contrary, as I argued above, characters in fiction are, proportionately to the extent that they are 'representative' of a supposed human nature, models upon whom selves in history must fashion themselves if they are to have a claim on being a 'reasonable' or 'enlightened' individual—a legitimate individual—within human nature. It is in these terms that the economy of identity assumes a political cast, for 'representation' here assumes the burden also of political re-presentation. It transpires that characters, acting on behalf of selves (functioning as 'representatives' in a manner akin to bourgeois parliamentary representation), act as the legislators for certain kinds of political practice. As Davis indicated, the novel reduces all political action to moral action undertaken by and on behalf of individuals; character, operating according to an economy of identity in which the character is assumed to function as the mimetic representation of a self which is equally assumed to be fully present to itself, fully self-identical, is the means whereby this morality of individualism supplants the possibility of political praxis in narrative.

However, postmodern narrative disturbs the neat equations of the economy of identity, reversing the trajectory described by earlier narratives. In postmodern characterization, the narrative trajectory is from the assumed homogeneity of identity (as in the nameable identity of Menelaus, say) towards an endlessly proliferating heterogeneity, whereby identity is endlessly deferred and replaced by a scenario in which the 'character' or figure constantly differs from itself, denying the possession of and by a self and preferring an engagement with Otherness. Every mention of the same proper name, for instance, operates to release a new narrative, one which is typically at odds with the narratives previously ascribed to that proper name in the fiction. Rather than the self being identified with one narrative (biography), in this postmodern model the self disappears under a welter of proliferating narratives, 'forking paths', which never cohere or become exactly commensurable with one another. *Vivre* does not equal *raconter* here, at least not in the sense that a life has one story: rather, there is the production of an *excess*, a *surplus* of narrative, and it is this surplus which disturbs the neat equalities of the economy of identity and which calls into question the function of representation in postmodern narrative. Representation is no longer conceivable as a simple 'duplication' or substitutive mimetic doubling: representation is now 'excessive' or economically dysfunctional.

We have thus a different economy, an 'economy of difference'. Postmodern narrative enacts the character as *Dasein*, the character who constantly escapes the fixity of identity by existing in and through the temporal predicament whereby the assumed or desired totality of a real self is endlessly 'dispositioned', always a 'being *there*', as opposed to a being here, a being present to itself. This is not so much a character, more a series of fleeting instantiations of subjectivity, a series of 'appearances' which do not act as the cover for a 'deeper' reality, for it is that very notion of a material or essential reality which postmodern characterization denies. At best, then, the progression of a postmodern narrative cannot move from appearance to the enlightenment of a reality, but only from appearance to disappearance to *different* appearance and so on. In such characterization, the idea of a reciprocity, according to which the character is seen as a representative of the self of the historical reader, becomes impossible, since it is just this notion of a totalized real and essential selfhood that the texts deny. The simplicity of a seemingly 'democratic' mode of characterization, based upon a liberal individualism and the category of 'representation', is called into question. Postmodern narrative reveals that it is not simply the case that earlier modes of reading fiction reduce the political to the moral; more importantly, in their delineation of social and political formations through the medium of 'representative' characters, they confuse a political category of representation with an aesthetic mode of mimesis. Criticism has always prioritized this aesthetic component, in its endless discussion of 'well-rounded', or 'vividly realized' or 'fully depicted' characters in fiction. In brief, there has been in this area a dangerous 'aestheticization of politics'.[39]

But postmodern narrative does not easily reverse this orientation. Instead, it introduces, through its mode of characterization, the category of *ethics*. The reader of postmodern narrative, as allegorized in Calvino's *Se una notte d'inverno un viaggiatore*, is fully implicated in the proliferation of narratives. However, unlike the reader of earlier fictions, she or he is denied the possibility and solace of producing a totalized self for the characters being processed in the reading; the totality of a supposedly enlightened truth or real essence of character is denied as a result of the proliferation of narratives which contradict such a totality. This also means that postmodern narrative attacks the possibility of the reader herself or himself becoming a fully enlightened and imperialist subject with full epistemological control over the fiction and its endlessly different or altered characters. In order to read postmodern narrative at all, the reader must give up such a singular position, for she or he will be endlessly 'disposed', displaced, in figuring a number of different narratives and different characters. She or he has to be seduced from the occupation of one position ('Othello's occupation's gone') into many positions; she or he has to give up a quasi- authorial position of a supposed access to the singular truth of character and move instead into a series of dispositions (ethics) in trying to deal with the proliferating narratives she or he hears. The reader, then, is denied access to a totalizing narrative which will allow her or him to identify herself or himself against the stable 'other' of a mysterious character. Rather, the reader replaces such a totalized enlightened narrative, proposing access as it does to a singular monotheistic truth, with the multiplicity of singularities, the multiplicity of different local narratives, having no claims on truth in any absolute sense at all. The reader becomes nothing more or less than an excuse for the proliferation of yet further narratives, further dispositions. The reader thus becomes as imbricated in a temporal or historical predicament as the characters in postmodern narrative, and, like those characters, has

[39] For the implication of such a state of affairs, see, of course, Walter Benjamin, 'The Work of Art in the Age of Mechanical Reproduction', in *Illuminations*, ed. Hannah Arendt (trans. Harry Zohn; Glasgow: Fontana, 1973).

no access to a totalized narrative of a true or essential selfhood according to which she or he orients her or his present being. The reader's 'temporality' or historical condition in the act of reading postmodern characterization is itself characterized by the notion of disposition, of being seduced or disposed from one position to another in the construction and deconstruction of a series of narratives. In this, there is no final or overall single position which would allow for a systematic ranging of the narratives; there is only an economy which, in its basic orientation to heterogeneity, endlessly produces more and more different narratives. Where the economy of identity produces a single totalized narrative or a priority among narratives which allows for the formulation of a narrative of the stable self, it also arrests the temporality of narrative and the notion of temporal change which is axiomatic to narrative. Postmodern characterization keeps the narratives going.

In so doing, postmodern narrative lures a reader into 'disposition', a translation of the Greek *ethos*. To this extent, the category of the ethical is introduced; and through this, which involves the reader in the search for 'the good' (as opposed to the mere subscription to a monotheistic truth), the political does in fact return. As MacIntyre indicates, there is a distinction between the ethical and the political, but it cannot be drawn too sharply:

> Such a distinction depends upon there being a distinction between private and public life of such a kind that I can consider what it is best for me to do without considering in what political order it is requisite for me to live, either because I treat the political order as a given and unalterable context of private action, or because I think the political order irrelevant for some other reason.[40]

Postmodern narrative of characterization, of course, in attacking not only the notion of a self but also the dichotomy on which it is based (interiority of 'reality' versus external ostension of 'appearance'), eradicates the distinction between the ethical and the political. A fundamental ontology is replaced by a first philosophy of ethical demands. To read postmodern characterization is to reintroduce the possibility of politics, and importantly of a genuinely historical political change, into the

[40] Alistair MacIntyre, *A Short History of Ethics* (London: Duckworth, 1967), 129.

act of reading; and this reintroduction is generated from the category of the ethical, from the disposition (mood, ethics) of the reading subject.

3. SEEMING OTHERWISE

What is at stake, then, in postmodern characterization is, first, the confusion of the ontological status of the character with that of the reader; secondly, the decentring of that reader's consciousness, such that she or he is, like the character, endlessly displaced and 'differing'; and, thirdly, the political and ethical implications of this 'seeming otherwise', shifting from appearance to different appearance in the disappearance of a totalized selfhood. The reading subject in postmodern characterization is, thus, exactly like Kristeva's 'subject-in-process', a subject whose very subjectivity is itself endlessly deferred, endlessly differing. The explicit political dimension of reading postmodern characterization is now clear: it involves a marginalization of the reader from a centralized or totalized narrative of selfhood, thus rendering the reading subject-in-process as the figure of the *dissident*. Among her types of dissident, Kristeva locates both the experimental writer, working with the 'diaspora of those languages that pluralize meaning and cross all national and linguistic barriers', and, crucially, *women*: 'And sexual difference, women: isn't that another form of dissidence?' What these two groups share is the impetus towards marginalization and indefinition; they are in a condition of 'exile' from a centred identity of meaning and its claims to a totalized Law or Truth. And she writes: 'Our present age is one of exile. How can one avoid sinking into the mire of common sense, if not by becoming a stranger to one's own country, language, sex and identity? Writing is impossible without some kind of exile.'[41] Exile, further, is itself a form of dissidence, since it involves the marginalization or decentring of the self from all positions of totalized or systematic Law (such as imperialist nation, patriarchal family, monotheistic language), and 'if

[41] Julia Kristeva, *The Kristeva Reader*, ed. Toril Moi (Oxford: Blackwell, 1986), 299, 296, 298; cf. also Kristeva, *Étrangers à nous-mêmes* (Paris: Gallimard, 1988).

meaning exists in the state of exile, it nevertheless finds no incarnation, and is ceaselessly produced and destroyed in geographical or discursive transformations'.[42]

In the terms which concern us here, those of experimental writing, the major source of such exile and its consequential political disposition towards dissidence is in the questioning of the system of language itself (though, as is clear now, this is not easily to be distinguished from the concerns of empire, family, and so on). Postmodern characterization, construed as a writing in and from exile, serves to construct the possibility, for perhaps the first time, of elaborating the paradigmatic reader of these new novels as feminized. Woman, as 'that which cannot be represented, that which is not spoken, that which remains outside naming and ideologies',[43] is always 'dispositioned' towards otherness, alterity. To read postmodern characterization is thus to begin to construct the ethics of alterity, to replace a philosophy of Identity with that of Alterity, to discover what it means—without yet *representing* what it means—to speak always from the political disposition of the Other, and hence to find *presentation* as itself a disposition (mood, ethics) towards alterity.

[42] Kristeva, *Reader*, 298. [43] Ibid. 163.

3. *Agency and Understanding*

From the foregoing pages, it should be clear that we now have a significant problem in criticism and theory regarding the notion of agency. If it is the case that the subject of consciousness is 'humiliated', as I argued in Chapter 1; if, further, it is the case that the subject is oriented towards a loss of identity and an embrace of alterity as I indicated in Chapter 2; then it follows that we must have an extremely austere version of subjectivity. It would appear to be the case that the postmodern prioritizes the object over the subject, and that the subject orients herself or himself towards the Other as objects. One word for this, of course, is 'consumerism'; yet I would hold that in the sociology of consumerism we still have a philosophy of Identity at work, for the subject finds itself replicated in its objects, even if the possession of and by objects simply generates the desire for further consumption. We also have the disturbing issue, in a philosophy of radical alterity, that the subject of consciousness, in seeing the Other in the form of objects, has no capacity to attend to the possibility of the other as subject. In this, we would have an ethical problem, adverted to by Kant, in which it would appear to be impossible to distinguish seeing other humans as ends from seeing them as means to ends.

Rather than think this problem immediately in terms of a politics of consumerism (which I think is a premature formulation of the nature of the problem), I propose to think it as an issue of *agency*. How and on behalf of whom does the subject act; how does consciousness interact with its others; how can intentional agency—or authority—exercise itself as such? In brief, what is the nature of authority in a postmodern mood?

An important duality lies at the very heart of the concept of authority. The *OED* offers the following definition: authority is 'the power or right to enforce obedience'. For authority to exist or to take place, there must, therefore, be two poles: on the one hand, there is the force to be obeyed; on the other, the obedient follower of such a force. This makes it clear from the outset that authority is always of the nature of some kind of event 'in history', in that it does not depend upon one transcendent individual, but is always necessarily realized in a social and historical situation involving an ethical relation. It is never accurately considered in a simply positivist fashion, but is always marked by what Bakhtin, in his debate with the Formalists, described as the 'tactical'. Even if the term is given an explicitly metaphysical resonance, implying a divine Law, then still the effects of authority—and hence the possibility of its existence as event, fact, or concept—depend upon a recognition, in history, by others who will subject themselves to such a Law. *It is in history that authority authorizes itself as such.*

My contention here is that a modernist conception of authority, which has dominated most thinking on the matter since broadly 1500 in Western Europe, implies a resistance to precisely the historical situating which I claim is necessary and implicit in the structure of authority. More specifically, there has been a consistent negation of the possibility of *intellectual agency*: in an idealization of the issue of authority, consciousness has been denied access to the historical and has consequently been denied the possibility of agency. In Chapter 1 I indicated the contemporary legacy of this in Paul de Man; but I wish here to account for the prehistory of this state of affairs.

Despite the necessarily relational—'tactical'—structure of authority (its dependence upon two opposed and materially situated polarities), authority is aligned in modernist cultures with an ideology of individualism which is primarily dependent upon an illusory self-present subject of consciousness, and which is eventually dependent upon a theology or an idealist and positivist version of agency. Most commonly, theorists have considered the issue in terms of a theme of 'influence' between individuals, a theme articulated most powerfully in the work of Bloom.[1] According to this, either authority is a

[1] See e.g. Harold Bloom, *The Anxiety of Influence* (New York: Oxford University Press, 1973), *A Map of Misreading* (New York: Oxford University Press, 1975), *Poetry and Repression* (New Haven: Yale University Press, 1976), and *Agon* (New York: Oxford University Press, 1982). Prior to Bloom, the most succinct theoretical statement concerning the issue of such influence is Walter Jackson Bate, *The Burden of the Past and the English Poet* (London: Chatto & Windus, 1971). Frank Lentricchia, in *After The New Criticism* (1980; repr. London: Methuen, 1983), 283, asserts a more direct influence on Bloom in the figure of Paul de Man's essay 'Lyric and Modernity', initially delivered to the English Institute in 1969 (in *Blindness and Insight* (2nd edn.; London: Methuen, 1983)).

more or less amorphous power to which an individual is subjected and whose laws the individual corroborates through explicit recognition or repetition (such power may be that of a government, a dictator, an artist, etc; but the most important factor for present purposes is that it can always be *identified,* even if only vacuously as an 'ideology', say); or, authority is considered in terms of an individual's ability to circumvent such submission and to inaugurate a rival set of 'authoritative' or authorizing laws. This (essentially Said's formulations of the question in *Beginnings*) is a drastically limited and falsified manner of thinking the problem of intellectual agency. It enables authority to be thought of as something experienced in the first instance always 'privately', divorced from history and its things, as an element in what Althusser would have called the ISA, whereas in fact authority is predominantly an effect of the RSA.[2]

There are three sections to the argument of this chapter. In the first, I indicate how modernist thinking is and has been idealist on the issue of authority, and that it therefore constitutes a resistance to historical agency—indeed to history itself—both in authority and in our critical thinking about it. Secondly, I explore the construction of authority as a mode of *transgression,* which is explicitly or implicitly the model with which most contemporary theory works (i.e. that authority is 'critical' and authentic only to the extent that it transgresses against the obvious, the ideological, the 'given'); yet I shall show that in fact there is a resistance to transgression within this model as it stands, and hence a resistance to authority within authority. This is important for the simple fact that we too readily and prematurely identify 'criticism' with 'transgression' or 'opposition'; hence what is at issue in this argument is not only the very

[2] See Edward Said, *Beginnings* (New York: Basic Books, 1975), and his 'On Repetition', in *The World, the Text, the Critic* (London: Faber & Faber, 1984). For some interesting recent work on repetition, see Gilles Deleuze, *Différence et répétition* (Paris: PUF, 1968; repr. 1985), Jeffrey Mehlman, *Revolution and Repetition* (Berkeley and Los Angeles: University of California Press, 1977), and J. Hillis Miller, *Fiction and Repetition* (Oxford: Blackwell, 1982). See also Louis Althusser, *Essays on Ideology* (London: Verso, 1984), where the distinction is made between ISA and RSA. That distinction owes something to Gramsci's distinction between civil and political society; and the present chapter is more inclined to the Gramscian inflection than the Althusserian one.

possibility or otherwise of criticism, but also the possibility of historical agency on the part of the intellectual subject. Finally, I shall offer a model of postmodernism which will release the historicity of authority and avoid these tendencies to idealism and complicity with a dominant—uncritical, unreflective, anti-historical—ideology.

1. MODERNISM: THE NOMAD UNDER ARREST

At an early point in *Orientalism*, Said writes that:

> There is nothing mysterious or natural about authority. It is formed, irradiated, disseminated; it is instrumental, it is persuasive; it has status, it establishes canons of taste and value; it is virtually indistinguishable from certain ideas it dignifies as true, and from traditions, perceptions and judgments it forms, transmits, reproduces. Above all, authority can, indeed must, be analyzed.[3]

In one way, all that this says is that authority is ideological, institutionalized, forceful, and yet available for critique or for ideological unmasking. But Said's terms are most instructive. One vital component here to which I will return is that of authority establishing 'canons of taste and value', alongside its relation to acts of judgement and criticism. But what is immediately apparent is Said's denial of mystery to authority; in common with his work elsewhere, Said here wants to establish the secular credentials of authority. In the work of *Beginnings* which appears to be influenced by Kermode and Eliade, this takes the form of the distinction between 'origins' (which are sacred) and 'beginnings' (which are secular). Said's distinctions are important because the prevalent manner of thinking authority has been precisely ideological and metaphysical—though not for the reasons suggested by Said. Theory has approached authority in an idealist manner (thereby ruling immediately out of court any question of material agency), frequently ignoring the specificities of authorities in their distinct historical situations. In this respect authority has been treated in much the same way as Foucault's 'power'. Foucault

[3] Edward Said, *Orientalism* (London: Routledge & Kegan Paul, 1978), 19–20.

himself always insisted on the necessity of analysing specific incidences of power to note the different ways in which powers could be articulated and resisted; but much *soi-disant* Foucauldian practice has been satisfied too easily by treating power as if it were some homogeneous, if slightly amorphous, entity, thus effectively collapsing all heterogeneous powers into the same mythic form, usually that of 'oppression'.

The distinction wanted by Foucault for power (and which I am stressing for authority), a distinction between heterogeneous specificity or singularity and the homogeneity of generalization, has occurred before in theory. Bakhtin, for instance, attacked the Formalists in similar terms. In order to authorize *ostranenie* and *literaturnost* as guiding principles, the Formalists had to construct a model of 'ordinary language' against which the autonomy of the aesthetic function could be asserted. This was fine, apart from the fact that, as Bakhtin indicated, their view of ordinary language was a fictional—even false—constructed hypothesis which bore no relation tothe specific and real conditions of how language worked in historical fact. Such conditions, of course, involved what Bakhtin called 'speech tact', a tact which acknowledges the real conditions of acts of communication in all their singular specificity:

Speech tact has a practical importance for practical language communication. The formative and organizing force of speech tact is very great. It gives form to everyday utterances, determining the genre and style of speech performances. Here tact [*taktichnost*] should be understood in a broad sense, with politeness as only one of its aspects. Tact may have various directions, moving between the two poles of compliment and curse. Speech tact is determined by the aggregate of all the social relationships of the speakers, their ideological horizons, and, finally, the concrete situation of the conversation. Tact, whatever its form under the given conditions, determines all of our utterances. No word lacks tact.[4]

[4] Mikhail Bakhtin and P. N. Medvedev, *The Formal Method in Literary Scholarship* (trans. A. J. Wehrle; Cambridge, Mass.: Harvard University Press, 1985), 95. By analogy with this argument, one might veer towards the kinds of propositions advanced by the later Baudrillard, that Marxism authorizes capital. See, in this regard, Jean Baudrillard, *Simulations* (trans. Paul Foss, Paul Patton, and Phillip Beitchman; New York: Semiotext(e), 1983), 36–7; and cf. my comments on this in my study *After Theory* (London: Routledge, 1990), ch. 9.

Hence the historical dialogicity of all language and all communication; hence also the necessity for attention to the singularity of each instant of such communication, for different instants will determine different enactments of this 'tact'. Authority has too often been analysed in the 'Formalist' mode, as some pure effect of the 'who is speaking':[5] that is, it has always been seen from the idealist position of the speaker/writer in monological isolation, and, as a result, authority has been idealized as an effect of an individual. The further consequence of this has been a simplistic 'juridical' theorization of agency: not the effect of 'who is speaking', but the effect of 'who is guilty or responsible', as if judgements regarding actions could be simply isolated from the historical situation determining those actions.

This situation obviously obtains in the kind of intentionalist theory of literary criticism advocated by Hirsch; but it is also the case in many modes of reader-response criticism (as in the early Fish, Iser, Jauss, or, most extremely, Bleich).[6] What makes both the intentionalist and reader-centred positions idealist is, finally, the (quasi-juridical) *identification* of authority: authority is located in a single proper name, distinguished from all other interfering historical factors. We are condemned in this thinking to work with that version of the word which Vico derived from the authority of etymology when he suggested that 'authority' was fundamentally a question of 'property'; and in a modern capitalist situation, this means that authority is a question of the individual, the owner of an action, she or he who 'owns' and 'owns up' to her or his commitments. In turn, such commitments or 'actions' are then seen as determinant of the character of the individual. The result is the impasse of existentialism, about which more later.

[5] The most sophisticated version of this is to be found in Roland Barthes's essay on 'The Death of the Author', in *Image–Music–Text* (ed. and trans. Stephen Heath; Glasgow: Fontana, 1977), 142.

[6] See e.g. E. D. Hirsch, *Validity in Interpretation* (New Haven: Yale University Press, 1967); Stanley Fish, *Self-Consuming Artifacts* (Berkeley and Los Angeles: California University Press, 1972), *Is There a Text in this Class?* (Cambridge, Mass.: Harvard University Press, 1980); Wolfgang Iser, *The Implied Reader* (Baltimore: Johns Hopkins University Press, 1974); Hans Robert Jauss, *Toward an Aesthetic of Reception* (trans. Timothy Bahti; Brighton: Harvester, 1982); David Bleich, *Subjective Criticism* (Baltimore: Johns Hopkins University Press, 1978).

Authority, however, like speech, never happens in a void. It is always inherently 'tactful', 'tactical': dialogical (to the point of being 'tactile' in some instances). It is thoroughly determined by a socio-historical situation which far exceeds the capacity of any individual consciousness (writer's or reader's; law-giver's or law-obeyer's) for intentionality or substance. It is thus a mistake to adopt an intentionalist position which ascribes a specific name to a specific authority or act. Authority—and (by now it should also be clear) judging and *justice*—is not a matter of individual intention, but is rather an effect of the interplay of various intentionalities.

Hartman proposed something close to this in *The Fate of Reading*, where he contemplated authority in terms of the issue of the 'exemplary text':

> it is hard to conceive of a literary reader who is not immersed in the search for an exemplary text: a text to be used against the wastefulness of living without concentration, or a text to support by one's life, given the need. So at the end of Ray Bradbury's *Fahrenheit 451* (as filmed by Truffaut) each exile from the book-burning state adopts the name of a text he has learnt by heart and which he represents: one person is now called *David Copperfield*, another *Emile*, or even *Paradise Lost* . . . The extinction in this symbolic situation of the personal names of *both* author and reader shows what ideally happens in the act of reading: if there is a sacrifice to the exemplary, it involves the aggrandizement neither of author nor of reader but leads into the recognition that something worthy of perpetuation has occurred.[7]

Once more, we hear in this a beginning modernism: Flaubert's 'Madame Bovary, c'est moi'; but 'moi' is also a deictic, shifting its value depending on the subject of its enunciation. This drive to the extinction of the proper personal name acknowledges the real relations between those who exert authority and those subjected to it. What is at stake is a transpersonal articulation of a play of forces which we call 'authoritative' and which tend to be located in the stronger or (logically and/or temporally) 'prior' force. For Hartman (as, indeed, for the American New Critics in their theorizing of the 1940s and 1950s), the transpersonal authority ('this thing that's bigger than both of us' as it

[7] Geoffrey Hartman, *The Fate of Reading* (Chicago: University of Chicago Press, 1975), 255.

were) is the authority of the text. Yet this too is still not counter-idealist enough, for in the case of Hartman, the intension of the text, *its* intentionality, becomes a determining and *originary* authority. It is precisely such a notion of the originary authority that constitutes the idealist falsification of the problem.

Given the simple fact that authority is an effect of history, that is, that authority is produced as a result of the socio-historical relations between two or more forces which are *a posteriori* assigned positions as 'author' and 'reader' (or, in wider terms, authority and its subjects, origin and derivation), it follows that there can be no originary moment of authority which simply subtends or effects a historical situation in the way that Hartman and other latently idealist critics require. In every case, authority is made into a 'property' which can be assigned (to) a proper name which appropriates it. It is this manœuvre—the construction, identification, and characterization of a single authorizing source or intention—which constitutes the fabrication deployed to maintain an implicitly idealist version of authority, an authority of origins rather than of beginnings or situations, an authority which bears no relation to the real state of historical affairs in which or through which authority and agency are produced.

Given the status of the text as a dialogical formation, the authority inscribed in it is intrinsically multiple and self-transforming; it is a multiplication of singularities; it is subject to modification or even substantial change depending upon the different socio-historical situations in which the text is articulated, enacted, produced, or—more simply—*understood*. That is a truism, of course. But it is this undecidability of the text, its 'nomadicity' as it wanders towards the occupation of a temporary stability (called 'understanding'), which the ascription of a proper name as its guiding authority arrests.[8] The manœuvre by which the nomadic text is arrested also serves the function, then, of making the text seemingly available to and for the understanding or consciousness. At least temporarily, it arrests the text and offers a *point de repère* from which a reader can identify herself or himself in an act of intellectual apprehen-

[8] The idea of nomadicity is here derived from the thinking of Gilles Deleuze and Felix Guattari in *A Thousand Plateaus* (trans. Brian Massumi; Minneapolis: University of Minnesota Press, 1987), esp. § 12.

sion, and can thus identify herself or himself as an authoritative agent or subject of consciousness even in the very instant in which she or he is subjected to the authority of the text. In short, the manœuvre is one which repeats the ideological interpellation of the subject as delineated by Althusser; any such reading, critical or unreflective, is caught in ideology and idealism precisely at the moment when it thinks it is free and 'authoritative' or self-determining.

The fact that we attribute a proper name or other designation of identity to an authority is indication enough that authority becomes a matter of 'distinction'; and, as Bourdieu has shown, acts of distinction such as this are never innocent. Bourdieu traces the way in which distinctions, especially aesthetic distinctions or matters of taste, serve the function of demarcating the social class of the individual who makes the discriminations. Until Bourdieu, 'no voice is heard pointing out that the definition of art, and through it the art of living, is an object of struggle among the classes'.[9] Ferry would corroborate this to some extent, though without the same notions of distinctions among social classes; rather, Ferry links the history of taste and its occasional revolutions to the history of forms of democracy and their intrinsic individualisms in the modern and postmodern worlds.[10]

In both instances, it is the authority given to works of art that is at issue. For Bourdieu, as for Lyotard, there is a close relation of analogy between the aesthetic and political dispositions, and acts of distinction are important in both. Here is where Said's idea of authority as something instrumental in the formation of 'canons of taste' has a greater purchase and specificity. Bourdieu argues that taste is affirmed through negation, through the refusal of other competing tastes as 'disgusting'. He writes:

> The most intolerable thing for those who regard themselves as the possessors of legitimate culture is the sacrilegious reuniting of tastes which taste dictates shall be separated. This means that the games of artists and aesthetes and their struggles for the monopoly of artistic legitimacy are less innocent than they seem. At stake in every struggle over art there is also the imposition of an art of living, that is, the

[9] Pierre Bourdieu, *Distinction* (trans. Richard Nice; London: Routledge & Kegan Paul, 1984), 48.

[10] See Luc Ferry, *Homo Aestheticus* (Paris: Grasset, 1990).

transmutation of an arbitrary way of living into the legitimate way of life which casts every other way of living into arbitrariness.[11]

Taste, the act of distinction which identifies an authority, is no mere aesthetic factor, but one which involves the formulation of socio-cultural distinctions, authorities, and hence one which also enables the possibility of legitimate agency for the subject. Further, the activity we call 'understanding' (and which is actually, as I have argued, merely ideological interpellation) lies behind the strategies which enable such 'taste' to become normative, institutionalized, and thus vested with a weight of authority which far exceeds the capacity of the individual bearer of taste. For in this case, the individual is aligned with a class or with an institution which validates her or his activity and agency and which grants her or him authority as the representative of that class or institution.

This is nowhere more the case than in the incidence of what I will call the 'parasitic citation', an appeal to some prior authority whose function is to invest the present speaker with the weight of history and tradition as vested in the prior authority, and also consequently with the similar status of an authority in her or his own right, as she or he becomes the representative not of themselves as individuals but rather of the *institutionally agreed* force of taste and, *ipso facto*, correctness and legitimacy. In this mode of citation, the present speaker identifies herself or himself closely with (in fact, identifies herself or himself *as*) the prior author, speaking the words of the prior author as if they were her or his own: e.g. 'I think it was Schiller (or X, Y, or Z) who once remarked that . . .', etc. (a kind of remark not usually precisely footnoted). When citations are attributed, we have the same situation. To demonstrate the point, I shall do it myself and cite Bourdieu:

A practical mastery of social significance, based on functional and structural homology, underlies and facilitates everyday reading of the 'classics', and, even more, since it is a practical use, literary quotation, a quite special use of discourse which is a sort of summons to appear as advocate and witness, addressed to a past author on the basis of a social solidarity disguised as intellectual solidarity. The practical sense of meaning, which stops short of objectifying the social affinity

[11] Bourdieu, *Distinction*, 56–7.

which makes it possible—since that would nullify the desired effect, by relativizing both the reading and the text—provides simultaneously a social use and a denial of the social basis of that use.[12]

Institutional authority, it follows from this, depends upon a self-contradictory notion of distinction. To be an author, one must distinguish oneself from those who merely obey and reiterate some already existing authority: one must be 'nonconformist'. Yet this distinction also involves an affiliation—more importantly, an identification—of the self with a class or institutional force; hence the extreme delimitation of distinction at the same time. Because one has more than an ethical disposition towards an Other, and instead *identifies* the Other with the self, distinction is eradicated even as it is being produced. In social terms, at least as these relate to questions of general cultural practice, this formulation of authority, vested in the names of certain authors, depends most immediately upon the class affiliations of those involved in acts of canon-formation, which is, of course, nothing more or less than parasitic citation writ large. To act in relation to such grand-scale parasitic citation is to delimit very circumstantially the possibilities of human agency: only those actions seen to conform with the norms of a canon are legitimate.

In the formulation of authority which comes in canon-formation, or in any such form of institutionalized authority, we have an exemplification of the very essentialism of authority which circumvents history: authority as transcendent Law. Those involved in such institutionalization of authority, as in the example of university literary canon-formation, say, pretend to be involved in a critical understanding of certain texts. In fact, of course, what happens is slightly different. A group shares certain class values, and then pretends that according to their understanding of specific texts those values are validated by the texts which are deemed to 'contain' those values. Their understanding, of course, is one which depends upon the ideological interpellation by which they recognize themselves and their values not in the texts as such but in what they call their understanding of the texts' real meaning and value. *Anagnorisis* constructs agency, in a word. The texts are thus vested with

[12] Ibid. 73.

authority as the bearers of such values. Axiomatically, of course, the group defines its own understanding of the texts as valid and legitimate, rejecting competing possible understandings as tasteless, disgusting misreadings, which simply show not the fallibility of their own judgements but rather the lack of proper understanding and acknowledgement of authority on the part of other tasteless readers (who, clearly, subscribe to different social norms and practices). This—the examination system which dominates education—is the manifestation of an aristocracy of culture, as Bourdieu calls it, an aristocracy which is profoundly essentialist:

> the holders of titles of cultural nobility—like the titular members of an aristocracy, whose 'being', defined by their fidelity to a lineage, an estate, a race, a past, a fatherland or a tradition, is irreducible to any 'doing', to any know-how or function—only have to be what they are, because all their practices derive their value from their authors, being the affirmation and perpetuation of the essence by virtue of which they are performed . . . Aristocracies are essentialist . . . The essence in which they see themselves refuses to be contained in any definition. Escaping petty rules and regulations, it is, by nature, freedom.[13]

This 'aristocracy', then, in its essentialism, is precisely the police who arrest the nomads. By this I mean to suggest that it is the very institutionalization of authority, constitutive of an aristocracy of culture, which serves to fix and identify authority automatically (though ideologically), and to lead to an idealist and anti-historical (essentialist) construction of authority. Those who would be 'free agents' under this (modernist) system of thought must subscribe to such authority; but this, of course, in its essentialism, is precisely the counter to any more genuinely emancipatory deployment or articulation of authority or agency on behalf of the subject who would be critical.[14] The parasitic aristocracy looks both ways: back to prior authors whom they claim as their 'legislators' (and whom they edit, pretending to know their work better than the authors knew it

[13] Ibid. 23–4.

[14] It would also be true to suggest that this affects the issue of postcolonial theory, in which the pedagogical formation of subjected peoples, and the consequent reactions to this, are increasingly important. For a fuller exploration of the theoretical issues involved in this area, see Homi K. Bhabha, *The Location of Culture* (London: Routledge, 1994).

themselves); and forward to those who will be subject to their legislation, the other 'disgusting' classes whose taste requires correction or, as we more frequently call it, education. Such education is nothing more or less than the policing of a thought which might threaten to proceed beyond the bounds controlled by the aristocracy of culture. The aristocracy, then, identify themselves firmly with and as the legislators of taste, value, legitimate cultural authority, and legitimate political agency. The essentialism of this aristocracy—its closed nature, and the fact that it is unanswerable to anything outside its own ideological formation and values—is instrumental in the denial of history, a denial of the possibility of historical change. Certain institutions of learning acquire part of their authority from tradition, that is, from the fact that they are five hundred or so years old; but some universities have *always* been, and always will be, 'five hundred years old': their authority is vested in tradition or heritage, but not in history, and their function is to control political agency.

2. UNDERSTANDING: AUTHORITY AS TRANSGRESSION

Before considering the dominant critical notion of authority as a mode of transgressive agency, it is first of all important to engage more fully the issue of understanding itself. I have been arguing so far that authority is in fact 'unnameable', and that attempts to identify it are complicit with an ideological falsification of the concept of authority, a falsification constructive of an aristocracy of culture with its corollary of class-oppressions. It is empirically as well as theoretically obvious that, in any act of communication, there is a tendency for authorities to proliferate, because of the conditions of the dialogicity of linguistic acts. One text is the site of innumerable dialogic situations which far exceed the capacity of any individual's intentionality. One text is a point from which there proceed innumerable 'lines of flight' or deterritorializations, as Deleuze would call them. Were this to be acknowledged, however, it would present a threat to the aristocracy of culture and its basis in two kinds of property: the wealth of commodities (including artworks) and educational capital (discourse and its mediation) manifested in the aristocracy's self-assured 'understanding' of the works and worlds which it owns. Property and understanding, then, are *both* modes of capital. Further, while capital thrives on exchange, its ideology depends upon a resistance to the critical agency which could effect real or substantial historical change. As Althusser argued, citing Marx: 'every child knows that a social formation which did not reproduce the conditions of production at the same time as it produced would not last a year. The ultimate condition of production is therefore the reproduction of the conditions of production.'[15] The resistance to history and agency which informs our prevalent idealist, positivist, and essentialist notion of authority, and which sustains a culture policed by an essentialist aristocracy, covers a more basic problem. That problem is the negation of history in understanding itself, an attitude sustained by what should be called an 'imperialism of understanding'.

Understanding—as we understand it—is fundamentally an act of intellectual appropriation. There is a phenomenological situation in which a subject of consciousness comes to inhabit a position from which the text makes sense, and thus she or he gains an 'authoritative' understanding of the text. 'Understanding' is, of course, in these terms really 'over-coming', mastering a text or controlling a situation through the relation to the text. In it, the subject identifies itself, as a subject of consciousness, with the immediate (unmediated) substance of its thought; it thus *recognizes* itself in a moment which is called free apprehension but which is actually the *anagnorisis* constitutive of ideological interpellation. More generally, to understand an enigma, one goes through certain moves. First, one recognizes it as an enigma because the language in which it is formulated does not immediately conform to the language in which we 'ordinarily' think. Secondly, one effects a translation so that the language in which the enigma is articulated is translated into something already known and recognizable within the rules and tenets of the language in which we formulate ourselves as authoritative subjects of consciousness. In this way, the alterity of the world is reduced to identity: consciousness expands to grasp that which was foreign or alien. Alterity is

[15] Althusser, *Essays on Ideology*, 1.

reduced to homogeneity: the world is not unknown, it is simply that which we have forgotten or repressed, which understanding will bring back into the light of self-evidence. The world becomes the unconscious of a subject whose act of understanding involves a colonization of the space of alterity and the collapsing of that complex and three-dimensional space into the narrow but reassuring confines of the two-dimensional and stereotypical mirror. It is in these terms, of course, that we 'understand' literary and other texts. We translate Chaucer into modern English; we translate the problems presented by that text called 'Shakespeare' into terms, values, categories—even dress—which we can at least recognizably comprehend. As Said has indicated, we 'understand' the pluralities of the Arab world by collapsing it into a myth in which we see the undesired face of the American; and so on.[16] In theoretical terms, the name for this procedure is that of Stanley Fish. According to Fish's later 'neo-pragmatist' thinking, it is impossible to step outside the programmatic habits of our located consciousness: we make the critical pronouncements we do simply because we are who we are; those pronouncements are what makes us who we are, what gives us our identity. Such neo-pragmatism, clearly, offers no threat to the aristocracy of culture, for its procedures and theoretical impetus share the same underlying philosophy of identity. In Fish's case, the identity in question is that of Fish himself; in the case of Rorty, the identity in question is that of the 'north Atlantic bourgeois democracies' or, in some more specific cases, 'America' or a nameable ethnic group.[17]

In every case of such understanding, there is an exercise in cartography. An alien terrain is redrawn as part of an extended 'home' terrain. The alterity constitutive of the world becomes merely a Lacanian Imaginary for the subject, who can then think the world as her or his unconscious. A simple act of

[16] See Said, *Orientalism*, and *Covering Islam* (London: Routledge & Kegan Paul, 1985). Said explicated this point further in direct relation to American foreign policy on the Iraqi Gulf crisis which 'started'—if we ignore its prehistory—on 2 August 1990 when he discussed the matter with Michael Ignatieff on BBC2's *Late Show* transmitted on 6 September 1990.

[17] See Stanley Fish, *Doing What Comes Naturally* (New York: Oxford University Press, 1992), and *There's No Such Thing as Free Speech* (New York: Oxford University Press, 1994); Richard Rorty, *Contingency, Solidarity, Irony* (Cambridge: Cambridge University Press, 1990).

bringing the Other into linguistic formulation confirms it as the mirror of the subject, who thus expands her or his consciousness by appropriating its Other. 'Understanding' a text, then, implies the drawing of a strictly policed boundary within which we can either agree or disagree with the 'author' of the text under discussion. But the crucial point is that the *parameters* of agreement and discord have already been fixed through the imperialism we call understanding. Such understanding is an act complicit with the aristocracy of culture and its falsifications and idealist non-historical tendencies.

Yet this is what modernity calls 'reason'; and the aristocracy of culture (not to mention Fish or Rorty) professes itself reasonable. As part of Enlightenment (Habermas's 'project of modernity'),[18] we ascribe authority to reason itself (and hence identify it, homogenize it). But there is, clearly, an aristocracy of reason which formulates itself in exactly the same 'distinctive' way as the aristocracy of culture. Such neo-Cartesian, 'self-evident' reason is one which arrests intellection, and which becomes fundamentally essentialist and class based; and, as Baudrillard has it, 'les masses font masse'.[19] Class reason provides the brake upon the authority of reason even as it formulates itself. Once more, this 'free' exercise of reason is not at all free but is rather predetermined and constrained in advance by class (and other) interests. This mode of reasoning is what Kant called 'determining judgement', a mode of thought which would have its basis in 'theory' as we would now call it (intrinsic rules of judgement, regulatory presiding questions, and so on). Its claims to a free objectivity are, however, contradicted by its inherent dependence upon a will which is introduced into reason and which perverts its free operations. There is, in short, a resistance to reason within the very Enlightenment reason that explains and underpins our 'understanding'.[20]

[18] See Jürgen Habermas, 'Modernity—an Incomplete Project', repr. in Thomas Docherty (ed.), *Postmodernism: A Reader* (Hemel Hempstead: Harvester-Wheatsheaf, 1993), and Habermas, *The Philosophical Discourse of Modernity* (trans. Frederick Lawrence; Cambridge: Polity, 1987).

[19] See Jean Baudrillard, *In The Shadow of the Silent Majorities* (trans. Paul Foss, Paul Patton, and John Johnson; New York: Semiotext(e), 1983), 1–2.

[20] See Jean-François Lyotard, 'Svelte Appendix to the Postmodern Question' (trans. Thomas Docherty), in Richard Kearney (ed.), *Across the Frontiers* (Dublin:

This mode of rationality, then, whose inherent imperialism of understanding renders alterity available for comprehension in terms which produce only the dialectic of mastery and slavery such that knowledge is always necessarily imbricated with power, might be countered by a different order of reason. A modernist rationality, contaminated by the introduction of the will into reason, leads only to the solace of a comforting imperialism of understanding in which the subject knows herself or himself to be axiomatically (or, we might now say, 'aristocratically') correct and tasteful in her or his judgements, both aesthetic and political. The counter to this would be an order of reason which eschews the world as Imaginary, and which prefers a Levinasian concern for the maintenance of alterity as alterity. Bachelard argued in quasi-Nietzschean fashion that 'One must return to human rationality its function as a force for turbulence and aggression. In this way sur-rationalism will be established, and this will multiply the occasions for thought.'[21] So, instead of there being a will to conformity in reason, a will which reduces the world to the known but merely forgotten part of the subject's identity and self-presence, we might have a contrary movement wherein there lies the possibility of a mode of agency or authority based upon a specific kind of transgression: a transgression against the very identity of the subject herself or himself. This would entail a situation which would transgress against 'understanding'. The subject of consciousness and thought itself would have to be separated such that it would become possible to think without mastery, to know without power.

But modernist authority is already, as I remarked, founded in transgression. Authority is linked in modernity to novelty, to what Said thinks as a 'heresy' or proposal of alternative beginnings to the narratives we live by. In order to be an author in modernity, one must do something avowedly 'new'; in order to be new, it must be in contradistinction to prevailing norms. Three things follow. First, such authority depends upon

Wolfhound Press, 1988), 263–7, in which Lyotard indicates that what is at issue in the debate he has with Habermas is not reason itself but the introduction of the will into reason, an introduction which is latent in Enlightenment philosophies.

[21] Gaston Bachelard, as cited by Said in *Beginnings*, 40. See also Séan Hand (ed.), *The Levinas Reader* (Oxford: Basil Blackwell, 1989).

distinction. Secondly, to be an author one must hypothesize a prior system of laws in the area in which one wants authority. Thirdly, once this hypothetical system is in place, one must intervene with some violation or transgression of its norms or laws. I set this out as if it were diachronic, but in fact it is synchronic: the three moves occur simultaneously, and their effect is the production of authority, of a position in which a subject claims the mastery of understanding/overcoming.

The synchronicity of this is important. The authority or law against which one will transgress is actually produced coterminously with one's own transgressive intervention. Both the new and the prevailing authorities are effected at once. But this means that the prior law is a hypothetical construction whose formation is deployed in the interests of a particular set of present requirements. When, for instance, one attacks 'the entire history of Western philosophy' in the name of something called, say, deconstruction or feminism, it is important to realize that this 'entire history of Western philosophy' proposed as the counter to or enemy of deconstruction or feminism does not exist as such until deconstruction or feminism has formulated and characterized it in the particular way which will enable Derrida or Irigaray (say) to distinguish themselves from it. 'The entire history of Western philosophy', thus, is a myth constructed for the sake of a particular authority; and, in turn, that authority is also, and equally, 'mythic'.

Two questions now propose themselves. In the first place, the hypothetical law against which I will transgress in becoming an author itself determines and constructs the possibility of this transgression, whose nature is thus drastically limited: the 'new' authority is predetermined and thus not very new at all. Secondly, something else now appears as a more primary determinant of authoritative agency, for it appears that my hypothetical prior law is constructed according to the requirements of a particular programme which states that, if I want to perform a particular action, then I shall have to construct an authority-model whose transgression will inexorably demand or at least enable that action to take place in a valid and legitimate manner. I shall deal with these two issues separately.

To be an author, I must consciously transgress against a prevailing law.[22] But this means that I must already understand that law. 'My' authority sets up the law against which I transgress; and it is *according to those laws* that my action is deemed to be transgressive. That is to say, the possibility of my transgression is written into the construction of this prior law or authority. Thus it is a transgression which, far from denying or negating that law, serves simply to corroborate it as a law, norm, or authority; and, by extension, to place me in the position of the renegade, the outlaw, the unconventional eccentric: the critic. But it is now apparent that this 'criticism' is hardly a differential serious or radical kind of criticism, if it implicitly serves to consolidate the very laws it aims to attack.

In the case of the second problem, that of there being some more primary drive to authority in my actions, we have a slightly different issue. If it is the case that my transgressive act is itself predetermined, then one has to ask from where does the decision to transgress come in the first place? What is it that wants to perform the particular action which my authoritative intervention enables? Here, we find the crux of the modernist problem of authority. For if I suggest anything to fill in this blank originary space (be it instinct, ethics, social demand, ideology, neurosis, biology, or whatever), then all I do is to repeat the first problem in a slightly different place, for I would then be forced to hypothesize a model of the authority of instinct, ideology, or whatever fills my originary space. It is this very demand for the location and *identification* of a source for authority that is the problem: it is a theological (or at least idealist) impetus which remains within so-called secular modernist or enlightened thinking. In Said's terms, it is the demand for an origin rather than a beginning. We

[22] Strictly speaking, the unconscious is not really admissible here. The issue is complicated by the reception of a transgression, itself of course to be transgressed if it is to become the source of an authority. Relevant examples would include the effects to which Nietzsche's writings were put by the Nazis or other later agents, or indeed the effects to which Enlightenment's instrumental forms of reason were put (on which see Zygmunt Bauman, *Modernity and the Holocaust* (Cambridge: Polity, 1989)). Other examples might be the controversies surrounding de Man and Heidegger in recent years. To what extent is an author responsible to or answerable for events which could not be in their consciousness?

should, therefore, simply junk the problem. After Wittgenstein, it should be clear that I do not know what I mean (and that I do not therefore know what 'I' means) until I have said it: my actions are necessarily undirected, experimental, 'avant-garde' in the sense of being 'untimely'. Their meaning, as they say, is not present to themselves. To pretend otherwise is to remain within the falsification and self-contradiction of modernity, whose secularism is here contaminated still by a residue of idealism and positivism. It is also to remain in the situation where authority is marked by 'ownership' ('my' meaning, 'my' text, and so on), and which falls into a Lockian politics where the right to a voice is given through the control of property or capital.

A modernist version of authority, which is determined to make meaning present-to-something, usually a proper name (of text or writer), is, in fact, a therapeutic inoculation against the seizure of authority and against the genuinely historical act or agency. It is an inoculation against the historicity of meaning with its drives towards deterritorialization, anonymity, and the untimeliness and 'impropriety' of the avant-garde. Modernist authority is, to borrow Baudrillard's term, a 'scenario of deterrence',[23] and what it wishes to deter—like capital and its aristocracies of culture—is the very possibility of history, mutability, and the concomitant threats posed to a social formation and a philosophy in which this aristocracy remains in explicit control and in which 'criticism' is locked away in that space reserved for dissidents: the institutions of the academy. In short, what is deterred is the possibility of consciousness being active, of intellection being itself an agent of change. In this respect, authority—which appears to involve a specifically historical intervention on the part of an author—is precisely the scandal which preserves laws, norms, and a principle of reality which is presented as fundamentally idealist and essentialist. If one task of Marxism was to get history started, we might add that one task of the postmodern is to get historical criticism—intellectual agency—started.

[23] Baudrillard, *Simulations*, 36.

3. REFLECTIVE AGENCY

Jameson writes of the 'effacement' in postmodernism of some 'key boundaries or separations, most notably the erosion of the older distinction between high culture and so-called mass or popular culture'. He goes on, in terms which should be placed alongside Bourdieu and Ferry, to suggest that:

> This is perhaps the most distressing development of all from an academic standpoint, which has traditionally had a vested interest in preserving a realm of high or elite culture against the surrounding environment of philistinism, of schlock and kitsch, of TV series and *Reader's Digest* culture, and in transmitting difficult and complex skills of reading, listening and seeing to its initiates. But many of the newer postmodernisms have been fascinated precisely by that whole landscape of advertising and motels, of the Las Vegas strip, of the late show and Grade-B Hollywood film, of so-called paraliterature with its airport paperback categories of the gothic and the romance, the popular biography, the murder mystery and the science fiction or fantasy novel. They no longer 'quote' such 'texts' as Joyce might have done, or a Mahler: they incorporate them, to the point where the line between high art and commercial forms seems increasingly difficult to draw.[24]

This, to rephrase it in Bourdieu's terms, is just that taste which reveals itself as 'bad taste' because it mingles tastes to the point of indistinction. It is also the taste which thereby threatens socio-political 'identity', the class-identities which depend upon the formation of an aristocracy of culture and of a 'proletariat' or those excluded from such an aristocracy.

If we begin from Jameson, we can see how postmodernism might help reinstate historicity to authority and thus restore the possibility of intellectual agency.[25] The *mélange* of tastes, the eclecticism, of postmodernism leads to an inherent tendency in the postmodern work to deterritorialization and immaterialization. For perhaps the first time, aligning oneself with a taste—for the postmodern—is not the articulation of a clearly

[24] Fredric Jameson, 'Postmodernism and Consumer Society', in Hal Foster (ed.), *Postmodern Culture* (London: Pluto Press, 1983), 112.

[25] But see Jameson's comments on the weakening of historicity in a later version of 'Postmodernism and Consumer Society', the much-cited 'Postmodernism: or, the Cultural Logic of Late Capitalism', in Docherty (ed.), *Postmodernism: A Reader*.

defined class position. On the contrary, it implies a refusal of any such clear, stable identification. There is no stable terrain from which or into which a colonizing act of imperialist understanding can take place; nor is there any 'essential' work, any 'essence' of a work, to be understood in the first place. In a particular sense, *the postmodern is not available for understanding*, at least in so far as understanding is actually the drive to mastery, to 'overcoming'.[26]

The modernist deployment of taste is instrumental in the legitimation of certain socio-political positions: it proposes that the knowledge invested in aesthetic and political practices by a specific group, the aristocracy of culture, is normative. But something happens to knowledge (to consciousness-as-agency) in the postmodern which makes such legitimation and normativity impossible.

Kroker and Cook, in *The Postmodern Scene*, describe postmodernity as 'the quantum age', one in which a Virilian 'hyper-speed' problematizes what we think of as normal epistemological procedures: 'If the Newtonian law of gravity could postulate a *real* body whose objectivity is established by its mass, the (quantum) law of postmodernity eclipses this body by flipping suddenly from mass to energy.'[27] This description of a slippage from mass to energy is a recurring figure in many descriptions which strive to explain the elusiveness, the svelte lissom nature of the postmodern. Lyotard thinks it in terms of the growing 'immaterialization' of culture; Virilio thinks it in terms of the effect of speed in technology and communications; Deleuze in terms of a Bergsonian inner temporality or historicity of what appears superficially to be a stable mass; Baudrillard in terms of the evasion of the masses and the questioning and problematization of the entire principle of reality through the parodic simulacrum. A formulation of the same effect in specifically literary matters might be the suggestion of MacHale, that postmodernist fiction is a fiction

[26] For a fuller elaboration of this argument, see my *After Theory*. On understanding as mastery and its consequent complications, see Barbara Johnson, 'The Frame of Reference', in her *The Critical Difference* (Baltimore: Johns Hopkins University Press, 1985).

[27] Arthur Kroker and David Cook, *The Postmodern Scene* (London: Macmillan, 1988), p. v.

which prioritizes ontology over epistemology, in a reversal of the modernist structure of relative priorities.[28]

There is something to all this. Lyotard describes the postmodern (seemingly paradoxically) as that which comes before the modern, as the founding condition of the possibility of being modern in the first place. The classic formulation of this is in terms of a future anteriority which is deemed the proper tense of the postmodern:

A postmodern artist or writer is in the position of a philosopher: the text he writes, the work he produces are not in principle governed by preestablished rules, and they cannot be judged according to a determining judgment, by applying familiar categories to the text or to the work. Those rules and categories are what the work of art itself is looking for. The artist and the writer, then, are working without rules in order to formulate the rules of what *will have been done*. Hence the fact that work and text have the characters of an *event*; hence also, they always come too late for their author, or, what amounts to the same thing, their being put into work, their realization (*mise en œuvre*) always begins too soon. *Post modern* would have to be understood according to the paradox of the future (*post*) anterior (*modo*).[29]

This can be briefly explained. The postmodern is the exercise of something rather like a Kantian 'reflective judgement', as opposed to a 'determining judgement'. In the latter, the subject of consciousness has merely to conform to some overarching theory or set of prescriptions which will tell her or him how to judge correctly (legitimately) in a particular case. The postmodern works without such rules or theory, experimentally: it is energetic, undirected, unprogrammed—and hence it lacks any *identifiable* authority. The modern is the moment in which this radical energy reifies in a work/object, which can then become a commodity, available for analysis and imitation. The 'event' that is the postmodern becomes the 'work' that is modern if and only if it begins to 'faire masse', to become massive, stable; and such massification arises from modernist critical claims to understand the work. Should this happen, the historicity

[28] See e.g. Brian MacHale, *Postmodernist Fiction* (London: Methuen, 1987); Paul Virilio, *L'Horizon négatif* (Paris: Galilée, 1984); and the works of Deleuze, Lyotard, Baudrillard.

[29] Jean-François Lyotard, *The Postmodern Condition* (trans. Geoffrey Bennington and Brian Massumi; Manchester: Manchester University Press, 1984), 81.

inscribed in the postmodernity is drained, as the event is given a location in space and time which can be identified and referred to, and, ultimately, made available for knowledge, for understanding/overcoming and the 'authority' that comes with it. The fundamental opposition, thus, is between what I'll call the 'eventual' (which is postmodern, full of historicity) and the 'punctual' (which is modern, and is an identifiable location which literally 'roots' the postmodern, gives it 'a local habitation and a name', allows it to form an earth).

This postmodern is 'avant-garde' in the sense that it provokes an 'untimeliness'; in its eventuality, it refuses punctuation, refuses a 'proper' moment. Most importantly, it refuses a collocation *or identification* between the subject of consciousness and the substance of her or his thought: it opens a temporal *décalage* between the subject of consciousness and the substance of that thought. It is this temporal *décalage* which is properly called criticism.[30] In this postmodern, texts, writers, and readers are all fundamentally 'displaced'. As a result, authority is also displaced, its interior energy released in 'lines of flight' or quanta. But this displacement is twofold. First, there is a displacement from the individual named author to a socio-political formation—the historical events—which make the formulation of a specific work possible; secondly, there is the displacement of those authors in history as well, in their own 'untimeliness' with respect to the substance of their thought. Like Lacanian subjects, authors are always thinking just precisely where they are not and they are not where they think; hence they are always historically out of step with themselves.

The terms of this chapter—agency and understanding—should now be afforded their full percussive resonance: fundamentally, their concern is that of the famous eleventh thesis on Feuerbach, in which Marx favours agency ('changing' the world) over understanding ('interpreting' the world). My point is that Marxist criticism has failed to do justice to this preference. Conventionally, Marxist criticism has concerned itself most fundamentally—and rightly—with historical accuracy. The problem is not with the exercises in 'dating' so prevalent in Marxist criticism: rather, the problem lies in what the critic

[30] This argument is elaborated more fully in my *After Theory*.

expects from such dating. My claim in this argument is that what is gained is, at best, mere interpretation; and, worse, that such interpretation serves the fundamental purpose of constructing a narrative of linked dates whose tacit teleology is always oriented towards the explication of the present: i.e. the point is to *preserve* the identity of the present (and that of its subject, the critic). Historical change—i.e. the *differing* of the present—is, paradoxically, precluded.

The task of a criticism which would be historical is to reveal those displaced authorities which enable the constitution of specific individuals at specific moments as 'authors'. It is only in this way that knowledge will cease to be merely 'punctual' (as it is in dating) and that it will be released as an event, a historical eventuality productive of intellectual agency. That is, knowledge will become inherently historical and *material,* and will produce an authority which is divorced from the totalizing pretensions of a modernist knowledge with its drives to power and mastery, a mastery which requires slavery as its correlative and which requires one individual to be recognized and identified as an essentially aristocratic master, an 'author', at the cost of the voices of alterity.

PART TWO

4. *Incipient Postmodernisms*

In the first section of this book, I have been at pains to stress that the postmodern is characterized by a specific 'mood', and not primarily by chronology. This should be clearly recognizable as the line taken by Lyotard, who argues that the meaning of the prefix 'post-' does not indicate a simple 'after', and further, that since the post*modern* is certainly a part *of* the modern, it indicates pre-eminently the necessity for a *rewriting* of the modern.[1]

It should also have been apparent that, in the first part of my study, the figures of Othello and Desdemona (in their jealousies, their surveillances, their beguilings, their attachments to each other as commodities) appear and disappear from time to time. In its concern for questions of visual perception and epistemology, and in its concern for the appropriation by one subject (Othello) of another (Desdemona) whose otherness is intolerable for a jealous subject, *Othello*, we might say, is organized around problems which have a particular purchase in the modern. Jealousy is Shakespeare's trope for the improper desire for appropriation by one subject of another, for the acknowledgement of the difficulty of attending to Desdemona's radical alterity as a differently centred subject of consciousness from Othello. Some 350 years later, a similar issue, addressed by Robbe-Grillet in *La Jalousie*, rewrites Othello's problem as a problem for subjectivity. The subject would traditionally define itself—and thus protect its identity—against a significant Other. In *Othello*, that Other is a gendered Other, productive of and subsequently threatening to masculinity. In the *chosiste* writing of Robbe-Grillet, the objects of the world against which the subject usually defines itself seem to be striking back all the more vigorously. Robbe-Grillet offers a text in which there is a problem for the very survival of subjectivity in the face of Others, Others who refuse to accept the status of

[1] See Jean-François Lyotard, *The Postmodern Condition* (trans. Geoff Bennington and Brian Massumi; Manchester: Manchester University Press, 1984), and *The Inhuman* (trans. Geoffrey Bennington and Rachel Bowlby; Cambridge: Polity Press, 1991), esp. 'Rewriting Modernity'.

objects for a subject and threaten to assume subjectivity themselves, against which the subject defines itself.

My point in making such an observation is to indicate that the question of the postmodern is not a question simply of recent date. It is rather the case that the question of the postmodern arises whenever a culture begins explicitly to consider itself historically, and whenever as a result it begins to consider the levels of its own modernity. Such moments would include the turning of the seventeenth century, when writers and artists began to deal seriously with the new configurations of the post-Copernican world, or the period of 'Enlightenment' in the eighteenth century when the epistemological progresses that mathematical procedures had enabled had also the effect that the culture was able to consider earlier moments as 'backward' and hence it was able to think itself 'modern'. I have intimated that, in both instances, this incipient modernity is not simply an aesthetic matter; rather, what appears to distinguish these moments is the easy familiarity of the relations between the aesthetic and the political or cultural. A specific attitude to empirical vision bolsters an imperialist politics; a specific construction of the avowedly and self-consciously 'modern' subject enables the development of institutionalized education and bolsters a particular aesthetic education; and so on.

In the present chapter I shall consider a paradigmatic case of John Donne, a poet who has assumed a dominant position in our thinking of literary modernisms, be it in his engagement with issues specific to the early modern period, or in his sponsorship by various writers who found his work useful for their own work in the fabrication of idiosyncratic 'traditions' in the early twentieth century. More specifically still, I shall focus attention on the ways in which Donne's texts address the human body, for one of the dominant philosophical questions of this period is that which focuses on the body as a kind of medium between consciousness and the material world. Having then shown an incipient postmodernism in Donne's poetry, I shall, in the subsequent chapters of this section, turn to the *located* body—the body in space and in specific geographical or geo-cultural spaces—in more recent poetry. Whereas the first section of this study was—sometimes silently—organized around the mood of jealousy, this second section will begin to articulate a specific condition of 'love'. It goes without saying that such terms are not intended in any simple metaphysical sense, even if I begin this second section with a reading of a poet frequently referred to as precisely a 'metaphysical' poet.

According to Maurice de Gandillac in *Genèses de la modernité*, it is in chapters 11 and 12 of the second book of his *Docte ignorance* that Nicholas of Cusa outlines the essential break constitutive of a veritable modernity. Here is the passage in which the argument is made:

> A la machine du monde on ne peut attribuer aucun centre fixe et immobile, que ce soit notre Terre sensible, l'Air ou le Feu ou quelque élément que vous vouliez . . . Si le monde avait un centre, il aurait aussi une circonférence . . . Le Ciel ne contient aucun pôle immobile et aucune étoile dans la huitième sphère ne décrit un cercle maximum, car elle devrait être équidistante des pôles, lesquels n'existent pas . . . Les habitants des antipodes voient comme nous le Ciel au-dessus de leur tête. Où que se situe l'observateur, il se croiera au centre de tout . . . Il est donc impossible de décrire le monde et de lui assigner une figure, car en aucun lieu il n'a centre ni circonférence.[2]

This geographical problem, fundamentally a problem of space, is also a problem of the subject and of representation. It is in the midst of this 'mechanical' problem, this problem with the 'machine du monde' (itself prefigurative of the later Newtonian models of physics), that Donne writes. I wish to argue here that we have in Donne a fine example not only of an incipient modernity, but also of a symptomatic emergence of a postmodern within that modernity. Both traditional and theoretical criticisms of Donne have attended in great detail to the status of the physical body, usually considered in terms of a somatic (if sometimes romantic) eroticism. But I wish to complicate this by thinking the body in terms of the problematics of the subject and of representation. Without necessarily entirely endorsing the theses of Artaud or of Deleuze and Guattari, I will show that Donne's engagement with the fundamental reassessments of space and time that are constitutive of the modern break is conditioned by an attitude which uncannily prefigures the notion of a 'body without organs'. Perhaps more importantly, I

[2] Maurice de Gandillac, *Genèses de la modernité* (Paris: Les Éditions du Cerf, 1992), 633.

will also be in a position to reassess the concept of 'love' in Donne (and hence of the emergence of this specifically modern configuration of a cultural arrangement of eroticism) as an early modern cultural problematic, related to philosophy and to criticism in general.[3]

I shall address this issue in three parts in what follows. First, I shall indicate some of the implications of Donne's engagements with the body as space. Secondly, I shall turn to the theme and theory of representation at work in the early modern period, taking Donne as a paradigmatic example. Thirdly, I shall open Donne to a kind of schizoanalysis more frequently associated with a more recent critical philosophy.[4]

1. DONNE'S BODY IN SPACE

One of the single most notable facts about the body in Donne is its spatial mobility: especially if the body is gendered female, it seems always to be able to accommodate a space which is ostensibly much greater than itself. No doubt some of this stems from the emblematic thinking which would, in Christian terms, characterize or symbolize the female body as some kind of 'temple', but Donne typically confuses the sacred dimensions of such thinking with their possible secular reconfiguration. The classic example of this, of course, is the woman represented in Elegy 19 as 'my America, my new-found land', a woman whose body expands to encompass a whole new world. In Donne's poems, this is not at all unusual. His attitude to space was highly imaginative: a flea becomes a marriage-bed or church, for example (in 'The Flea'); the ghostly body of Elizabeth Drury can contain a history of the world ('The First

[3] On the 'body without organs', see e.g. Antonin Artaud, *Le Théâtre et son double* (Paris: Gallimard, 1964), 101, on the importance of the eye. But cf. Jacques Derrida on Artaud, in two essays in *L'Écriture et la différence* (Paris: Seuil, 1967); Gilles Deleuze and Félix Guattari, *Anti-Oedipus* (trans. Robert Hurley, Mark Seem, and Helen R. Lane; London: Athlone Press, 1984). On the issue of 'love', see Alain Badiou, *Manifeste pour la philosophie* (Paris: Seuil, 1989), and *Conditions* (Paris: Seuil, 1992), esp. 253–74, and cf. his *L'Éthique* (Paris: Hatier, 1994); and cf. Ch. 9 below.

[4] Some of what follows is a development of earlier arguments elaborated in my study, *John Donne, Undone* (London: Methuen, 1986). Yet in the present argument, the development is such that it moves away from a—by now relatively straightforward—poststructuralist engagement.

Anniversary'); a room becomes a universe ('The Sun Rising'). The last example here is particularly interesting, for in it we see repeated the Shakespearean concern with the manipulation of space as a weapon of cultural appropriation. One of the things 'The Sun Rising' is about is colonialism, linked once more to the possibilities of the visual:

> If her eyes have not blinded thine,
> Look, and tomorrow late, tell me,
> Whether both th' Indias of spice and mine
> Be where thou left'st them, or lie here with me.[5]

In these lines, we have the rehearsal of the sun's intimate relation to vision as such; but, more pertinently, we also see an act of appropriation of the world, an otherness to be colonized, in the appropriation of the woman. As in Shakespeare, who laid the theme most bare in *The Tempest*, the construction of a masculinist and self-identical space for the human self or body is an abiding concern.

I have previously argued, elsewhere, that the compressions of space indicated in a text such as 'The Sun Rising' are themselves really an attempt to deal not so much with simple space as with the encroachments of a secularized consciousness, and thus are attempts to face up to the vagaries of time and with the sense Donne had of history beginning.[6] That sense of time is Augustinian through and through. It is a sense of time driven by the evacuation of self-presence, as described in Augustine's *Civitas Dei*:

> It is evident that as long as the soul is in the body, especially if sensibility remains, a man is alive, his constituent parts being soul and body. Consequently he must be described as being still 'before death', not 'in death'. But when the soul has departed and has withdrawn all bodily sensation, a man is said to be 'after death', and dead.
>
> Thus between these two situations the period in which a man is dying or 'in death' disappears. For if he is still alive, he is 'before death'; if he has stopped living, he is by now 'after death'. Therefore he is never detected in the situation of dying, or 'in death'. The same thing happens in the passage of time; we try to find the present

[5] John Donne, in *The Complete English Poems*, ed. A. J. Smith (Harmondsworth: Penguin, 1973), 80. All subsequent citations from Donne are from this edition.

[6] See Docherty, *John Donne, Undone*, esp. 17–51.

moment, but without success, because the future changes into the past without interval.[7]

There is in this an uncanny prefiguration of some of Derrida's thinking: in Augustine's magicking away the fact of death as an event or experience for the subject of consciousness, there is also an incipient attack on the metaphysics of presence. Such a thinking is characteristically modern in its imbrication of knowledge in its most intimate form of self-consciousness with power over one's own biography or history, fundamentally with power over the self construed as a form of bodily presence. Lyotard brings together the major themes here:

Modernity is not an era in thought, but rather a mode (this is the Latin origin of the word) of thought, of utterances, of sensibility. Erich Auerbach saw its dawnings in the writing of Augustine's *Confessions*: the destruction of the syntactic architecture of classical discourse and the adoption of a paratactic arrangement of short sentences linked by the most elementary of conjunctions: *and*. Both he and Bakhtin find the same mode in Rabelais and then in Montaigne.

For my own part, and without attempting to legitimate this view here, I see signs of this in the first-person narrative genre chosen by Descartes to expound his method. The *Discours* is another confession. But what it confesses is not that the ego (*moi*) has been dispossessed by God; it confesses to the ego's attempts to master every *datum*, including itself. The *and* that links the sequences expressed by his sentences leaves room for contingency, and Descartes attempts to graft on to it the finality of a series organized with a view to mastering and possessing 'nature'. (Whether or not he succeeds is another matter.) This modern mode of organizing time is deployed by the *Aufklärung* of the eighteenth century.[8]

What I wish to add to this is that the syntactic construction here can be linked very clearly to the sequential acquisitiveness, by the eye, of a world perceived as a threatening alterity. The self-preservation involved in the texts of confession is one which is predicated upon the power of speculation, in all of its senses. Donne was writing at the moment of the incipient empiricism based upon the 'truth of the eye' or upon Othello's

[7] Augustine, *City of God* (trans. Henry Bettenson; Harmondsworth: Penguin, 1972), 519–20.

[8] Jean-François Lyotard, 'Universal History and Cultural Differences', in *The Lyotard Reader*, ed. Andrew Benjamin (Oxford: Blackwell, 1989), 314–15.

'ocular proof'; and in what follows here I shall explore the relation of such colonialist empiricism to the power of a disembodied eye, an eye whose task is to arrange in sequence (or on a map) its possessions, and thereby to render a body in which the eye can be situated.[9]

The ideology in question states that what is before the eye is what is true: what is before the eye or what can be seen here, now, is true. This is clearly a somewhat dubious claim for philosophy in the early modern period (and it is, of course, subsequently figured as a central issue at the start of Hegel's *Phenomenology*); and the notion that one can found a truth upon a positioned subjective perception has to find ways of strengthening itself. There is clearly a nagging doubt in this mode of thinking that truth is becoming dangerously 'positional' (i.e. dependent solely upon the site or position from which it is spoken) rather than 'transpositional' (which is how one might expect truth to be considered in a culture so heavily weighted by a theological thinking). Donne's playing with space and time is an attempt to fix or stabilize a here and now, it would seem: he wishes to arrest the flux of time and space, to control his environment, to generate a stable—and self-legitimizing (i.e. quasi-transpositional)—subject-position for the 'I', the 'confessor' who in confessing produces himself.[10] His means of achieving this is to focus on the eye and on what is present to it. Notably, when Donne compresses space into a here or when he reduces time to a now, the deictics find their stable point of reference in the eye or the visual sphere itself.

'The Good Morrow' is a useful example of this in operation. Like many of Donne's Songs and Sonets, this is a poem set at a temporal turning-point, an Augustinian moment of the present through which past and future are traced. The 'present' is characterized not only as a moment of 'linking' or bringing

[9] The simple fact that the issue of 'ocular proof' is rehearsed in *Troilus and Cressida*, reiterated in *Othello*, and reconsidered in the guise of surveillance in *Measure for Measure*, indicates that it was an important matter at the turn of the seventeenth century. See my comments on scopophilia in 'The Flea' (Docherty, *John Donne, Undone*, 53–9). Cf. also the work of Luce Irigaray, *Speculum* (Paris: Minuit, 1974), on the centrality of the visual to modern philosophy; and see also David Michael Levin, *The Opening of Vision* (London: Routledge, 1988), in this same regard.

[10] Cf. Artaud, *Le Théâtre et son double*, 132, on the instability of time.

together (as with the 'and') two separate entities, but also as a moment of vision, a moment when the 'waking souls'

> watch not one another out of fear;
> For love, all love of other sights controls,
> And makes one little room, an every where.

It is, further, a moment of the discovery of truth in the *regard* or in the gaze:

> My face in thine eye, thine in mine appears,
> And true plain hearts do in the faces rest . . .[11]

Here, the eye is the location of truth. But, more importantly, truth is in an eye which is marked with a specific kind of power, fundamentally the power to reduce alterity to identity or, in the terms in which I am currently describing the problem, the power to conceive of the subject-position as transpositional and to assume for what is basically a localized perception the status of generalized legitimation or consensus. The world of the Other (in this case, the woman as object of the gaze) is translated into the terms of the self (the lascivious eye of the persona speaking the text).[12] This is not only a general pattern in Donne, it is also paradigmatic of the writing of the early modern period. We see it laid bare in 'The Flea', a poem whose organization depends upon the telescopic play of distances or of space; but, crucially for the present argument, the play with space and time in 'The Flea' is engaged simply to stress the power of the scopophiliac subject of vision, the meshing of the 'I' with the 'eye'.

If the eye controls space and truth, we have here a peculiar confusion of visual empiricism (testing against the eye) with imperialism (the control of space, the reduction through cartography of alterity to identity). This—a modern collocation of empire and empiricism—depends upon the primacy of the disembodied (quasi-transpositional) eye. In a word, this aspect of the modernity of Donne depends upon the construction of 'point of view', and upon a proto-phenomenological construc-

[11] Donne, 60. This poem is one which uncannily prefigures the texts of the anti-psychiatrist R. D. Laing. Cf. Laing, *Knots* (Harmondsworth: Penguin, 1969), 17, 27, for random examples of a writing which is tantalizingly similar to that of Donne. In both instances, what is at stake is the transpositionality of truth-statements.

[12] See Badiou, *Conditions*, 263, on the resulting impasse in the phenomenology of love.

tion of exterior space in relation to an identifiable 'I'-centred point in space, that of the empirical eye. Such an eye cannot see alterity at all, in fact; rather, it sees only a mirrored reflection of the self, or it so successfully interiorizes alterity as to reduce it to identity. This is the *mimetic* ideology of Hamlet who, holding the mirror up to nature, sees himself therein: mimesis, in this modernity, eradicates the very world of material history which it ostensibly claims to present. Space, *as extension* (and hence, of course, the world itself), is fundamentally lost or erased in this claustrophobic manœuvre: the 'real', as a result, becomes nothing more or less than what Badiou would call a 'masturbatory' eroticized body.[13]

2. REPRESENTATIONS

Prior to Donne, it was a fairly common practice to consider the body allegorically in spatial terms. Augustine metaphorically aligns the body with a house: 'My soul is like a house, small for you to enter, but I pray you to enlarge it. It is in ruins, but I ask you to remake it.'[14] Charles d'Orléans picks up on the common metaphors of his moment and establishes the conceit of the body as house in a number of poems and songs, like 'Se Dieu plaist, briefment la nuee':

> Par les fenestres de mes yeux
> Le chaut d'Amour soulois passer;
> Mais maintenant que deviens vieux,
> Pour la chambre de mon penser
> En esté freschement garder,
> Fermees les ferai tenir.

A similar kind of figure appears in Spenser (e.g. Book 2, Canto 9, of the *Faerie Queene*) when Guyon enters the 'house' of Alma, a house allegorically intimately linked with the body of Alma.[15]

[13] Badiou, *Conditions*, 266. Cf. Taylor Stoehr, 'Pornography, Masturbation and the Novel', *Salmagundi*, 2 (1967–8), 28–56, for the ways in which point of view and masturbation are linked.

[14] Augustine, *Confessions* (trans. R. S. Pine-Coffin; Harmondsworth: Penguin, 1961), 24.

[15] Charles d'Orléans, in Brian Woledge (ed.), *Penguin Book of French Verse* 1 (Harmondsworth: Penguin, 1961), 274–5. See my comments on these examples in Docherty, *On Modern Authority* (Brighton: Harvester, 1987), 74–7.

Clearly, Donne shares much of this attitude to the body as a site of spatial exploration. But his difference lies in his complication of a spatial consideration of the body with a temporal one: his 'modernity' lies in the prioritization of the temporal present over the spatial present.

He frequently tries to establish what I have elsewhere called a 'scene of recognition', a scene in which the Other can be reduced to a factor of the self, a situation in which alterity becomes a factor of identity, and difference a factor of the same.[16] But it would also be the case that his 'scene of recognition' is always threatened: when he looks into the lover's eyes, he finds himself reflected there, yes; but he also finds the possibility that (like Charles d'Orléans) the lover will close her eyes or will look elsewhere. The object of the gaze may always turn out to be the subject of another, different gaze. Philosophically expressed, the problem is that Donne is aware of the fallacious basis on which the desired transpositionality of his truth is grounded. In other words, he finds a stable subject-position built upon the sands of impermanence, of change and mutability. Like the characters in R. D. Laing's hypothesized dialogues in *Knots*, he finds the Other as a factor of the self, certainly; but this is only at the cost of seeing the self threatened by alterity, by a becoming different, and thus threatened also with the loss of all capacity for truth and its consequent replacement with a paranoia endemic to modernity.

This proposes a problem of the body, and specifically of the eye, as a site of temporal change rather than of spatial control. For the colonial mentality, it is never enough to control space, one must also control the history of the Other as well. We find perhaps the clearest example of what I'm talking about in Donne in a poem like 'A Lecture upon the Shadow'. This poem is organized around the issue of the relation of truth to visual representation. Truth is seen in the text as a function of the visual, as a function of what can be seen: the shadow, as a representation (and, of course, as an extension into space) of the presence of the body. As in 'The Good Morrow', we find ourselves at a turning-point of the Augustinian present: a noon which stands uncertainly and undecidably between past

[16] See Docherty, *John Donne, Undone*, *passim*.

(morning) and future (afternoon). Donne's task is to 'Stand still', to fix this moment of recognition which, in its stability, he will be able to call 'love', a moment in which there is an expansion of the space of the subject to encompass its Other. The shadows cast by the body are its extensions into space. Donne wishes to control this, to 'map' such extension: but to control the space of the body is also to control the time of the body here. It is love's minute, love's day, that concerns the poet in this instance.

I suggest that what Donne wants here is an uncanny prefiguration of the body without organs. Deleuze and Guattari characterize the body without organs as 'the identity of producing and the product': in one succinct instance it is described as 'the body without an image',[17] or, as Donne might have it, the body without its shadow. For present purposes, the body without organs as a concept should be understood in its limited sense as the 'body without organization'. For Deleuze and Guattari, we start from the principle of movement, from the fluidity or flux of energy or *kinesis*. But kinetic energy, a kind of pure activity of producing lines of flight (or in the present case a pure exponential production of more and more strained 'conceits'), is frequently arrested or interrupted, rendered *static*, by an 'organ' whose function it is to organize the energy into—among other things—a material body capable of producing and isolating a 'point of view', a locus for positional truth.

> It is at work everywhere . . . Everywhere *it* is machines—real ones, not figurative ones: machines driving other machines, machines being driven by other machines, with all the necessary couplings and connections. An organ-machine is plugged into an energy-source-machine: the one produces a flow that the other interrupts. The breast is a machine that produces milk, and the mouth a machine coupled to it.[18]

The body without organs is a body prior to its organization in these machine-couplings, an organization which enables the production of the fallacy of stable identity. The body without organs is basically a body experienced entirely as time, as fluency or currency, as the site of exchangeability or mutability, rather than as self-presence.

[17] Deleuze and Guattari, *Anti-Oedipus*, 8. [18] Ibid. 1.

Donne's disembodied eye operates as the producer of flows or of energy. Paradoxically, the body which is the erotic object of such energy, the body which is the object of the gaze, must always escape the vision if the erotic impulse—and with it the self of the subject—is to be maintained. Were it to be fixed, were Donne to allow himself the kind of stability he ostensibly desires in the object of the erotic gaze, it would serve to kill the energy of the subject. For Donne as subject—indeed, for subjectivity itself—to exist at all, it has to be unhinged, unfixed, unstable: all of which is precisely the threat which criticism (allied as it is to the presentation of transpositional and verifiable truth) finds it difficult to bear.

Donne's poems bear the same relation to truth as does some surrealist cinema (in films like Buñuel's *That Obscure Object of Desire* or *Un chien andalou*). Such a cinema delights in the questioning and destabilizing of any truth-claims whatsoever. The Donnean body-without-organs is an anarchic body, which fails not only to fix its erotic object but also thereby fails to establish an identity for itself. Thus, the desire to reduce alterity to identity, to see difference as a factor of sameness, finally turns back upon the perpetrator: 'Donne' is contaminated by difference, by alterity, and even (perhaps paradoxically) by weakness and victimization. His very construction of the scene of recognition under the rubric of a scopophiliac love undoes his ostensible aim to construct a stable identity. His desire for a stable truth is itself diluted by the production of temporality: in striving to control the history or time of his Other, he succeeds only in giving that Other a history in the first place. Such a production of a secular relation constitutes the very modern break characteristic of Donne's writing.

3. INCIPIENT POSTMODERNISM

We might say, then, that in Donne, the body without organs appears in the form of the body without somatic or erotic organization. It is a body in time rather than in the stability of a space. It thus figures in the texts as a body which is somewhat dysfunctional with regard to representation. Because it prioritizes the temporal over the spatial deictic, because it produces the secular through exerting a linguistic pressure upon the conceits of space, the body enters in Donne into the function of an almost alchemical *mécanique des fluides*,[19] itself prefigurative of Irigaray. It is a body which cannot be represented because it can never have been present—'here'—in the first place.

Once more, the roots of this modern body are to be found in Augustine. Pondering time, Augustine is faced with the situation where all time is reduced to a fleeting series of instants, linked, at best, by the ampersand. According to Maurice de Gandillac:

C'est alors qu'intervient, avec toute sa polysémie, la mystérieuse faculté qu'Augustin nomme 'mémoire'. A la rigueur, le mot ne devrait désigner que la remémoration d'un passé disparu; en fait, intimement liée à cette *mens* qu'Augustin définit comme 'ce qui est excellent dans l'âme' . . . la *memoria* concerne pour lui toute forme supérieure de présence à soi . . . Conservatoire de l'instantané et de l'éphémère, si elle est aussi 'l'immense capacité' de toute expérience et de tout savoir, c'est parce que Dieu lui-même y fait son demeure et que par elle, en quelque sorte, l'Éternel confère au temporel, au-delà de la dispersion et de l'impuissance, une valeur positive de rassemblement et de l'énergie.[20]

For Donne, however, the body without organs is a body which lacks this *memoria*. To that extent, it also lacks a monotheistic attitude and a self-identical God (the God of 'I am that I am'): there is no possibility here of an allegory between the poet's body and the temple of God, such as we find in Herbert, say. Donne occupies more the position of 'Desdemonism', replacing 'I am that I am' with 'I do beguile the thing I am by seeming otherwise' (or, on occasion, with the Iago-like 'I am not that I am'). The position here, however, need not be atheistic: rather, it appears to confound the identifiability of a monotheistic attitude through the multiplication of points of view; and, to that extent, it is a 'pagan' attitude. The body is that of a pagan, or that of the schizophrenic. Schizophrenia such as this is to be understood not in strictly clinical terms but rather as a defining characteristic of a disjunctive relation between the subject and its language: the disjunction in question arises whenever the

[19] See Luce Irigaray, *Ce sexe qui n'en est pas un* (Paris: Minuit, 1977), on the mechanics of fluids as part of a debate around gender and philosophy.

[20] De Gandillac, *Genèses de la modernité*, 18.

subject 'beguiles' or seduces itself by speaking from a non-identifiable position, from the position where 'I' am not (or where I am not that I am).

In so far as this is the case, Donne's poetry can be considered in fact as being less clearly 'modern' and more as the site in which an incipient postmodernism impinges on the text. Not only is the text contaminated by a proto-Nietzschean 'active forgetting' (which endows it with its active energy), but it is also contaminated by the drives towards the multifariousness of paganism which Lyotard associates with the postmodern, and with that schizophrenic mood which Jameson has characterized as a recurring element in the postmodern conditions of textuality.[21]

Yet the final conclusion may be even more telling than this. Donne is widely regarded still as a poet whose writings invite comment in terms of a theorized eroticism, gender, sexuality, or, as more traditional criticisms might have it, 'love'. What the foregoing argument shows is that, in the early modern European culture of which Donne's writing is a symptom, such love was profoundly problematic. The visual basis on which such love was frequently predicated (a scopophiliac desire for a specific object) binds love intimately to the issue of truth, and also binds truth to the issue of aesthetic beauty. Here we see the first taste of that aesthetic which culminates in Keats, where 'Beauty is truth, truth beauty', in which the beauty in question is gendered and somatic, and the truth in question is based on visual representation. For truth to be truth, it must be transpositional; and yet a truth which is based in the eye (in the self-evidential) is firmly located in space to a single subjective point of view. Hence the self-evidence of truth, its power of self-legitimation, is now called into doubt even in the instant when it is being advanced for the first time in the beginnings of empiricism. The body, as the site for the inscription of truth, is rendered crucial in the operation of reason. But, in the primacy of the eye and in its intimate links with the construction of a

[21] On such paganism and its relation to the postmodern, see Jean-François Lyotard, *Rudiments païens* (Paris: Union Générale d'Éditions, 1977), and *Instructions païennes* (Paris: Galilée, 1977). On the specific aspect of schizophrenia in question here, see Fredric Jameson, *Postmodernism: or, the Cultural Logic of Late Capitalism* (London: Verso, 1991), ch. 1.

sexual love based on affective individualism, truth finds its predicament as a physical and material problem, not simply a problem of language or 'truth-telling'. For the first time, truth can be inscribed on the body in a specific way (deployed to great—almost self-parodic—effect by a writer such as Crashaw), its experience rendered as immediate as the odour of a rose, as the modernist Eliot would have it. But truth has lost its transpositionality and self-legitimacy. As Donne is only too aware, it has degenerated into the merest 'knowledge', a knowledge which is entirely place-specific, relativized, and schizoid. It is at this moment, thus, that knowledge becomes contaminated by power and by the will-to-power. As Lyotard has indicated, this is one major quibble the postmodern mood has with modernity: 'what was and is at issue is the introduction of the will into reason.'[22] Another way of putting this is to say that what was and is at issue is the introduction of the will into an eroticized vision, of love into knowledge, and of knowledge into truth.

[22] Jean-François Lyotard, 'Svelte Appendix to the Postmodern Question' (trans. Docherty), in Richard Kearney (ed.), *Across the Frontiers* (Dublin: Wolfhound Press, 1988), 265. For the relevant arguments in the debate around the relation of postmodernism to truth, see Christopher Norris, *The Truth about Postmodernism* (Oxford: Blackwell, 1993), and my (unsympathetic) review of this text in *Textual Practice*, 8/3 (1994), 503–7.

5. *Ana-*

'Back—up—again'; or, in Greek, 'ana-, ana-, ana-'. 'The Grauballe Man', ostensibly about a man who is 'back up again', is an exercise in what I shall call 'anagrammatology': it is a writing elaborated in various modes of this 'ana-': anamnesis, anagogy, anamorphosis, and analysis. In the present chapter I will show the poem as a writing which occurs as an *event* in these four modes. This status of the writing, as an event and not a work, nor even a 'text' in the conventional sense, is important. 'Eventuality' opens writing to a postmodernism, as an anachronic or untimely meditation, countering the 'punctuality' of the modern, which is concerned to map two points in time as if they were two stable points in space. Eventuality releases the interior historicity of those 'spots of time'. To think this writing as event enables an analysis which will be, literally, a setting free of its elements into a movement of emancipation. A philosophy of postmodernism will raise the stakes of the poem, disabling the conventional reading of it as a neo-modernist exercise in myth-making and replacing the usual banal reading of its politics with something literally more compelling. Three elements construct the argument: the issue of historicity; an exploration of the poem's cinematism; and a consideration of the poem as an engagement with the issue of justice, judgement, and criticism: a 'cutting' which attempts to *trancher la question*.

1. 'THE BEARINGS OF HISTORY'

Once imagined, he cannot be seen
(Seamus Deane, 'A Killing')

On the face of it, Heaney's 'The Grauballe Man' seems an unlikely contender for the title of 'postmodernist poem'. In terms of obvious theme and style, it seems that most critics would think of it in terms of a 'late modernist' text, Heaney as a late modernist poet, the ephebe influenced by Yeats and by a

Romantic tradition which was crucially concerned with landscape and a particular kind of eco-relation to the land.[1]

This 'economy', or law of space, however, is no longer available in the same way to Heaney as it was to the Romantics or even to the modernists who were all so famously concerned with the issue of 'exile'. Contemporary space is what Virilio thinks as an 'espace critique', a space in which geometry is giving way to chronometry: our socio-political being is organized not primarily by spatial or geo-political mappings, but rather by temporal, chrono-political determinations.[2] Heaney lives in this different eco-consciousness of the aesthetic of space proposed by (for examples) Beuys and Long, sculptors whose work is uncannily 'temporal' in that it is marked by its internal historicity and temporal mutability. A typical piece by Richard Long, say his 'A Line Made by Walking, England', is, in a certain sense, no longer 'there', except in the photographic record or image. Heaney's 'sense of place' is also—inevitably—now a sense of time. He writes: 'We are dwellers, we are namers, we are lovers, we make homes and search for our histories. And when we look for the history of our sensibilities I am convinced . . . that it is to . . . the stable element, the land itself, that we must look for continuity.'[3] This land is also a

[1] See e.g. Seamus Deane, 'The Timorous and the Bold', in his *Celtic Revivals* (London: Faber & Faber, 1985; repr. 1987); Elmer Andrews, *The Poetry of Seamus Heaney* (London: Macmillan, 1988); Neil Corcoran, *Seamus Heaney* (London: Faber & Faber, 1986). In their 'Introduction' to *The Penguin Book of Contemporary British Poetry* (Harmondsworth: Penguin, 1982), Blake Morrison and Andrew Motion made a polemical claim for Heaney as '[t]he most important new poet of the last fifteen years', one in the forefront of a new 'departure' in poetry 'which may be said to exhibit something of the spirit of postmodernism'. The hesitancies in this final phrase reveal the fact that their notion of postmodernism was extremely underinformed and untheorized. Antony Easthope trounces their suggestion in his piece, 'Why Most Contemporary Poetry is So Bad', *PN Review*, 48 (1985), 36–8, where he also argues that 'The Grauballe Man' is, in fact, 'resolutely *pre-modernist*'. Both views miss some essential points of what is at stake in the postmodern, as I shall argue here.

[2] Paul Virilio, *L'Espace critique* (Paris: Christian Bourgois, 1984). At the simplest level, this corresponds to an organization of life in terms of 'quality time' or 'labour time' rather than its organization in terms of the 'metropolis' and the 'suburbs'. Cf. the work of Gilles Deleuze, especially with regard to the idea that social, political, and psychological life are all organized around 'lines of flight', making territorializations and deterritorializations.

[3] Seamus Heaney, *Preoccupations* (London: Faber & Faber, 1980), 148–9. For a more detailed explication of this aesthetic in Long, see my *After Theory* (London: Routledge, 1990), 22–4.

repository of history and continuity across time. It is the case that, for Heaney, space has become critical in precisely another way close to this. Ireland itself is, of course, a 'critical space', a space built upon a 'critical difference' called 'the border' between North and South; it is built on that *stasis* or civil war which problematizes any sense of its identity, specifically any sense of its historical identity. It is for this reason, of course, that the Field Day company, with whom Heaney has worked extremely closely, is crucially concerned to forge a history, to *remember*, as a therapeutic—and political—act which aims to 'suture' the wound to Ireland which is the border.

'The Grauballe Man' is, in a sense, a poem on poetry itself; its writing is precisely this kind of therapeutic anamnesis: 'I have always listened for poems, they come sometimes like bodies come out of a bog, almost complete, seeming to have been laid down a long time ago, surfacing with a touch of mystery.'[4] But it is a poetry which lies uncertainly between image (the photograph which prompted the poem) and memory (where 'now he lies / perfected'), between history and its representation. If anything, then, this is a poem which is about poetry as mediation or about a specific act of reading. Heaney is confronting the bog as 'the memory of a landscape', the palimpsest record of history which is now conceived of as 'a manuscript which we have lost the skill to read'.[5] Most importantly, 'The Grauballe Man' is what we should think of as a kind of 'interstitial' event, a writing half-way between image and text, figure and discourse.

For the neo-Romantic and modernist traditions with which Heaney is conventionally aligned, 'imagination' forges a link between the subject of consciousness and history as its object. This enables the formulation of a transcendental subject in Romanticism or—less gloriously—a self capable of persistence in modernism. This transhistorical or mythic subject is, however, no longer easily available to Heaney, for the postmodern has problematized the relation between the subject and history, or between the 'real' and its 'representation'. If, in the 'society of the spectacle' or the 'hyperreal simulacrum', everything is

[4] Heaney, *Preoccupations*, 34.
[5] Ibid. 54, 132; the latter phrase is attributed to John Montague.

now of the status of the image, then the 'real' has simply disappeared. The reality which is supposed to ground our representations, be it the presence of history as exterior fact or the presence-to-self of the supposed transcendental subject, has itself become an image.[6]

This, in fact, is Heaney's problem, both a political and an aesthetic problem. The 'ground' for his poetry—history itself in the Irish context—has disappeared, gone underground. As a result, a series of reversals takes place in 'The Grauballe Man': what seemed a tomb is a womb; what seemed a man gives a kind of birth while also being the baby itself; to dig is to discover not the past at all (history) but rather 'the presence of the past' (anamnesis). When Heaney wrote the poem, he was deeply aware of the presence of the past, not just in terms of his search for 'images and symbols adequate to our predicament',[7] but rather in terms of the very historicity of the present, his present as a moment in flux, his spatial present as a moment bifurcated, divided, a moment when space has gone critical, differential, historical rather than antiquarian. As Deane suggests, the mythologization of history is more of a wound than a salve.[8]

The poem's crucial turn lies in a stanza which is itself an interstitial stanza:

> Who will say 'corpse'
> to his vivid cast?
> Who will say 'body'
> to his opaque repose?

[6] See Guy Debord, *La Société du spectacle* (Geneva: Champ Livre, 1967); Jean Baudrillard, *L'Échange symbolique et la mort* (Paris: Gallimard, 1976), *Amérique* (Paris: Grasset, 1986). This tendency in poetry is perhaps most marked in the work of John Ashbery. But it has been there in a great deal of Modernist writing, where there was a marked interest in the 'interstitial'. Modernist writers did not chart the 'death of the Self': they were interested in the self-in-time, and in the interstitial moments between those significant moments of assured selfhood or supposed self-presence. Hence Proust was interested not in the heartbeat itself but in the 'intermittences du cœur'; Woolf was interested not in actions but in what goes on 'between the acts'; Bergson was interested in the time 'between' marked instants; Eisenstein in the dialectical relation 'between' the images which constitute montage in cinema; Saussure in the relations 'between' signs rather than in signs themselves; Einstein in 'relative' rather than absolute measure; and so on. It is this 'interstitial' area which determines Heaney's writing here.

[7] Heaney, *Preoccupations*, 56. 'The presence of the past' was the title of the 1980 Venice Biennale which initiated the 'postmodern debate' in architecture.

[8] Deane, *Celtic Revivals*, 179.

This stanza asks: is history dead, a thing of the past; or is it alive, vivid, a presence of the past? It is the very posing of the question which opens the text to a postmodernism, to what I shall call its postmodern cinematism.

2. THE CINEMATISM OF THE POSTMODERN

'Postmodern' is frequently misunderstood: many follow a particular inflection of Fredric Jameson, who, while theoretically aware of the complexity of the postmodern, takes it in his practice to mean a rag-bag of the art produced since 1945. But postmodernism, if it is to be taken seriously, is not to be understood as a simple periodizing term like this. Rather, the postmodern calls into question this very manner of thinking history. Lyotard, for instance, asks:

> What, then, is the postmodern? What place does it or does it not occupy in the vertiginous work of the questions hurled at the rules of image and narration? It is undoubtedly a part of the modern. All that has been received, if only yesterday . . . must be suspected. What space does Cézanne challenge? The Impressionists'. What object do Picasso and Braque attack? Cézanne's. What presupposition does Duchamp break with in 1912? That which says one must make a painting, be it cubist. And Buren questions that other presupposition which he believes had survived untouched by the work of Duchamp: the place of presentation in the work. In an amazing acceleration, the generations precipitate themselves. A work can become modern only if it is first postmodern. Postmodernism thus understood is not modernism at its end but in the nascent state, and this state is constant.[9]

Postmodernism is, as it were, the moment in the modern work when a critical difference becomes apparent; it is, for instance, the critical distance between Cézanne and Picasso when the latter paints in such a way as to call even the experimentalism of Cézanne into question; Picasso—postmodernist to

[9] Jean-François Lyotard, *The Postmodern Condition* (trans. Geoff Bennington and Brian Massumi; Manchester: Manchester University Press, 1984), 79; cf. Fredric Jameson, 'Postmodernism; or, the Cultural Logic of Late Capitalism', *New Left Review*, 146 (1984), 53–92; and Jameson, 'The Politics of Theory', in his *The Ideologies of Theory*, 2 vols. (Routledge, 1988), ii. 103–13.

Cézanne—becomes modern when a critical space is introduced by the works of Duchamp, and so on.

'Postmodern' describes not a work, but rather an event; it is not a point in history, but an event in its historicity. The effect of this is to question a prevalent understanding of history itself. One view of history suggests that the past can be 'sliced into', and that certain nodal 'points' can be identified and epistemologically understood: thus, say, the 'history' of '1848'. Call this the 'modernist' view, one shared by Jameson whose periodizations necessitate the location of some crucial 'points' in history. Another view suggests that this 'point' is merely an epistemological hypothesis: '1848' is not a point in time, but is itself internally historical, in the sense that within 1848 there is only a series of differing 'becomings' or events whose flux and mutability cannot be arrested. There is, as it were, an overlap between, say, January and February 1848, and it is this *overlap* or interstice which is history, not the points 'January' and 'February' between which the overlap eventuates. Call this the postmodern view: in this, epistemology becomes difficult; but the historicity of history is maintained. The modernist view is, properly, the very contradiction of history.

This can be more easily explained in terms of a kind of cinematism which is extremely appropriate to Heaney's poem, which itself hovers undecidably between discourse and figure, between the photographic still and the properly cinematic moving image. Heaney's task in the text is not to discover an archaeological remnant of the past in its antiquarianism, but rather to write in the interstices of history itself, to *be historical* and to be aware of the flow and movement of history, history as 'becoming', even as he writes—or because he writes—the poem. It is an attempt to make movies out of the still image, which is, of course, one of the reasons why most of the descriptions of the body describe it in fluid movement or flux.

Cinematism is precisely aligned with the postmodern. Bergson characterized 'old philosophy' as the belief that the flow of Being could be reduced to a series of 'coupes immobiles' or 'stills'. Deleuze follows Bergson in the rejection of the still and its replacement with the 'coupe mobile', a 'cut' which releases the temporality or cinematic heterogeneity (akin to 'l'espace critique' of Virilio) held within the apparently still or homogeneous photographic image itself. For Bergson, according to Deleuze,

> le mouvement ne se confond pas avec l'espace parcouru, l'espace parcouru est passé, le mouvement est présent, c'est l'acte de parcourir . . . les espaces parcourus appartiennent tous à un seul et même espace homogène, tandis que les mouvements sont hétérogènes, irréductibles entre eux.[10]

The reading of Heaney as a modernist has to view this text as one in which there is an established homogeneity—a late symbolist *correspondance* à la Baudelaire—between Jutland and Ireland which, as Deane has pointed out, can be maintained only by some 'forceful straining'.[11] Such a reading, further, has to ignore the literal *movement* of the text, which delineates not the past but the presence of the past as a living present and the mutability of that present, its fluidity or flux.

'The Grauballe Man' is an example of a kind of montage, which Eisenstein had described as a dialectical process. Montage 'arises from the collision of independent shots';[12] as, for example, the collisions between Jutland and Ireland, the Iron Age and the IRA, the description of the man prior to the 'corpse/body' stanza, and the child hinting at a Christian iconography, raising the issue of justice which dominates the latter half of the poem, and so on. Montage such as this gives what Deleuze calls 'l'image indirecte du temps, de la durée. Non pas un temps homogène ou une durée spatialisée, comme celle que Bergson dénonce, mais une durée et un temps effectifs qui découlent de l'articulation des images-mouvement'.[13] It is a common misconception, deriving from much literary criticism, to suggest that Bergson had argued for the prioritization of some kind of subjective time, a time which was to be measured within the subject. Deleuze points out the fallaciousness of this. Far from time being within the subject, the subject is—that is to

[10] Gilles Deleuze, *Cinéma 1: L'Image-mouvement* (Paris: Minuit, 1983), 9.

[11] Deane, *Celtic Revivals*, 179.

[12] Sergei M. Eisenstein, *Film Form* (Cambridge, Mass.: Harcourt Brace Jovanovich, 1969), as quoted in Gerald Mast and Marshall Cohen (eds.), *Film Theory and Criticism* (2nd edn.; New York: Oxford University Press, 1979), 104.

[13] Deleuze, *Cinéma 1*, 47.

say, the subject 'becomes'—only through the agency of time itself.[14] Virilio raises this to a sociological status: 'Au temps *qui passe* de la chronologie et de l'histoire, succède ainsi un temps *qui s'expose* instantanément. Sur l'écran du terminal, la durée devient "support-surface" d'inscription, littéralement ou plutôt automatiquement: *le temps fait surface*.'[15] Time surfaces, a little like the body in the bog, which is also, for Heaney, the poem itself in which time—or, in my preferred term here, historicity—exposes itself.

This 'temps qui s'expose' is prefigured, as Virilio points out, in the techniques of photography and cinema.[16] Those techniques, of course, were precisely the techniques which Benjamin feared, on the grounds that they would make history less accessible, would derealize it in some way. However, this derealization is nothing more nor less than the denial of the availability of the *coupe immobile*, the denial of the still; and it bears repeating that the still itself is the very opposite of historicity as such; the still, or the *coupe immobile*, which enables a stable knowledge of the past, the pastness of the past, is a kind of epistemological myth, however necessary. Heaney's text, however, is not about the pastness of the past but its presence. This is in accord with the living in a critical space of Ireland which Virilio's philosophy would see as a paradigmatic postmodern condition. As a result of the movement away from perspectivism and its pieties towards cinematism, the inhabiting of time has supplanted the inhabiting of space itself. It is this issue which Heaney's poem is addressing: the anamnesis of history.

In anamnesis, according to Plato in *Meno*, we have something which modernism articulated much later as a Proustian *souvenir involontaire*. In this, there is not so much a moment of knowledge of the past, but rather an actual recreation of the past, now present fully: it is, as it were, the actualization of the virtual.[17] It is this process of 'actualization' which is central to

[14] See Gilles Deleuze, *Différence et répétition* (Paris: PUF, 1968; repr. 1985), 116, especially the passage on Kant and what Deleuze thinks as the 'je fêlé' which marks the becoming of the subject, its existence in historicity or in the form of time.

[15] Virilio, *L'Espace critique*, 15.

[16] Ibid. 77

[17] See e.g. Georges Poulet, *Proustian Space* (Baltimore: Johns Hopkins University Press, 1977).

Heaney's poem. The body in the photograph starts off as a fluid being:

> As if he had been poured
> in tar, he lies
> on a pillow of turf
> and seems to weep
>
> the black river of himself

As the poem continues the description, we have what is in fact a process very like Robbe-Grillet's well-known description of a painting, 'La Défaite de Reichenfels' in *Dans le labyrinthe*, which, as it elaborates itself, becomes less static painting and more mobile scenario. A soldier, described fully as an image, begins to talk with a little boy, himself fully delineated within the frame of the painting; but as the description progresses the frame is transgressed and the boy and soldier leave 'La Défaite de Reichenfels' (the title of the canvas: figure) and engage with each other in a fully narrative situation, 'dans le labyrinthe' (the title of the novel: discourse).[18] This tendency towards the mobility and the mutability of narrative, the actualization of the virtual, of that which seemed to be merely a representation—in short, the presentation of the unpresentable—occurs also in Heaney. The poet describes the corpse/body to the point where it is unclear whether it is alive or dead, unclear on which side of the grave it is; then recalls the photograph; and moves towards the perfection of the man in the memory of the poet, at which point the presence of the past becomes all the more telling in the issue of justice which the poem is addressing. It is 'the actual weight | of each hooded victim' which the poet feels. 'Actual' means 'current; present'; and the issue of justice is itself realized as now and present for the writing or reading of the poem. Through anamnesis, the virtual or hypothetical issue of justice which is proposed by the atrocity of the Northern Irish situation, is made actual, current, an event. Its currency or fluency is also, of course, realized in the fluidity of the bog man, who is seen not as a still but as a moving image: as a *coupe mobile*.

[18] Alain Robbe-Grillet, *Dans le labyrinthe* (Paris: Minuit, 1959), 24–31 *et seq*.

3. 'CURT CUTS'

the curt cuts of an edge
Through living roots awaken in my head
(Heaney, 'Digging')

In this cinematic poem, then, there is an arrangement around a crucial 'cut' or rupture. Within the text itself, that cut is the slashed throat of the bog man; and a slashed throat is also a throat which cannot speak. Heaney writes a poem about the difficulty of writing poetry within the problematic of injustice which determines the situation of the poet and his poem; both live in a terrain marked by a savage cut or critical space which lodges them in history rather than in place. If people have no clearly demarcated terrain within which to identify themselves, they must turn to time and live in it. But the time is 'out of joint', in the sense that the history of Ireland is itself 'cut' or slashed, interrupted by a long colonial sojourn. These are Heaney's 'living roots', which quicken or come to life in his head. As Virilio indicates, 'le temps n'est un temps vécu . . . que parce qu'il est interrompu'.[19] The poem enacts this living time through its cut and montage organization.

But this slashed throat raises another issue: that of justice and revenge. The text is clearly related to Heaney's 'Trial Pieces', poems exploring Viking culture in relation to his own:

I am Hamlet the Dane,
skull-handler, parablist,
smeller of rot

in the state, infused
with its poisons,
pinioned by ghosts
and affections,

murders and pieties,
coming to consciousness
by jumping in graves,
dithering, blathering.[20]

[19] Virilio, *L'Espace critique*, 103; cf. Gilles Deleuze, *Kant's Critical Philosophy* (Minneapolis: University of Minnesota Press, 1984), pp. vii–viii.
[20] Seanus Heaney, 'Viking Dublin: Trial Pieces', in *North* (London: Faber & Faber, 1975), 21–4.

The Jacobean revenge motif in Heaney is closely related to the idea of 'finding a voice', with 'Feeling into Words', those 'words, words, words' which Hamlet reads/says when confronted with the not so wily spy, Polonius, who finds a 'pregnancy' in Hamlet's talk.[21]

Heaney's first prose collection, *Preoccupations*, opens with the word 'Omphalos' repeated three times ('words, words, words'), with which he 'would begin'. This is important to the Oedipal impetus in Heaney. In his poetry, the land frequently occupies the position of the maternal womb, a womanly space to be 'quickened by penetration' as Deane puts it.[22] Heaney 'speaks daggers' to this Gertrude earth, this 'Bog Queen'. Oedipalization is, of course, a setting of time 'out of joint', for it enables the mythic attempt of the son to be simultaneously son and father of himself. In Heaney, this temporal *décalage* is made more evidently a 'presence of the past' in the ghostly apparition of Hamlet in 'The Grauballe Man' and his other 'Danish' poems.

This bog man is strangely androgynous. First, we find that a 'ball' is like an 'egg'; there is a dark linguistic hint here that the testicle is like an ovary; and this linguistic slippage or ambivalence, this metaphor itself, merging ball and egg, produces that theme of pregnancy which dominates the latter half of the poem. Further, even his body takes on a female cast:

> His hips are the ridge
> and purse of a mussel . . .

There is a kind of *anamorphosis* going on here, as the male character mutates into something female. A mussel typically is a container of sorts; and here it is as if the man's hips contain a 'currency', a pearly fluency. This fluency or fluidity in the cast of the body makes it an example of what Irigaray thinks as a *mécanique des fluides*,[23] a 'mechanics' which enables the poem to become mobile, a mutable *coupe mobile*. It is also a mechanics which enables the poem to articulate a 'becoming womanly'; and, again, the drive towards becoming rather than being is a

[21] See Seamus Heaney, 'Feeling into Words', in *Preoccupations*; the references here are to *Hamlet*, II. ii.

[22] Deane, *Celtic Revivals*, 177.

[23] Luce Irigaray, *Ce sexe qui n'en est pas un* (Paris: Minuit, 1977).

drive towards the historicity of eventuality rather than to the fixity of a punctuality. This engagement with gender places the text in the mode of anamorphosis.

The man is 'pregnant' in these lines: but what he is pregnant with is, of course, the presence of a future. The poem, then, is written in this peculiar future anterior tense which, according to Lyotard, describes the typically postmodern event. Further, it again recalls Deleuze who cites Augustine's notion: 'il y a un présent du futur, un présent du présent, un présent du passé, tous impliqués dans l'événement, enroulés dans l'événement, donc simultanés, inexplicables. De l'affect au temps: on découvre un temps intérieur à l'événement . . .'[24] This slipperiness of the 'actual', the constant and fluid actualization of a virtual which organizes the poem, is manifest in all the slipperiness which threatens to be arrested but which the text constantly strives to release or to loosen. If the man is in a sense giving birth to himself from the female bog in which there lies a 'Bog Queen', then it follows that the poetry is in a sense also giving birth to itself, originating itself or authorizing itself in this peculiar act. The poet is Hamlet giving birth to himself, the poet as ephebe delineating a birth to himself through a violent act of self-wounding. For the poem is itself paradigmatic of poetry for Heaney; it is a poem about his own writing, which comes from the bog or from anamnesis, but it is also thus a poem which delineates how the poetry must derive from an act of self-wounding anamorphosis.

In my epigraph to this section, Heaney has described himself as the man suffering from the cut or bruise to the living root which is not in the Grauballe Man's head but in his own. The poem is his epithalamium in a sense: the wedding text which tries to wedge together the wounding, a suturing which is involved in the act of love. It is the 'Wedding Day' on which

> I am afraid.
> Sound has stopped in the day
> And the images reel over
> And over . . .[25]

[24] Gilles Deleuze, *Cinéma 2: L'Image-temps* (Paris: Minuit, 1985), 132.

[25] Seamus Heaney, 'Wedding Day', in *Wintering Out* (London: Faber & Faber, 1972), 57.

It also brings to mind his dream of freedom:

I had to read from Martin Luther King's famous 'I have a dream' speech. 'I have a dream that one day this nation will rise up and live out the full meaning of its creed'—and on that day all men would be able to realize fully the implications of the old spiritual, 'Free at last, free at last, Great God Almighty, we are free at last.' But, as against the natural hopeful rhythms of that vision, I remembered a dream that I'd had last year in California. I was shaving at the mirror of the bathroom when I glimpsed in the mirror a wounded man falling towards me with his bloodied hands lifted to tear at me or to implore.[26]

The Grauballe Man is, as it were, the image in Heaney's mirror: it is his Imaginary, his dream of freedom. As an Imaginary, it fits in with the idea of *anamnesis* in the poem. For what we have is a situation in which the world, that alien space, turns out according to the logic of the poem not to be an unknown alien realm at all, but rather simply what the poet always knew but had simply forgotten: it is as if the world is, as it were, a latent unconscious for the poet, his Imaginary; and the writing of the poem is the therapeutic act of recovering what had been repressed, and facing it. In these terms, the atrocities of violence in Ireland are a return of the repressed pagan rites of sacrifice. Paganism, of course, is itself aligned by Lyotard with a certain postmodernism.[27]

But there is another image which fits this in the text as well. That image is an image of Robert Lowell, who ghosts this poem. Lowell ghosts the poem in the stanza which describes the head of the Grauballe Man:

> The head lifts,
> the chin is a visor
> raised above the vent
> of his slashed throat . . .

What we have here is a situation again reminiscent of Hamlet, especially that Hamlet who tests the veracity of Horatio when the latter is testifying to seeing Hamlet's dead father, returned

[26] Heaney, *Preoccupations*, 33.

[27] See Jean François Lyotard, *Rudiments païens* (Paris: Union Générale d'Éditions, 1977), and *Instructions païennes* (Paris: Galilée, 1977), *Tombeau de l'intellectuel* (Paris: Galilée, 1984), *Le Postmoderne expliqué aux enfants* (Paris: Galilée, 1986).

from the grave rather like a proto-Grauballe Man. In that scene, Hamlet asks whether the ghost was armed:

HAMLET. Armed, say you?
ALL. Armed, my lord.
HAMLET. From top to toe?
ALL. My lord, from head to foot.
HAMLET. Then saw you not his face.
HORATIO. O, yes, my lord. He wore his beaver up.[28]

This can be easily translated back into Heaney's text. Here, the idea of the chin as a visor which is raised above the throat suggests a literal 'disfiguration' in the sense that the face—the 'figure'—disappears in a particular way. It implies a closeness of the eye and the mouth, or, as Lowell would have thought this, a closeness of 'Eye and Tooth'. In Lowell's poem of that name, we have an examination of a particular kind of justice, the justice of a biblical mode (eye for eye, tooth for tooth, etc.) which is placed at the service of a political ideology, that which is identified in Lowell's poem by the imperialist American eagle:

> No ease from the eye
> of the sharp-shinned hawk in the birdbook there,
> with reddish brown buffalo hair
> on its shanks
>
> clasping the abstract imperial sky.
> It says:
> *an eye for an eye,*
> *a tooth for a tooth.*[29]

In a certain sense, then, Heaney's 'bog poems' become his version of a text *For the Union Dead*: a volume which is, of course, a validation of America's 'North'. Heaney's 'Act of Union' sees the relation of imperialism in precisely the same Oedipal terms which 'The Grauballe Man' explores.

In the interstices of the poem, then, there comes a pressure which breaks it from within. It is, in a sense, an allegory of Ireland's situation. But, whereas the modernist reading would see this in terms of a spatial allegory in which the text would be

[28] Shakespeare, *Hamlet*, I. ii.
[29] Robert Lowell, 'Eye and Tooth', in *For the Union Dead* (London: Faber & Faber, 1965), 18–19.

regarded as falling into two halves, marked by the interstitial line of Lowell and/or Oedipus, and would thus think this breakage or interruption in spatial terms, what my own reading shows is that this Irish situation, this 'curt cut', is itself a temporal out (hence allegory as *anagogy*), one which involves history and which sees the poem as itself a historical event. Heaney here is not map-making, but history-making: one of the 'history boys'.[30] When Lowell appears as the ghostly father figure in the way I have described, we have 'the presence of the past', not its pastness.

Lyotard suggests that the 'post' of postmodern be understood in terms of 'ana-': it is a 'procès en "*ana*" ': 'Tu comprends qu'ainsi compris, le "post-" de "postmoderne" ne signifie pas un mouvement de *come back*, de *flash back*, de *feed back*, c'est-à-dire de répétition, mais un procès en "*ana-*", un procès d'analyse, d'anamnèse, d'anagogie, et d'anamorphose, qui élabore un "oubli initial" '.[31] Heaney's poem is precisely such a process. It is analysis: literally a setting free and into mobility of elements which had seemed to be irreversibly conjoined. It is anamnesis, in its articulation of and actualization of the presence of the past, even of disparate pasts. It is anagogical in its allegorical enactment of the historical split which is the *espace critique* of Ireland. It is anamorphic, a distorted drawing or representation with its abnormal transformations of Heaney into Oedipus, Oedipus into Lowell, Ireland into America, *North* into *For the Union Dead*, Jutland into Ireland, and so on: all those montage effects of this cinematic poem. It is in short the elaboration of an 'initial forgetting', a forgetting of the violence of origin itself.

[30] Seamus Deane, 'Send War in Our Time, O Lord', in *History Lessons* (Dublin: Gallery Books, 1983), 12.

[31] Lyotard, *Le Postmoderne expliqué aux enfants*, 126.

6. *Initiations, Tempers, Seductions*

McGuckian's poetry is pointless, in a sense akin to the way in which Molly Bloom's soliloquy is without point, unpunctuated or unpunctual. A typical sentence meanders around a point, apostrophically veering from it whenever it seems to be about to touch ground, so to speak:

> You call me aspen
> Tongue, but if my longer and longer sentences
> Prove me wholly female, I'd be persimmon,
> And good kindling, to us both.[1]

It has become fashionable to read McGuckian as a poet whose language, grammar, and syntax all serve to question masculinism, and to see her as a poet in a literary lineage deriving from Joyce's Molly. There may be some truth in this, but at the outset it might be worth suggesting that the lines from 'Aviary' just quoted provide strong circumstantial evidence for a hunch one has while reading McGuckian. Like another predecessor aligned with a feminist poetic, Emily Dickinson (and also like McDiarmid), McGuckian seems to be a keen reader of the dictionary. The *OED*, for instance, under 'aspen', gives an etymology linking the word to 'asp' and offers, as an example of a particular usage of the word, 'aspen tongue', meaning 'the tongue of a woman'. It looks more than likely that these lines were dictated not by any specifically feminist intention preceding the poem, but rather by a reading of the dictionary.

The verse often reads as if the language itself, a language devoid of a consciousness, were directing it:

> Asleep on the coast I dream of the city.
> A poem dreams of being written

[1] Medbh McGuckian, *Venus and the Rain* (Oxford: Oxford University Press, 1984), 21 (hereafter referred to in text as *VR*). All subsequent references to McGuckian's poetry are to this and the following collections: *The Flower Master* (Oxford: Oxford University Press, 1982), hereafter *FM*; *On Ballycastle Beach* (Oxford: Oxford University Press, 1988), hereafter *BB*.

Without the pronoun 'I'.
('Harem Trousers', *BB* 43)

Often it is difficult to locate any single position from which the poem can be spoken. In philosophical terms, we have a kind of 'blank phenomenology': the relation between the speaking subject or 'I' and the object of its intention is mobile or fluid. It reads as if the space afforded the 'I' is vacant: instead of a stable 'persona', all we have is a *possibility*, a potential of personality, a voice which cannot yet be identified. The poetry becomes a poetry of 'villainy':

This house is the shell of a perfect marriage
Someone has dug out completely; so its mind
Is somewhere above its body, and its body
Stumbles after its voice like a man who needs
A woman for every book.
('The Villain', *VR* 19)[2]

A recurring feature of McGuckian is an 'untimeliness', the sense of a gap between what is said and the voice which says it. There is a fractured 'unpunctual' consciousness here. That 'untimeliness' is consonant with a current in contemporary philosophies of the postmodern. Deleuze, for instance, often relates his philosophy to the notion that 'the time is out of joint', and he considers a Nietzschean untimeliness to be inherent in anything which can be genuinely called 'thinking'. Similarly, Lyotard indicates that the postmodern artwork exists in a 'future anterior' tense and is always contaminated by the artist's own unreadiness for it. If the ripeness or readiness is all, then the artist and philosopher is she or he who is never 'ripe': 'work and text . . . arrive always too late for their author, or, what amounts to the same thing, their being put into work always begins too soon.'[3] Here, I argue for a postmodern McGuckian. She offers the availability of a poetry which is not defined by its

[2] It is as if a Cartesian *cogito* here has been replaced by a *loquor* as the subject of the voice. For a fuller argument documenting this as a trait in contemporary writing, see my *Reading (Absent) Character* (Oxford: Oxford Univeristy Press, 1983), 34–6, 87–123, and *passim.*

[3] Jean-François Lyotard, *The Postmodern Condition* (trans. Geoff Bennington and Brian Massumi; Manchester; Manchester University Press, 1984), 81. Cf. e.g. Gilles Deleuze, *Kant's Critical Philosophy* (Minneapolis: University of Minnesota Press, 1984), and *Nietzsche and Philosophy* (London: Athlone Press, 1983).

relation to a tradition or place; rather, her writing offers a way of breaking away from the 'place-logic' which is central to the formulation of a national culture, tradition, or lineage.[4]

The first three major collections construct a specific trajectory. *The Flower Master* (1982) is an initiatory collection. Many of its poems are concerned with different kinds of initiation rites and with the transgressions of borders or boundaries. These borders, however, are not the expected geographical border (though that one is here too), but are more symbolic borders, such as the boundary between infancy and adulthood; the border between an Edenic garden and a secular world, and so on. A concern for our secular ('fallen') condition is apparent from the earliest poems such as 'Problem Girl', with its Eve-like girl, eating her apple; or in 'Lychees', with its delineation of a degeneracy from religious life into secularity. From these and other poems, it becomes clear that McGuckian's real 'Flower Master' is none other than the nineteenth-century poet of diabolism, Baudelaire, whose *Fleurs du mal* ghost this text.

Venus and the Rain (1984) has as its dominant trait a concern for space, both inner and outer. The 'inner space' is that of the vacuous subject of the blank phenomenology; the outer space that suggested by the planetary turn of the title poem. Here, one finds traces of another French thinker, the mathematician, philosopher, and Catholic Pascal, whose *pensées* were both thoughts and flowers (pansies), and whose writings interlace in the same fragmentary fashion as McGuckian's poetry, with overlaps from one text into the next. Pascal, of course, was a man terrified by 'Le silence éternel de ces espaces infinis'.[5]

One might immediately be tempted to think of *On Ballycastle Beach* (1988) as McGuckian's *North*, for its title refers to a geographical location at one of the northernmost points of Ireland, in County Antrim. But, once again, if the reader searches here for the kind of explicit or mythic politics found in other contemporary Irish poets, she or he will be disappointed. These poems are organized around a 'French-born' idea, *le temps perdu*.

[4] On 'place-logic' in the thinking of Rudolph Agricola, see Walter J. Ong, *Ramus: Method and the Decay of Dialogue* (Cambridge, Mass.: Harvard University Press, 1958), 121. The present chapter characterizes such place-logic as 'modernist'. For an argument describing the modifications of space and time in postmodernity, see David Harvey, *The Condition of Postmodernity* (Oxford: Blackwell, 1989).

[5] Blaise Pascal, *Pensées*, in *Œuvres complètes* (Paris: Seuil, 1963), 528, no. 201.

Temps, meaning both time and weather, allows McGuckian a trope which organizes poems obsessed with seasonal change. Here, it is as if the rituals which interest her are the pagan rites which have been latent in all her writing. There is also here a governing figure of 'seduction' or *temp*-tation, as if the texts were written by a Lilith figure, and as if the texts were an attempt, or essay, at constructing a literary lineage deriving from Eve and her apples.

The present argument falls into three sections. First, I chart some 'initiations', to demonstrate McGuckian's concern for ritual and artifice and to probe the resulting idealism in the writing. Secondly, I 'take the temperature' or temper of the verse, exploring the ethos of McGuckian's blank phenomenology, her vacuous 'idealist' subjectivity. Thirdly, I link her writing to surrealism and superrealist movements, and through this describe a politics of her postmodern questioning of the real.

1. INITIATIONS

A prevalent conception of art is that it occupies a different order from the secular world. Many, following an Arnoldian argument, subscribe to the notion that art is a substitute for religion and that it therefore sets up an opposition between the secular and the sacred. In its crudest forms, this is pure idealism; yet, as Eliade and Girard argue, with some sophistication, there is a sense in which the ritualization of everyday life is crucial: societies require rituals as markers of time's passage. A simple unmarked flow of time would be difficult to understand as time at all. Time and history have to be narrativized; and narratives organize themselves around temporal markers such as birthdays, funerals, anniversaries, solstices, and so on. Kermode argues that the endings of narratives cast sense retrospectively upon them; but these endings are movable feasts.[6]

[6] See e.g. Mircea Eliade, *Le Mythe de l'éternel retour* (Paris: Gallimard, 1949); Erving Goffman, *The Presentation of Self in Everyday Life* (Edinburgh: Edinburgh University Press, 1956); Frank Kermode, *The Sense of an Ending* (New York: Oxford University Press, 1967).

McGuckian is concerned with two such deictic moments. The first is what we call puberty, a shift from infancy into adulthood, from 'non-speaking' (*infans*) into a voice. Hence the first initiation rite is one concerned with sexuality and with language, the acquisition of a voice, the possibility of 'being listened to'. The second such instant, often located within the first, is a mythic moment of a beginning or birthing of sorts. She often writes of maternity or pregnancy; but these are related to another beginning, the mythic biblical beginning in the fall from grace. This second initiation moment, then, is the moment of the entry into history as such. Both moments of initiation are tantalizingly implicated with each other in the opening poems of *The Flower Master*.

'That Year' opens with a description of a young woman's discovery of some aspects of her body:

> That year it was something to do with your hands:
> To play about with rings, to harness rhythm
> In staging bleach or henna on the hair,
> Or shackling, unshackling the breasts.

A memory, linking 'that year' with another, earlier one, follows, introducing the two colours which are important here:

> I remembered as a child the red kite
> Lost forever over our heads, the white ball
> A pin-prick on the tide, and studied
> The leaf-patterned linoleum, the elaborate
>
> Stitches on my pleated bodice.
> It was like a bee's sting or a bullet
> Left in me, this mark, this sticking pins in dolls,
> Listening for the red and white
>
> Particles of time to trickle slow . . .

The memory, linking a moment of childhood play with 'that year', hinges on a red kite and a white ball like a pin-prick. The girl looks at her own body with its elaborate—or laboured—stitches. Then there is the wait for 'red and white | Particles'. Given the suggestion in 'Slips' (*FM* 21) that poetry operates partly by metaphor and partly by euphemism, it becomes impossible—if we 'listen'—to miss the allusion here to red and white corpuscles, and hence the suggestion that what is being awaited is a menarche. The ritual nature of this moment, 'that year', is hinted at in the linking of the menarche with magic, the voodoo of 'sticking pins in dolls'. Yet there is, of course, also that other year being hinted at: the later year of a birthing, as suggested in those laboured stitches on the bodice, themselves 'slips' for a Caesarean birth. The poem closes with the image of a curtained, cushioned woman, brought to bed.

This pubescent initiation is reiterated in 'Tulips'. Here is the first tacit appearance of a 'master', who is not, as might be expected in this poem, the Wordsworth whose daffodils are tacitly alluded to by the poem's description of flowers dancing 'ballets of revenge'. Rather, the second stanza offers an elaborate intertextual weaving into Henry James's novella, *The Turn of the Screw*, itself a thoroughly ambiguous tale of frustrated sexuality and of a young woman's relations with a 'Master'. The governess in James was 'raped' or 'carried away' in London at the Master's house; but this sexual overtone, apparent in the tale as in the poem, is also linked to a linguistic issue. The word 'metaphor' means 'carrying across' or 'carrying away': the sexual initiation is also a linguistic initiation, as here in 'Tulips', another poem in which the reader must listen for the slips.

The poem constantly displaces its reader, and is difficult to read because of the elongation of its sentences and the resulting complexity of syntax. The first part of the first sentence (lines 1 to 6) tempts the reader to come to syntactic and semantic rest some seven times, as she or he searches more and more desperately for the ending of the sentence (its 'that year') which will enable the retrospective making of sense. The tulips have the presence of mind to defend themselves against the unwanted intrusion of rain which falls into the daffodil. If McGuckian is a reader of the dictionary, we might be aware that the *OED* offers a definition of 'tulip' alongside its meaning as a flower with phallic stem: a 'tulip' is 'a showy person; one greatly admired'—a kind of flower-master, in short. The poem, with this allusion to James's novella, enables the reader to hear the difficult phrase 'grocery of soul' as an echo of Mrs Grose, whose own 'grossery of soul' is that she is illiterate: the one character in the James text who cannot read and yet also the one who knows what's going on. Letters—mislaid, stolen, intercepted or unread—form the focus of *The Turn of the Screw*, a text whose whole *raison d'être* is the paralysis of interpretation, the stymying of understanding, as has been argued by Felman and Brooke-Rose.[7] The same difficulty arises here, and one suddenly has to read the letters which constitute the poem differently.

Its opening phrase, 'Touching the tulips was a shyness', is an odd phrase as it stands; yet, if one listens to the flower, one can also make a different sense: touching the *two-lips* was a shyness. Heard in this 'American' inflection (*à la* James), one has the image of a speaker demonstrating her shyness by actually touching her finger to her lips. But, at this point, and given the 'absence of mirrors', one can also begin to hear the feminist input into this dense, complex poem.

Irigaray, especially in *Speculum* and in *Ce sexe qui n'en est pas un*, has proposed that the entire history of Western thinking has been inescapably masculinist for the primary reason of its prioritization of the specular gaze and of the sense of vision. If we replace this with tactility, she suggests, we might be able to counter the inevitability of masculinist thinking, which is complicit with a denial of subjectivity and a denial of the voice to woman. Irigaray argues that, while men require some external effect to articulate their sexuality (woman, hand, object of sorts), women are always in touch with themselves, for their genitals are formed by two lips in continual tactile arrangement. It is the intrusion of the male tulip-like stalk of the phallus which arrests auto-erotic pleasure and self-presence (or present-mindedness). Given the absence of mirrors in 'Tulips', one might realize that the tactile overcomes the visual here. But now, 'touching the tulips | two-lips' is thoroughly ambiguous. On the one hand, touching the tulips might suggest an obvious touching the phallus; but, on the other, it also suggests the woman touching her own lips, both mouth and vagina. The poem thus becomes one of covert masturbation, a 'womanliness of tulips'.

[7] Shoshana Felman, 'Turning the Screw of Interpretation', in Felman (ed.), *Literature and Psychoanalysis* (Baltimore; Johns Hopkins University Press, 1982), 94–207; Christine Brooke-Rose, *A Rhetoric of the Unreal* (Cambridge: Cambridge University Press, 1981), 128–87.

The feminist problematic is that of 'not being listened to' (*BB* 51). Hence the necessity for circumlocution or 'slips', most obviously in the euphemistic language of flowers deployed by other unheard women such as Ophelia or Perdita in Shakespeare. In 'Tulips', the touching of the fingers to the oral lips describes the woman as silenced. But, listening to the slips here, the availability of a 'womanliness of tulips', a womanly voice, can be discovered. To hear this voice is the critical task. This poem simply describes the moment of a ritual transgression in which the poet loses infancy in the articulation of sexuality (literally: for sexuality is articulacy, literacy, here).

Initiation, and with it linguistic and gendered authority, implies a rite of passage or transgression of a boundary. This symbolic boundary in McGuckian replaces the geo-political border in other poets' work. She thinks the boundary symbolically, which is conventional enough, deploying a Christian mythology of the expulsion from a paradise into history, the theme which dominates *On Ballycastle Beach*, where the sands of time replace the gardens implied by *The Flower Master*, after the journey through space in *Venus and the Rain*. But the symbolic geography opens another issue which haunts the poetry: the construction of an 'economy' or law of the household.

This begins in the first collection, where it is as if 'Admiring the Furs' gets too close to the political situation for comfort. The passage across the checkpoints in this poem brings to the speaker's mind her 'measurements at nine', a memory of a pre-pubertal state. But this is related to the furs in the window and the violence which brings them there for human warmth and comfort. The animal skin—our own covering—is produced through an act of violence; and in this poem it is as if the 'preoccupation', as Heaney would think of it, causes a pain, the pain which 'tells you what to wear' (*VR* 40). The Irish state, bifurcated on a boundary, *is* an agonizing death, a wounded skin which has to be sloughed off. The checkpoint is, like the window-pane, a boundary which serves to cover the presence of pain, that pain which is the wounding of Ireland, the killing of Ireland through the act of partition.

The transgression of this very political boundary is rare in McGuckian. More frequently the boundary to be transgressed takes on a more ritualized and sacral aspect, and operates under a symbolism of domesticity. One example is 'Mr McGregor's Garden', which alludes—as do all gardens in this poetry—to a primal garden, an edenic state once lost and always remembered with nostalgia.[8] The poem starts darkly, with 'Some women save their sanity with needles'. On the one hand, this might be an item from a domestic lexicon, suggesting knitting-needles used with the pin as in the 'pin-prick' of 'That Year'. But there is a darker side to this, with the hint of a witch-like injection, and hence the idea of saving sanity through drugs. Attention immediately turns to the mode of saving sanity proposed by the speaker:

> I complicate my life with studies
> Of my favourite rabbit's head, his vulgar volatility.

This 'Bunny' becomes her furry comforter later in the poem. But the 'vulgar volatility' is the essential issue here. The rabbit's head, of course, is classically used in theories of visual perception to demonstrate a particular boundary in the way we see. The drawing of a rabbit's head is also a drawing of a duck, depending on how we choose to view it. It is impossible to see both at once, yet it is also impossible to see the volatility, the shift, as the rabbit crosses the threshold of perception to become a duck.

Perception, sight itself, involves us in a transgression of the very same kind of boundary which caused the pain in 'Admiring the Furs'. Here is an articulation of those Irigarayan theories which acknowledge the pain caused to women by perception as we think it, by the prioritization of the visual as the determining element of modern Western culture. McGuckian answers this directly in 'Painter and Poet', where she seems to favour not the replacement of vision with tactility as in Irigarary, but rather the replacement of vision with words, language, poetry.

This perceptual transgression operates in much of her domestic imagery, where doors and windows are forever being opened and closed, indicating a threshold boundary which invites danger. Similarly, letters frequently go unread, whether the envelope remains whole or is violently torn open. It is as if

[8] This poem works in the tradition of the 'garden-poem', which dates at least from the Renaissance.

the act of reading her letters were itself an act of violence or transgression, an act of the same kind of initiatory violence which causes the personal pain described in 'That Year'. Such windows and doors appear, for fine examples, in 'The Sofa' or 'The Sitting'.

But the window, as Bachelard might say, produces the house.[9] The threshold which is a doorway immediately implies not just a threatening outside, but also a domestic interior, of the kind described in 'The Flitting' (which also 'has cost me' much discomfort) or throughout the poetry in incidental references to domestic scenes, furniture, the architecture of rooms, beds, and so on. This becomes of some importance in 'The Sun-Trap'. In the greenhouse whose hygroscope says 'orchid', the flower associated with testicles (from the Greek *orkhis* = testicle), the speaker is

> touched by even the strange gesture
> Of rain stopping, your penetration
> Of my mask of 'bon viveur', my crested notepaper,
> My lined envelopes. From your last letter
> I construed at least the word
> For kisses, if not quite a kindred spirit.

Reading this last letter, then, there is the suggestion first of the 'penetration' of the envelope, a transgression of a lining, together with the idea of a sexual relation in those kisses. However, something is not quite right in that the letter cannot easily be deciphered: it is misread, and the reader is searching for a 'kindred spirit' while finding only the 'word | For kisses'. The letter clearly brings disturbing news, of 'the magically fertile German girl | Who sleeps in the bunk above you', and who

> seems
> To me quite flirtatious
> Though you say she's the sort of girl
> You'd rather have as a daughter.

This reminds the speaker of some previous 'near-tragedy' of a weekend spent with a 'cousin once-removed'. And, at this moment, three things coalesce. First, the trapping of the sun, its

[9] See Gaston Bachelard, *La Poétique de l'espace* (Paris: PUF, 1957).

capturing within the space of the house, and hence its transgression of a boundary, produces the warmth of an interior set against the sickly rain and threatening weather of the outside: the house, thus, as a site of a mutation or transformation. Secondly, this relates to the search for a 'kindred spirit', with its hint of some familial or domestic relation. Thirdly, there are the near-explicit references to incest, in the idea of the German girl as the flirtatious daughter sleeping in the same room (actually, technically the same bed) as the correspondent, and the unspoken event between speaker and cousin once-removed. Transgression, then, involves the building of a house as a ritual or sacral space called the family which exists as an apotropaic warder-off of death and history. But the production of the house and its interiorized space, together with the necessity of sexual relations as the mode of initiation which makes the house possible in the first place, produces what Freud well knew about, the taboo of incest.

The domestic poems of McGuckian are contaminated thus by the dark and guilty question of endogamy; and it is the guilt associated with this tribal sectarianism which brings *The Flower Master* more clearly into line with Baudelaire's *Fleurs du mal*, a collection also dotted with domestic imagery, but a book which was gothically obsessed with the revelation of an evil which lay behind—and indeed founded—the decorous nature of a bourgeois existence. In McGuckian's case, there is a link between the necessity of transgression (sexual initiation and entry into secular history) and the inevitability of an evil introspection, an 'endogamous' looking inwards towards a guilt perceived in the space 'within', the interior produced by the transgression and its threshold. 'Look within', urged the modernist Woolf, famously; and when McGuckian does, she sees guilt. The much-vaunted erotics of her writing are all tinged with the sense of a maleficence, a diabolism, and with the need to find a pure genealogy, but one which in its purity would be uncontaminated by this taboo of interiority, this incestuous thinking and introspection.

A postmodern sublime lies available here. We have the necessity of a transgression, the idea of a breakthrough across some threshold of perception, together with the recalcitrance which that transgression provokes: this is the pleasurable pain of interpretation in McGuckian. It is like the seduction of a letter unread, a letter which remains tantalizingly visible beneath or within its envelope; but the tearing open of the envelope reveals that the letter is not there after all: what we thought was a meaningful missive turns out to be a pattern on the envelope. Throughout the verse, it is precisely at the moment of taking root, or of finding a single place from which to understand a poem, that it melts away again into ambivalence and ambiguity. 'A newly-understood poem will melt | And be hard again' ('Mazurka', *BB* 22). And even the point of transgression, the threshold, cannot be properly or adequately identified: 'The point when I sleep is not known | By me, and words cannot carry me | Over it' ('A Dream in Three Colours', *BB* 44).

The reader of McGuckian is in the position of the person who moves from the state of being awake to that of being asleep: either she is awake or asleep, and it is impossible to locate her at the precise moment of the change between the two. The 'checkpoint', in this way, magically is made to disappear, in exactly the same sophisticated way in which death is made to disappear in Augustine or Wittgenstein or Camus.[10] Yet, of course, the checkpoint undeniably exists: this hovering uncertainly between existence and non-existence is its 'sublimity'. It is both there and not there, like Venus herself who is described like a Malevich painting: 'White on white, I can never be viewed | Against a heavy sky' ('Venus and the Rain', *VR* 31), precisely the heavy sky which dominates the 'sickly Irish weather' ('The Sun-Trap', *FM* 24).

The letter in McGuckian, the text or poem as well as its very constituent letters, is the site of this refusal of representation. Each poem is, as it were, a threshold inviting the initiation of its reader into some meaning; yet it also denies that meaning at the very instant of its perception. This is McGuckian as Malvolio, a McGuckian who does not play ducks and drakes so much as ducks and rabbits. Initiation promises change; and it is the precise moment of initiation which McGuckian wants to locate. Yet, because of its very characterization as the site of mobility

[10] See Augustine, *City of God* (trans. Henry Battenson; Harmondsworth: Penguin, 1972), 519–20; Ludwig Wittgenstein, *Tractatus Logico-Philosophicus* (trans. D. F. Pears and B. F. M'Guinness; London: Routledge, 1961), 6. 4311; Albert Camus, *Le Mythe de Sisyphe* (Paris: Gallimard, 1942), 29–30.

and mutability, as a point of transgression or change, the locus of initiation cannot properly be identified, represented, or described. It is, as it were, immaterial, invisible as Venus in the rain. The point of initiation, the 'checkpoint', is itself pointless.

2. TEMPERS

One neat mutation central to McGuckian is the linguistic slippage between 'tempt' and 'temporal'. In Christian mythology, Eve, eater of the apples that figure so widely in McGuckian, tempted or tried or tested the apple and Adam's resistance to it. This temptation by and of the woman provokes the fall into temporality, the condition in which McGuckian must now write what Stevens would have called 'The Poems of our Climate': that is, poems in which she takes a secular 'temper' or temperature, measuring the flow and sequence of the seasons which co-ordinate or order secular life. But, because of the 'blank phenomenology' of her writing, she is condemned to live in a kind of temporal absence. She is always—temporally and temperamentally—at odds with herself: the poems chart a dislocation in their speaker, who always occupies some different temporal moment from the moment actually being described in the poem. There is a gap, a *différance*, between the moment of the enunciation and the moment of the enunciated. As in Heidegger, the poet is always living alongside herself. She is like the character who lives in a cold climate in 'Minus 18 Street':

> I never loved you more
> Than when I let you sleep another hour,
> As if you intended to make such a gate of time
> Your home.
>
> (*BB* 19)

As a being-in-time, and one living that time as a gate or threshold of transgression, the poet is never present-to-herself. Caught in a late or neo-romantic predicament, her voice is always temporally out-of-step with what it says. Her time, like that of Hamlet, is 'out of joint'.[11]

[11] In romanticism itself, of course, this predicament was that of idealism. The poet typically desires an ontological empathy with the world of the natural

On Ballycastle Beach, despite its parochial title, is among the more exotic of McGuckian's collections, delighting in words derived from Eastern Europe, Africa, and Asia as well as the more domestic kinds of detail expected after her earlier work. But it is worth starting closer to home, in the poem 'Not Pleasing Mama', whose only 'foreign' phrase is the French 'à la belle étoile', meaning 'under the open sky'. This poem opens with the odd suggestion that the weather is unsure:

> If rain begins as snow, then the weather
> Has slipped down as between walls, is not
> To be trusted any more
> Than any other magic.
>
> (*BB* 20)

This weather is out of its proper place.[12] The French speaker who interjects might hear an interlingual pun here: *temps* as both weather and time. This text, thus, is not to be trusted for it is the site of another 'slipping' between meanings, between languages and countries, between cultures. If the weather is misplaced, it is also—to the French voice of the text—a *temps perdu*; and this opens the text to its interrelation with Proust, whose text begins not only with not pleasing Mama but also with not being pleased by the Mama who withholds the good-night kiss. Proust, if he is about anything, is about the loss or waste of time, about a time out of joint.

'Not Pleasing Mama', with its tempting apple, is a key poem: it casts retrospective light on the opening poems of the collection, 'What Does "Early" Mean?', 'Staying in a Better Hotel', 'Apple Flesh', and 'Grainne's Sleep Song', all texts which share

which—it is claimed—was enjoyed by the rustic; but the poet, blessed or cursed (or both) with consciousness, can enjoy, at best, an epistemological empathy with nature, an empathy gained, however, precisely at the cost of her or his ontological alienation from that world. The autobiographical impetus is thus produced from a project in which the subject aims temporally to coincide with itself, a project doomed, as Sterne had clearly prefigured, to a sublime failure. For an argument characterizing this as also a 'modernist' predicament, see my 'Anti-Mimesis', in *Forum for Modern Language Studies* (1990).

[12] There is here a Rabelaisian joke, audible to the francophone speaker in the poem. 'Between walls' is between 'mur' et 'mur': 'ou mur y a et davant et derriere, y a force murmur, envie et conspiration mutue' (François Rabelais, *Gargantua*, in *Œuvres complètes*, i, ed. P. Jourda (Paris: Garnier Frères, 1962), 189).

the Proustian and Wordsworthian seduction by time and weather.

'What Does "Early" Mean?' It means 'before the proper or appointed time'. The poem describes a temporal displacement in which a house is out of step with the season: 'Yet I think winter has ended | Privately in you' (*BB* 11). This is related to McGuckian's own writing, which is equally 'untimely':

> None of my doors has slammed
> Like that, every sentence is the same
> Old workshop sentence, ending
> Rightly or wrongly in the ruins
> Of an evening spent in puzzling
> Over the meaning of six o'clock or seven . . .

'Early' is a deictic term, depending for its meaning upon a situation: 'six o'clock' is not by definition early. Hence the meaning of the term is itself untimely, as if the meaning of the word resided elsewhere or in a different time from that of the word's actual articulation. It also demands a relation between at least two times: to be 'early' implies an appointment; yet it also demands a disappointment, a failure of correspondence between the two or more elements destined to coincide at the proper moment. To be early is to be out of place as well as out of time: it is to be 'flitting', to be on the nomadic move, between situations. No echoes of Hardy ghost this verse.[13]

Moreover, 'early', in its implication of (dis)appointment, also demands narrative, for it demands a link to be forged in the plotting of two disparate moments. The narrative of 'early' is produced in 'Grainne's Sleep Song' (*BB* 16), in which untimeliness is directly related to 'a novel rough to the touch', presumably the narrative referred to later, that 'Uncompleted story, something sterile | I contracted fourteen years ago on the beach, | Entitled "Wild Without Love" '. The speaker steps out of this narrative, a past moment, to enter a present relation; but the temporal relation between the fourteen-years-old narrative and the situation of 'The day that I got up to' is fused and

[13] Hardy's poetry, especially in the famous instance of 'The Convergence of the Twain', is about keeping an appointment with fate; cf. Beckett, whose characters in *Waiting for Godot* pride themselves on keeping their appointment, but an appointment which is, by the play's formal definition, necessarily a disappointment.

confused. The narrative is incomplete, as the meaning of the poem is also incomplete, falling back to 'initials' or beginnings. The sleep song, then, is once more about the temporal relation between beginning and end; the sleep is a mediation or meditation between the two states or two times, and mutability or uncertainty becomes the order of the day.

It is this which makes McGuckian's poetry a 'critical poetry', in the same senses as Kant's philosophy was a 'critical philosophy' or Frankfurt School political theory is a 'critical theory'. All are formulated in a mode of proleptic difference. Deleuze offers the most succinct description of what is at stake here in Kantian and post-Kantian (for which read postmodern) thinking:

> Time is out of joint, time is unhinged . . . As long as time remains on its hinges, it is subordinate to movement: it is the measure of movement, interval or number. This was the view of ancient philosophy. But time out of joint signifies the reversal of the movement–time relationship. It is now movement which is subordinate to time. Everything changes, including movement.[14]

Movement, the movement of transgression across the 'door' hinged by time, is what McGuckian was after in earlier poems. Here, she has discovered the reversal which makes movement itself subordinate to time, secularism. An allegorization of this in terms of the political scenario—if one is needed—might run like this: there will be no movement over the border so long as time remains on its hinges—so long, that is, as a particular relation to secularity is maintained whereby the secular is but a pale shadow of the eternal or sacred. Movement will not come so long as Ireland remains 'pre-critical' or 'pre-historic'. A critical reversal of priorities is needed which acknowledges that movement over the border will only be possible if such movement becomes subordinate to time—that is, if the being of people on both sides of the border becomes a being-in-time, a being determined by historicity and not by fixed, eternal, or transcendental claims upon a true identity, a 'chosen ground' for a chosen people. The poetry is a call to a critical historicism: not just an awareness of time past, but an awareness that one

[14] Deleuze, *Kant's Critical Philosophy*, p. vii.

must 'disappoint' the history or narrative seemingly determined by that time past: time past must be misplaced, *perdu*.

3. THE FORCE OF SEDUCTION AND THE PLAY OF SURREALISM

The crudity of that allegory of politics in McGuckian does not do justice to the force of her poetry, which finds more indirect—but, I shall argue, more powerful—ways of intervening in the political culture in which she writes. As might be expected in any literature which might be called a literature of decolonization, there is in much contemporary Irish poetry a concern with power: the ambivalent desire for an autonomous national power even in the very instant when the culture is striving to escape the legacy of a suffering caused by such a power. Mastery, in *The Flower Master*, is the shape this takes in early McGuckian; but this quickly comes under speculative pressure in the writing.

Power, like temporality, depends upon relation and narrative: power is, as it were, shaped deictically. Specifically, it depends upon 'under-standing'; yet it is precisely understanding that McGuckian mistrusts. She replaces understanding, with its inherent notion of the availability of stable positions of 'mastery' (she who speaks enigmatically) and 'subjection' (she who would understand and subscribe to the master), with a notion of mere interrelation. The form this takes is one of seduction. Seduction here is taken in a sense close to that proposed by Baudrillard: it is not simply a sexual event; rather, it describes a state of relation between powers or forces, and one which explicitly excludes production. Production would here mean the end of seduction. Seduction is, for instance, the play of forces which keeps the planets in mutual interrelation: one subject of *Venus in the Rain*.

'Venus and the Sun' (*VR* 9) describes the pull which the Sun exerts on Venus, and an opposing pull, in the opposite direction, exerted by Mars. Seduction is the play of forces, attraction and repulsion, which enables such relation. The resulting tension *produces* the entity we call 'Venus', or that we call 'Mars', and so on. In other words, to identify something as 'Venus' is artificially to arrest the play of forces: to make a fiction from a *mécanique des fluides*.[15] The important thing is that the forces come first: there is no essence of 'Mars', 'Venus', or the 'Sun' which generates a specific force: those names are but the effect of a configuration of forces. To stabilize them with such a name or identification is a fictive arresting of time itself; McGuckian reverses the priorities of 'modern' thinking.

To put things this way, of course, is to add the corollary to the Kantian revolution described by Deleuze. In conventional thought, there already exists a mass called the Sun which exerts a force on other stable and identifiable masses called the various planets. This enables a belief in the stability and identity of 'Venus', 'Mars', and so on; and by extension, a belief in some essential 'meaning' for all the elements of the universe, some intrinsic nature. But McGuckian, who writes in a line deriving from the postmodern thinking of Deleuze, Baudrillard, and others, reverses this set of priorities. There is no Venus without Mars; there is no Sun without these and the play of forces by which they are constituted. Rather than subscribing to some desire to identify what is produced, McGuckian prefers to work at the level of the seduction itself. This way, she questions the modern belief in the availability of identity. The arrangement of matter we call 'Venus' is, as it were, the taking root or forming an earth of a play of forces which McGuckian wishes to keep in play and in place; the arrangement of matter may appear stable, but it is invisible ('white on white'); by extension, of course, 'North' would also have no intrinsic meaning, nor would 'Ireland', nor would 'McGuckian' and so on. 'Le monde n'est qu'une branloire perenne.'[16]

'Venus', then, is held together, instant by instant, only through a kind of *stasis*, internal dissent and tension or civil war. This kind of seductive attraction depends upon gravity, or *mass*. Much of McGuckian's imagery is drawn from the pull she feels towards a Christian iconography and lexicon. But it is a corollary of her post-Kantian poetry that her aesthetic world must be guided not by a Christian onto-theology, but rather by a pagan consciousness. Paganism, of course, is not atheist, but

15 See Luce Irigaray, *Ce sexe qui n'en est pas un* (Paris: Minuit, 1977).

16 Michel de Montaigne, *Essais*, 3 vols. (Paris: Garnier-Flammarion, 1969), iii. 20.

prefers a heterotheology, a multiplicity of forces called 'gods' which activate the world.

A number of poems reveal this paganism and relate it to a hieroglyphic questioning of the letter. 'Vanessa's Bower' (*VR* 10) is a poem with a misunderstood letter, specifically the letter 'E':

> Dear owner, you write,
> Don't put me into your pocket: I am not
> A willow in your folly-studded garden
> Which you hope will weep the right way:
> And there are three trains leaving, none
> Of which connects me to your E-shaped
> Cottage. Alas, I have still the feeling,
> Half fatherly, half different, we are
> Travelling together in the train with this letter,
> Though my strange hand will never be your sin.

This E-shaped cottage is like a railway station, from which there run three parallel lines of flight. Seduction here is the gravitational pull away from the cottage and its folly-studded edenic garden with its weeping tree. That journey is taken with 'this letter', meaning both a missive (the poem, perhaps) and also the letter 'E'. Interestingly, the Hebrew letter ש, which looks like an E on its side, is pronounced 'sin'. This letter in Hebrew, the language of the Bible, provokes the weeping. But another intertext appears here. Erasmus, in *Praise of Folly*, describes this Hebrew letter and its pronunciation in a passage demonstrating the folly of a belief in an original or God-given language (the Word, the logos).[17] We are always in flight—or in multiple lines of flight—from such a language, always out of step with it in time and space. It is not the case that the apple-laden language of woman is folly or madness; rather, what is folly is the garden itself and the belief that there ever was one pure or original language of sanity, one Word which was there in the beginning and which was God.

Frequently in her poems, McGuckian makes a turn towards nomadism, towards a chosen ground which is, strictly speaking, nowhere in particular. The nomad simply moves around,

[17] Desiderius Erasmus, *Praise of Folly*, in John P. Dolan (ed.), *The Essential Erasmus* (New York: Mentor Books, 1964), 151–2.

with no specific home except a 'Querencia' (*BB* 25), the idea of a home, occupying whatever space is needed and available at any given moment. This attitude clearly marks McGuckian off from other Irish poets, like Deane, Montague, or Heaney, who have questioned the geography of Ireland as a specific and historically determined plot of earth or rough field. McGuckian is more interested in symbolic space and in the occupation of a language or a voice. Always in flight, her poems—like her own voice and identity—are never fixed in historical time or geographical space: their meaning is always untimely, never present-to-themselves, and hence never 'available'. In this way, her text is always 'temperable', marked by a promiscuous mingling of different meanings held together in a play of internal forces which allows her never to lose her 'temper'.

Given this difference from her contemporaries, it becomes apparent that, if one were to look for predecessors for McGuckian, it would be an error to search among the Irish poets of the twentieth century. In terms of linguistic styles, she has more in common with both nineteenth-century decadence and twentieth-century surrealism, both internationalist movements. Much of her imagery could be derived from Neruda or Aragon rather than from Clarke or Kavanagh. Yet there is one way in which she overlaps with a thematics of flight which dominates much Irish writing this century. Yeats, for instance, starts by looking west, then makes successive leaps eastwards to Greece and Byzantium for the sources of his poetry; Joyce and Beckett, famously, exile themselves; Heaney begins from an archaeology of Irish soil, and then, like Yeats, makes a symbolic geographic move eastwards in his alignment of himself with the dissident poets of Eastern Europe. Heaney also leaves the soil in another sense, becoming 'Mad Sweeney', the bird among the trees which Yeats had also dreamt of becoming.[18] It is this 'line of flight' which McGuckian adopts, and in her it becomes a structural determinant of the language and syntax of her writing.

There is an exoticism in McGuckian, very apparent in the vocabulary of *On Ballycastle Beach*, for instance, which literally

[18] For a more detailed argument making this point, see my *After Theory* (London: Routledge, 1990), 173–90.

'unsettles' the text and its readers. The predominantly Latinate and Anglo-Saxon vocabulary of the first two collections is interrupted here by words like 'Ylang-Ylang' (Malaysian), 'vetiver' (from African languages), 'Mazurka' (Polish), 'Querencia' (Spanish), 'balakhana' (Persian), and so on. McGuckian here reiterates some of the symbolic geographical manœuvres of Yeats, Heaney, and others; but its effects are different.

'Querencia', for instance, suggests a kind of 'land of heart's desire', or desired homeland; but it is odd that an Irish poet should use a Spanish word to describe this. The word is actually used in Spanish to describe the terrain of the bull in a bull-fight: it is the 'stamping-ground' of the threatening and dangerous animal. The term thus provides her with an ambivalent word describing her relation to 'home', a home which is 'elsewhere', a home riven by *stasis* or dissent, a home which is desired but which also threatens. 'Balakhana' is the word describing the upper storey of a Persian house, the room in which nomadic travellers would be put to pass the night. This balakhana (a near homonym for Ballycastle, of course) is not a stable home either, but a nomadic place of encampment, a temporary abode.

This kind of language works to suggest an alienation in McGuckian's own relation to her language. Like her, the reader has to become a reader of dictionaries in the endless search for meaning, and the language is thus always at odds with the mouth speaking it, always untimely, always a blank phenomenology. There is no single governing Logos, no monotheology of Truth here, no originary language: McGuckian, like the 'character' in Christine Brooke-Rose's 'novel' *Thru*, lives increasingly in the space between languages. She does not live between English and Gaelic, but between English and the languages of Europe, Asia, Africa. This linguistic internationalism contributes to the instabilities which enable her work to be characterized as late surrealist.

In the present century, surrealism has had a chequered history. Initially an art dedicated to revolution, it became more and more explicitly reactionary. Yet it has always served one critical purpose well: it always questions the nature of the real. In its later development into superrealism, it is not the nature of reality so much as the very principle of ontological reality which is questioned. A superrealist painting, say, proposes the question: which is more real—object or image? The postmodern simulacrum, as Baudrillard points out, can question the very principle of reality itself by its parodic duplication; and this is its potentially most radical function. McGuckian is close to this, though her means of achieving it are not through the 'more perfect than perfect' mimesis of superrealism, but rather through the contortions of surrealism. Reality in her writing constantly slips away, leaving a reader to puzzle where she or he stands. Her sentences meander from *étrangeté* to *bizarrerie,* dislocating metaphor and being 'easily carried away' in this language which is dictated by no consciousness, and leaving a reader stranded in flight from multivalent realities. The early writing is concerned with a fall into temporality or secularity; the later with finding a means to cope with that 'fall' not by fleeing history but rather by fleeing the principle of a monotheological reality, which is seen to be imprisoning. All here is image: there is no presence, only representations. It is worth remembering that, in Ireland, there are several Ballycastles.

PART THREE

7. *Discourse and Figure: The Resistance of/to Cinema*

'In the cinema the modern is already history.'[1] Thus begins John Orr's study of *Cinema and Modernity*. Orr is at pains to argue, however, that it does not simply follow from this that cinema is somehow inherently postmodern. I have argued, in preceding pages of this book, that there is a specific problem of the visual and of representation at the core of the postmodern mood, none the less. It is important now to turn attention to a consideration of the specifically visual art of cinema in relation to alterity and postmodernism. Broadly, I shall examine the relation of narrative space to narrative time in cinema. I argued previously, following Moretti, that in the classical *Bildungsroman* there is a tendency to circumvent temporal development in the interests of establishing spatial metonymy or proximity, that there is an evasion of the historical in the establishment of consensus. I shall question some cinema in these same terms; and what I will show is a tendency which reverses this structure to some extent: in some instances a potential celebration of the spatial is diverted into an elaboration of temporal narrative, and consequently the prioritization of the visual is replaced by an attention to aurality.

This can be properly construed as a central theoretical (even technical) aspect of cinema which has assumed a thematic status in recent times: the relation between sound and image, the relation, if you will, of discourse to figure.[2] One of the questions which has recurred in previous pages relates to the status of ontology—that sensuous materiality of the real which appears on occasion to be called into question by contemporary technologies of the simulacrum. Further, it has been clear that

[1] John Orr, *Cinema and Modernity* (Cambridge: Polity, 1993), 1.

[2] The allusion here is to Jean-François Lyotard, *Discours, figure* (Paris: Klincksieck, 1971), which initially suggested to me the terms in which to think this cinematic problem. Some of what follows is philosophically indebted to Lyotard's argumentation in that book, though it should be said that I have somewhat freely adapted his suggestive terminology for my own ends here.

the Subject is in question or on trial (*en-procès*) in relation to its scopophiliac tendencies: it is as much the eye which is on trial as it is the 'I' in the postmodern mood. Cinema, clearly, addresses these issues fundamentally as a determining factor in its construction. In what follows, I shall argue that there is a certain tendency in contemporary cinema (affecting both mainstream fiction film and art film) to resist the internal implications of cinema itself: there is a resistance to cinematic culture within cinema. In brief, the argument will be summed up by saying that the films to which I attend consistently prioritize their discursive aspects over their figural; that, paradoxically, the visual field in this cinema is less important than the aural. In writing of Raymond Chandler, Jameson argues that the film versions of the great detective stories are contaminated thoroughly by the 'omnipresence of a radio culture as it resonates out into other genres and media'. He writes that

> the visual is presumably always incomplete while the auditory determines a synchronous recognition that can be drawn on for the construction of the new forms of a radio age. The thirties aesthetic—which has stereotypically been grasped as a kind of return to realism, a reaction against the modernist impulse, and a renewed politicization in the period of depression, fascism, and left-wing movements alike—needs to be reconsidered in the light of this most modern of the media, whose possibilities fascinated Brecht and Benjamin and not much later generated the lugubrious Adorno-Horkheimer vision of the 'culture industry'. The triumph of Hollywood seems to have fused many of these aesthetic developments into an undifferentiated mass, which it might be desirable to disentangle by thinking of the 'talkie', for example, as being, initially, a kind of radio film.[3]

Contemporary cinema is, in many instances, revisiting this Thirties aesthetic, and is reconsidering the relation of image to sound. This in itself, of course, is not a new observation: Godard, in many of his films (but perhaps most successfully in *Weekend*), disrupts the neat convergence of image and soundtrack in order to make the political gesture of questioning the ontological status of the real or of history. Godard's project coincides with criticism's emergent structuralist and semiotic

[3] Fredric Jameson, 'The Synoptic Chandler', in Joan Copjec (ed.), *Shades of Noir* (London: Verso, 1993), 36.

engagement with cinema, in which the image is viewed as a sign; and Godard works within such notions the better to disrupt them.[4] What is at stake, thus, is not simply a style of cinema, but rather the entire institution of cinema and its critical appropriation; and hence, what is at issue here is, once more, a postmodern question regarding the 'mood' or disposition of criticism towards this primarily visual art.

Writing about Godard, MacCabe indicates that the institution of cinema (by which he means the relations obtaining between the filmic production and an audience) is a major determinant of the organization of sounds and images in specific films themselves:

> Crucially this requires a fixed relation of dependence between the soundtrack and image whether priority is given to the image, as in fiction films (we see the truth and the soundtrack must come into line with it) or to the soundtrack, as in documentary (we are told the truth and the image merely confirms it).[5]

Godard plays constantly with this relation, disturbing it, using sync-sound to make it difficult to hear what 'central' characters are saying at crucial turns in the plot, establishing discrepancies between soundtrack and image, as in *Weekend* where a Black rubbish-collector speaks 'for' his Arab colleague, and vice versa. When the face of each character is on the screen, it is the voice of the other which is heard. The intimate link, usually presented as 'seamless', of voice to face, of subject to body, is thus ruptured; and, consequently, the very notion of the free inhabiting of one's own body or of one's own voice is called into question.

Yet in Godard, discrepancies such as these are almost always entirely *ironic*: the discrepant elements are set against each other in a dialectical (montagist) opposition which implies, but never necessarily directly states, a unified presence or identity of sound and image elsewhere: the synthesizing, by an informed critical audience, of the film's contradictions into an implied unification elsewhere and at some other time. It is this which, in the final analysis, renders the films of Godard

[4] See Colin MacCabe, *Godard: Images, Sounds, Politics* (London: bfi publications, 1980).

[5] Ibid. 18.

essentially 'modern' (or, in John Orr's terms, 'neo-modern'). They offer 'the solace of good forms', even if they do not display such good form.[6] Things can be different in some other cinemas.

It is important to note the further development of my earlier 'literary' arguments here. Earlier, drawing on Moretti's discussion of the *Bildungsroman,* I scrutinized the tendency in modernism towards the prioritization of spatiality, as a means of controlling, through abstraction and form, the disruptive tendencies of an incipient or latent postmodernism whose determining characteristic is its openness to a temporality which refuses the reduction of its force into signification. The different medium that is cinema allows for a furthering of the argument. In the literary form of the *Bildungsroman,* time collapses into space, certainly; but the space in question is not characterized by an ontological depth or *figural* sensuous substantiality or ontology: it is not visualizable but is rather space precisely considered as a form which strategically contains the disruptiveness of history. In other words, the space in question here is purely conceptual: it is the network of social relations as a *concept* rather than as a historical fact. Cinema offers the possibility of addressing more directly the issue of spatiality, *not merely as conceptual space*: its whole form depends upon the imaging of a three-dimensional—*figural*—visual field, not considered as concept but rather precisely *viewed* as substance. Once more, then, the postmodern is determined by a specific attitude to ontology or to the materiality of history (as well as to the historicity of the material order of things). Yet what one might add in the turn to this different medium is the notion of a postmodern spatiality that is characterized precisely by its disruptive force, and which thus differs from a modern spatiality whose business is to act as a strategy of containment against a disruptive historicity.

In literature, the disruptiveness that is history is contained under an abstract spatialization; in cinema, the question is whether sensuality—as a force resistant to conceptualization or to theorization—is contained under language or narrative.

[6] On the modern and its production of 'the solace of good forms', see Jean-François Lyotard, *The Postmodern Condition* (trans. Geoffrey Bennington and Brian Massumi; Manchester: Manchester University Press, 1984), 81.

In what follows, I shall attend firstly to what I shall posit as the explicit postmodernism of some contemporary cinema, and in this I shall concentrate on the particular example of Wim Wenders's *Paris, Texas*. The argument will be that the postmodern mood is evoked in cinema which stresses the sensuality of the image as a deep spatial phenomenon over the soundtrack. I take *Paris, Texas* as a paradigmatic example because it both offers and yet resists such an exploration of narrative space. Here we see a resistance *to* cinema. Following this, I shall turn to the (non)genre of *film noir* in order to explore the resistance *of* cinema to a conservative 'containment', and here I shall take the paradigmatic example of Billy Wilder's *Double Indemnity*.

1. THE REFUSAL OF FIGURE

The terms of this argument—discourse, figure—are taken from Lyotard's relatively early work of that title, *Discours, figure*. The argument of that study is long and complex; and all I wish to borrow from it for present purposes is a brief, but telling, series of observations, some of which Lyotard returned to in succinct form in 'Figure Foreclosed', written in 1984.[7] Part of the burden of *Discours, figure* is an attack on the philosophical bases of the entire structuralist (and latently poststructuralist) project, especially in regard to that project's pretensions to a semiotic scientificity legitimized by modes of thought which Lyotard stigmatized then as 'Western' and later as 'modernist'. In both *Économie libidinale* and *Discours, figure*, Lyotard indicated that the semiotic project depended on two questionable things: (1) the premature translation of 'things' into 'signs' (the translation, thus, of a material historical reality into something whose essence is that it is formally available for understanding); and (2) the prioritization of the 'readerly' over the merely 'visible', in a way which denies the visibility of the visible, always translating it into a material whose essence is that it can be processed as 'text'. Such—unjustified—procedures, Lyotard argued, served to erase the force or desire which was intrinsic to seeing, and to lose that force or desire under a more neutered

[7] Jean-François Lyotard, 'Figure Foreclosed', in *The Lyotard Reader*, ed. Andrew Benjamin (Oxford: Blackwell, 1989), ch. 4.

form of reading. For Lyotard at this moment, 'Lire est entendre et non pas voir.'[8]

In 'Figure Foreclosed', Lyotard discusses the 'origins' of a Western rationality, in the conflicts of Judaism and Hellenism, both of which thought of themselves as advances from or modernizations of an Eastern 'irrationalism' which was characterized as 'savage' or primitive. Judaism and Hellenism can thus be thought of in some way as being at the root of a specifically Western notion of modernity. In Judaism, as Freud indicated, there is one major and basic injunction: the injunction against making images: 'the prohibition against making an image of God—the compulsion to worship a God whom one cannot see.'[9] This, Lyotard argues, marks a huge shift in the way of conceptualizing, representing, or living the world. It necessitates a proportionate increase in discourse (talk about God) at the cost of the relative decrease in figure (seeing or sensing God). For Freud, the injunction against images meant that 'a sensory perception was given second place to what may be called an abstract idea—a triumph of intellectuality over sensuality';[10] and in Freudian analysis, of course, discourse—or the talking cure—increases precisely at the cost of the experience (images in the dreams). The imaginary is verbalized, in a word; the sensuous is rendered abstract.

I shall base what follows on this point: modernity is that which, while seeming ostensibly to offer a sensuous reality, has none the less in fact consistently prioritized the abstraction of such sensualities. In the development of modernism, from, say, the example of *Othello* to the texts of Conrad, there is a trajectory which moves steadily from the acceptance of the visual as a source of legitimation towards the visual or self-evident as

[8] Lyotard, *Discours, figure*, 217.

[9] Lyotard, *Reader*, 71. On the relation of this mode of thinking to Enlightenment (and, by extension, to modernity), see Peter Gay, *The Enlightenment*, i (Oxford: Oxford University Press, 1966), 33: 'As the Enlightenment saw it, the world was, and always had been divided between ascetic, superstitious enemies of the flesh, and men who affirmed life, the body, knowledge and generosity; between mythmakers and realists, priests and philosophers. Heinrich Heine, wayward son of the Enlightenment, would later call these parties, most suggestively, Hebrews and Hellenes.' Matthew Arnold was also later to make use of this distinction, as was Freud, and, most significantly for our present purposes, that other 'wayward son of the Enlightenment', Lyotard himself.

[10] Lyotard, *Reader*, 71–2.

precisely that which is dubious. Correspondingly, the discursive has been seen as the proper seat of reason and of self-evidence, of self-evident truths, with the result that there is a consistent inability to accept the alterity of the world as alterity and instead to see it as comprehensible sign, a sign whose evidential value and truthful meaning is located less in the (self-evidential) object itself and more in the linguistic subject of consciousness. This is the sense of McLuhan's famous dictum that 'the medium is the message': truth, in our time, has been increasingly located in the *mediation* of the world of objects by the subject of consciousness with its appeals, in a mode of thinking called 'rational' but actually instrumental and merely mathematical, to the self-evidential. Such thinking is less sustainable when the self or the subject of consciousness has become itself an area of dubiety, a site for the denial of the self-evidential or self-present.

These issues relate almost directly to cinema, most obviously in two questions of cinema: that of space and that of narrative.[11] In preceding chapters, it has become clear that the act of understanding, as it is construed in modernity, requires a spatialized mode of thought: to understand means to grasp from a 'point of view'; and understanding has been, in many instances, precisely conterminous with the construction of such a point of view, a place or position, from which understanding takes place and in relation to which the subject of understanding 'identifies' itself. This is called the phenomenology of perception, and it has its roots in a neo-romantic and specifically 'modern' philosophical framework. The problem arising here, as we have seen, is that the construction of the subject (especially in its most developed form as precisely *self-consciousness*, or 'identity') requires a prioritization of space; yet at the same time this subject is also conditioned thoroughly by its secularity or historicity (for such a temporal dimension is precisely the essence of its modernity as such). The resolution of this lies in the great paratactic form of narrative, the 'and'. Narrative, which links ostensibly divergent instantiations of subjectivity across time through the judicious linkage of the 'and', enables the construction of the modern subject (explicitly an

[11] The problem I am about to address could be described in terms of the development in philosophy from Merleau-Ponty to Paul Virilio.

autobiographical subject, one whose autonomy is guaranteed by the fact that it is the subject of its own narrative), and gives it its stability. Narrative *is* the condition of modernist understanding.

It is at this point in cultural history that the technology of cinema enters to disrupt modernity itself. From its earliest days, cinema has faced its own internal pressure as a mimetic art-form to find ways of creating the illusion that a flat two-dimensional image has the same depth or three-dimensional volume as sensual reality itself. This, essentially a technical problem dependent upon the construction and development of sophisticated kinds of camera lens, is also no less a philosophical problem regarding representation, and hence also a cultural problem regarding modernity.

The concern of mainstream Hollywood production has been the ideological construction of a representation which, it is assumed, exists in a seamless continuity with the reality of the spectator's world. This is a cinema which strives to avoid drawing attention to its own mechanical or technological constructions. One way in which it is consonant with the demands of a modernist culture is through the prioritization of narrative and causality. David Bordwell has pointed out, almost incidentally, the effect of such a procedure: 'In making narrative causality the dominant system in the film's total form, the classical Hollywood cinema chooses to subordinate space.'[12] There is less concern for the voluminous sensation of a three-dimensional ontological world than there is for the narrative drive of cause-and-effect whose temporal motion situates the audience as a subject in control of history or of personal development. The alterity of the world, as a site of resistance to such a subject in space, is elided in this framework. Yet space is, of course, not entirely ignored: technical tricks deployed in montage, and, later, with the aid of new lenses, the construction of a depth-shot, give the illusion of space; but classical cinema prefers not to linger on the voluminous field as such, always inserting its constituent action into a narrative drive towards making epistemological sense. Further, while movement (which is, of

[12] David Bordwell *et al.*, *The Classical Hollywood Cinema* (London: Routledge, 1985), 50.

course, of the essence of cinema) would always seem to imply space, cinema typically does not celebrate movement as such.[13] Rather, movement in cinema is always inserted into a specific *economy* of movement: it has to *signify*, and can only do so in relation to counter-movements elsewhere. So, for instance, in early films such as Lumière's *Repas de bébé*, all the movements of the parents and of the baby whom they are trying to feed refer in the first instance to each other: it is just such an internal structure which allows the viewer to see this film not just as random movements of three individuals but as a 'repas de bébé'. In other words, the structure and economy of movement are what make sense in the film. However, as Méliès noted while watching this outdoors scene, there *is* just such random movement on screen: Méliès was fascinated by the movement of the leaves on trees being blown randomly by the wind and making what is effectively an unplotted visual scene. We might suggest that it is this latter kind of movement, a random and 'non-sensical' movement, which constitutes a pure cinema; and, further, that such pure cinema is compromised by that kind of movement which is characterized as 'economic', a movement which exists in a primary relation to other movements which give it its economic status and epistemological significance. It is such an economics of the cinematic movement and image which contributes most essentially to the refusal of figure.[14]

I propose to analyse this refusal of figure in some contemporary cinema, and in what follows I shall concentrate attention on the paradigmatic example of Wim Wenders's *Paris, Texas*. I stress from the outset the paradigmatic nature of this example, for the movement which I shall trace, essentially a movement from eye to ear, is one which is exerting a pressure upon a great deal of contemporary cinema. There are numerous such examples. Beineix's *Diva*, for instance, is a film fundamentally about the capture of a voice. Modelled on the *film policier*, the film attends to a voice recorded in the opening sequence, and then

[13] Lyotard, 'Acinema', in *Reader*, ch. 8.

[14] The textual equivalent of this might be found in what Jean-Jacques Lecercle, following Gilles Deleuze, calls 'délire'. See Lecercle, *Philosophy through the Looking-Glass* (London: Hutchinson, 1985), *The Violence of Language* (London: Routledge, 1990), and *The Philosophy of Nonsense* (London: Routledge, 1994).

follows it all over Paris until, finally, it returns to the ear of the Diva, who hears herself sing 'for the first time' at the close of the film. Lynch's *Blue Velvet* sets its gothic scene in an opening sequence in which the camera lingers through the labyrinthine passage of a severed ear, and depends at crucial turns in the plot not so much on voyeurism as upon *auralism*. Some contemporary revisions of *film noir* depend crucially upon the voice-over (as in Scott's non-directorial cut of *Blade Runner*). Coppola's *The Conversation* is precisely a film about the voice and aural surveillance, and it attends not upon what can be seen but rather upon what can be heard. In the opening sequence of this film, we begin from an extremely scopic long-range shot of a city square, implying a huge depth of voluminous field; but the camera moves slowly and inexorably inwards, focusing eventually on one figure, the mimic who is doing a bit of street theatre. His act is to imitate passers-by; but whenever he is 'between the acts', he struts around in a parody of Chaplin's trampish walk, making the explicit allusion to an actor whose heyday was in the silent cinema. The *mise-en-scène* of this film is organized such that the space of the image is increasingly constricted; and, at the crucial turn in the plot, Harry Caul (played by Gene Hackman) finds himself crouched, foetally, in a ludicrously small space under a wash-basin while trying to hear what is going on in the next room. Whatever does go on is then drowned out by the noise of a television production of *The Flintstones*, played excessively loudly. The film closes with Caul playing his sax in a room which he has demolished (as if striking the theatrical set), and with the camera playing from left to right and back again in an evocation of the contemporary surveillance camera: but the single most important point for my present purpose is that the space thus produced is heavily circumscribed and restricted; Caul's only solace is in sound, his saxophone. Another relevant example is Moorhouse's *Proof*, which describes the existence of a blind photographer who depends upon aural descriptions both to take and to 'see' the photographs he takes. A similar structure obtains as a guiding principle of the narrative in Wenders's *Until the End of the World*, in which Sam Farber (William Hurt) and then Claire Tourneur (Solveig Dommartin) wear 'spectacles' which record the brain's responses to what they see so that Farber's blind mother will be able, on wearing and 'playing-back' the same spectacles, to see a world whose visual sensuality she has been denied. Campion's *The Piano* focuses on a mute (Holly Hunter) who comes slowly into language and who, paradoxically, frames the film's narrative with a retrospective voice-over. The trajectory I describe in this kind of film is one which comes to its most extreme form in Derek Jarman's *Blue*, a film which avowedly and determinedly eschews the cinematic image, giving only a blue screen for about seventy-five minutes, and in which the soundtrack is raised to an elementary status. All such films can be said to be at the opposite pole to that 'tradition' in cinema which contains films whose function is to problematize voyeurism, a tradition whose paradigmatic example is *Peeping Tom* by Powell and Pressburger, in which the violation of the specular is itself thematized.

Paris, Texas is an example which allows me to theorize more fully what is at issue here. The plot of this film is fairly simple. A man, Travis (played by Harry Dean Stanton), crosses the border between the USA and Mexico, in the desert, walking seemingly determinedly, and mute. His brother Walt (Dean Stockwell) comes to collect him, and drives him to Los Angeles, where, after an absence of four years, he is reunited with his son, Hunter (Hunter Carson), now 'adopted' by Walt and his wife, Ann (Aurore Clément). There is a gap here waiting to be filled: Travis's story. As the film unfolds, he gradually, slowly, and falteringly speaks and, as is common in Wenders, forms an allegiance with a child, Hunter. These two then go off in search of Travis's wife, Jane (Nastassia Kinski), whom they discover working in a peep-show in Houston. Travis and Jane never meet directly, though they communicate in a fashion at the peep-show. Travis narrates to her a lengthy and detailed story of two lovers in which Jane recognizes herself and her own story. Hunter and Jane are reunited; and Travis leaves.

The plot thus charts the development, in Travis, of language: he moves from mutism to positive garrulity and eloquence. The film is organized around a typical 'deferral' structure: an enigma is posed at the start in the proper name 'Travis', and is answered only much later, as the character of Travis comes to inhabit his own narrative and to narrate it. It is as if the film charts Travis's coming to a kind of linguistic self-presence, a kind of positive identity, a logocentric or phonocentric selfhood. Indeed, Wenders has declared that 'Cinema is, in a way, an art in which things and persons come to be identical with themselves';[15] and it is to some extent precisely such self-identification, importantly in a linguistic medium, that is enacted in this film.

At the opening of the film, narrative space is treated in a conventional fashion. We have a number of panning shots whose function is to stress the enormity of the desert-space across which Travis walks. These are intercut with a series of point-of-view shots taken from the vantage-point of a predatory vulture, and consequently drawing attention to the precarious position in which we find Travis. The first 'intimate' shot follows this, when Walt (and the camera) approaches Ann, filmed from behind and caught in a facial close-up only when she looks back over her shoulder in a sequence proleptically looking towards the first clear shot of Jane. When Wenders films both these sequences, the camera moves steadily towards its framed woman; and the movement is extremely conventional in its production of the illusion of spatial—ontological—depth within the frame. What will happen in the rest of the film, however, is a refusal of such figural depth, its collapsing back into the two-dimensionality of discourse, and its redrawing under the heading of temporal narrative.

Whereas, in the classical *Bildungsroman* form discussed earlier, there was a refusal of time and its collapsing into conceptual space, what we have here is the collapsing of sensual, three-dimensional space and its re-elaboration as narrative time. This is especially noticeable in Wenders, a filmmaker whose most dominant form has been that of the road-movie, and whose most frequent shot is the travelling shot.

On the way to Los Angeles, Travis and Walt stop at a motel. Travis, alone, starts to hum, and appears thus to be leaving his mutism behind, to be entering at least into sound if not yet

[15] This point, or variants upon it (drawn from an interview with Wim Wenders), is reiterated at various moments in Kathe Geist, *The Cinema of Wim Wenders* (Ann Arbor: UMI Press, 1988), and in Robert Phillip Kolker and Peter Beichen, *The Films of Wim Wenders* (Cambridge: Cambridge University Press, 1993).

quite into talk. But he stops very abruptly at the moment when he catches a glimpse of himself in the shaving mirror, retreats into silence, and runs off. At this point, then, the point of a hesitant move into discourse or, more precisely, towards making discourse and figure coincide, the move is ruptured by the force of the figure itself. As in Godard, the 'solace of good form' in which face and voice might coincide is here ruptured. In this film, things and places are not quite where they seem to be, and cannot be thus easily located in a mirror. Paris is in Texas; persons are neither where they seem nor who they seem to be. But, for Wenders, cinema is an art in which things and persons come to be identical with themselves; and thus we can see the desire for 'good form' which this film will attempt to satisfy, even if in an only superficially satisfactory fashion.

On the car journey to Los Angeles, Travis haltingly mentions the 'Paris' of the title (to be complemented later by the other 'road-movie' in the journey to Texas), and begins to tell the tale of why he has bought the patch of land represented in his photograph: the photo generates the narrative. As he elaborates the tale, we have a classic Wendersian *mise-en-scène*. Travis drives, and the sequence is filmed from his point of view, looking forwards out of the front windscreen of the car. But the top half of the screen comprises the rear-view mirror, in which we see, constantly, the eyes of Travis. There is, here, a sequential voyeurism: Travis, watching the road ahead, watches effectively the first 'road-movie' here, figured in the bottom half of the screen. We watch this, and also watch Travis watching this, in the image of the top half of the screen, the eyes in the rear-view mirror. This sequence, like a structure of desire in which the desired object is always elsewhere, always turning out to be a subject in its own right with a desire directed towards a subsequent object in turn, is an important part of the disjunction between discourse and figure here. It is as if Travis can speak if and only if he is not seeing himself, not availing of the mirror: discourse comes at the expense of figure. It is also during this road sequence, when Walt takes the driving-wheel again, that Travis explains the joke of the film's title; and, interestingly, he has enormous difficulty with his lines. Without a fractured screen such as I have described it, Travis has problems with language.

This leads into a crucial sequence in the film, that of the film-within-the-film (an obvious and not startlingly new device, used—theatrically—in *Hamlet*, for instance). The single most important point for present purposes is that the Super-8 home movie watched by Travis, Walt, Ann, and Hunter is *silent*. It is a film in which the viewing characters are invited to identify with themselves and to provide a running commentary, silently if need be, which completes their act of self-recognition and gives them the solace of the good form of identity. Such recognitions are played out in various ways: from the start, for example, Travis looks at the film and sees its reflection in Walt, ontologically present behind him; we are invited to repeat this structure immediately on seeing Travis on film. The sequence continues with the characters setting up a chain of surveillance which works in a fashion exactly akin to that described in the split-frame sequence with Travis driving discussed above. Characters do not so much watch the movie as watch each other's viewing and responses to the movie. But this establishes a *figural* community around the screen: it is figural because, in the movement from Super-8 to *Paris, Texas*, there is a movement which goes from epistemological recognition *silently* to ontological verification of the image. The illusion of a space or depth around the screen, a volume which requires dimensions and locations 'Before, behind, between, above, below',[16] is produced. Only two moments of commentary are made explicit. In the first, Hunter says 'me driving'; in the second, Hunter acknowledges Travis for the first time as his father, saying 'Goodnight, Dad' to *both* Walt and Travis. At this second point, we have the moment of 'making sense', a moment in which a discursive relation 'flattens' the sensuousness of the film's implied narrative space or volume: it is as if the film which has given the illusion of sensuous space cannot leave it in its brute or crude state, but must rather 'reduce' such force to sense in the linguistic relation.

[16] The allusion is to John Donne, 'Elegy 19: Going to Bed', in Donne, *The Complete English Poems*, ed. A. J. Smith (Harmondsworth: Penguin, 1973), 125. Cf. 'Incipient Postmodernisms', Ch. 4 above, and my comments on this poem in Docherty, *John Donne, Undone* (London: Methuen, 1986), 78–83.

Immediately after this sequence, Travis confidently looks at himself in the mirror and asks the Hispanic maid for advice on how he can make himself look like 'a father'. This enables the mimesis in which Travis and Hunter come together, imitating each other on a walk home from school, and drawing attention thereby to their links across time. Later, such mirrors and vision are abjured entirely. Travis makes a tape for Hunter, who listens to it while staring out at a view entirely occluded by low clouds. Here, as a complement to the silent Super-8 film, we have sound without image; and the ongoing playback of Travis's voice on tape continues, linking three disparate locations, making sense of them in an implied narrative structure. But this itself leads into the climactic sequence in the peep-show, in which Jane cannot see Travis, and Travis speaks to her, narrating the story, only *after* he has turned his back to the screen/window in which Jane appears. The screen is again split, this time in exactly the same way in which Wenders had split it when Travis and Hunter were on the road, communicating with each other by walkie-talkie, separated by the rear-windscreen of the truck, with Hunter in the position later adopted by Travis, and Travis in that of Jane. In a sequence, then, which more or less explicitly demands a sensuous response, however pornographic the structure of the peep-show may be, we have a film which avowedly refuses to indulge the sensuous demand for the illusion of depth. Wenders turns a room into a screen, and turns the sensuous visual reponse into an aural, epistemological, abstract moment of recognition in which Travis and Jane recognize each other only through the narrative told by Travis, only through this discursive device. This climax of the film, then, is *discursive*, an exercise in narrative, a refusal of the figural visual depth which cinema explicitly exists to explore.

That refusal of figure is also a refusal of the postmodern. Yet a mood has been constructed, a desire for the postmodern has been produced; and it is this which cinema is currently exploring in the many instances already cited in which the radical alterity of a figural space in all its sensuousness and immediacy is denied in the interests of a specifically 'modern' epistemology, driven by the paratactic impulse of a univocal narrative demand.

2. A LECTURE UPON THE SHADOW

Cinema, then, is a potentially highly compromised visual artform (at least in the talkie era). Yet there is a kind of film in which we might find an incipient postmodern appeal to the priority of figure, and a critical resistance to univocal semiotic sense-making. *Film noir* has a specific visual determination in the quality of its lighting which draws attention first and foremost to the visual field. It is in this cinema that we might find a critical postmodernism emerging; and it is perhaps for this reason that *noir* is currently being rehabilitated and reworked in some contemporary films.

The *noir* film typically has certain repeated characteristics, even if, as most criticism suggests, it is not quite a specific genre of film. Foremost among these characteristics is the voice-over. As in a film like Wilder's *Double Indemnity*, the voice-over operates in the mode of confession. This film lays its cards on the table from the outset, for Walter Neff (Fred MacMurray) reveals immediately in his dictated letter to Barton Keyes (Edward G. Robinson) that it was he, Neff, who committed the murder at the centre of the film's plot. This confessional voice-over gives the film the same orientation towards truth that we see in documentary films, in which, as MacCabe indicates, 'we are told the truth and the image merely confirms it'.[17] Yet there are clear distinctions between *noir* and documentary.

The voice-over implies a point of view, but not in a spatial sense. The voice-over always implies a temporal distinction between the time of the action displayed before us and the time of its recall or verbal narration. *Noir* is essentially determined by a *temporal* structure, driven by the narrative offered and authorized by the voice-over. Yet that narrative is never *clearly* 'confirmed' by the image, in the way in which documentary would validate itself. On the contrary, the visual domain in *noir* is typically dark, obfuscatory, occluded, offering at best a shadow of clarity. The narrative told is, in the most common detective-story forms of *noir*, a narrative of enlightenment and revelation. The result is that light itself becomes a central character. Indeed, Richard Schickel describes *Double Indemnity* as 'a

[17] MacCabe, *Godard*, 18.

drama about light, about a man lured out of the sunshine and into the shadows'.[18]

Light, as the impressionist painters knew as well as John Donne or Goya, is an indicator of time and its passage; but in *noir*, I shall argue that it enters the frame precisely as an indicator of space, volume, and figure. In *film noir*, the ostensible prioritization of discourse in the voice-over is disrupted by the emergence of a cinematic visual field characterized by the sensuality of the voluminous figure; and the emergence of such a field is enabled by lighting.

The character in *noir* is almost always accompanied by a shadow, and this cinema in many ways offers a lecture upon the shadow in the same way as Donne proposed in the early seventeenth century. In his poem of that title, he proposes a kind of 'high noon' of love, suggesting that it is only at the moment of utmost clarity when there are shadows neither before nor behind that lovers can find an entirely true instant or experience of love: 'Love is a growing, or full constant light; | And his first minute, after noon, is night.'[19] The poet wants in this text to arrest the flow of time and to control it as an ever-presence, a self-presence: 'Stand still' is how the text begins, as the poet hypothesizes the possibility of this temporal arrest. Yet the poem also rehearses that typically Donnean problem, questioning the spatial boundaries of the body. Precisely the same effect is to be seen in *noir* film, where the shadows of characters act as an extension, and sometimes an expression, of their bodies.

Consider, for instance, the sequence in *Double Indemnity* in which Phyllis Dietrichson (Barbara Stanwyck) sees for the first time the possibility of working with Neff to get rid of her husband. They sit together in the lounge of the Dietrichson house, with Neff explaining the reason for his call, the reinsurance of the two family cars. As he talks, beginning himself to explore the erotics of their relation ('That's a honey of an anklet you're wearing'), the camera adopts a fairly conventional position for the shooting of a dialogue. But, at one moment, Phyllis stands up and walks towards the fireplace. The camera follows

[18] Richard Schickel, *Double Indemnity* (London: bfi publications, 1992), 10.

[19] Donne, 62–3. Cf. Docherty, *John Donne, Undone*, 97–104.

her, leaving Neff out of shot entirely, but for his voice; and as he talks on (in what we might call a kind of sub-voice-over), we watch Phyllis pacing back and forth, accompanied by her shadow cast over the fireplace. This signifies, of course, at one level the rather basic fact that she is communing with herself, thinking to herself; and such a reading is confirmed when she returns towards Neff and asks about 'accident insurance', the camera at this point reassuming its more conventional framing of both characters.

The point is that this shadow signifies *more* than the character thinking to herself. It is crucial in drawing attention, by its superfluity or excess (a 'dyseconomy' in the visual field), to the physicality of Phyllis and thus in contributing to the sensuous eroticism of the scene as a whole. The presence of a shadow on the screen itself already draws attention to volume and space; in 'doubling' the body of the characters it also serves to present the theme of duplicity which runs throughout *noir* films, and it suggests a *haecceitas*, a 'being there' for the body in all its material and sensuous—figural—volume. The lighting in *noir* films, through its dependence upon having a body *between* the source of light and a surface upon which a shadow is projected, stresses the three-dimensionality of the narrative space of film. The shadows, in encouraging a sense of doubleness or duplicity, contradict, in Donnean fashion, the discourse, the voice-over.

It is in such an attention to light—and more precisely to the refusal of 'enlightenment' in its narratives—that *film noir* enables the possibility of a resistance within cinema, a resistance to the omnivorous and homogenizing power of a certain *discourse*. By offering images of the real, in all its spatial and voluminous banality, such film offers the possibility of arguing that the world is not immediately available as text, and hence not always immediately available for understanding.

This resistance is a critical resistance which wishes to attend to the specificity of the particular, refusing to situate a particular instance within a general theoretical framework of understanding which makes its comprehension possible. Copjec, following Pascal Bonitzer, argues that 'Speech, as we know—language—is the death of the thing'.[20] And it is to the sensuality

[20] Joan Copjec, 'The Phenomenal Nonphenomenal: Private Space in *Film Noir*', in Copjec (ed.), *Shades of Noir* (London: Verso, 1993), 183.

of the thing that *film noir* draws attention. Bonitzer makes a distinction between the 'disembodied voice' of documentary (in which the voice-over is never located in a body seen on screen) and the embodied voice-over more often seen in *film noir*, in which the speaker appears on screen, the voice hinged to a specific body. Copjec comments on this that:

> The distinction between the disembodied voice, which conveys knowledge and power, and the embodied voice, which conveys the limitation of both, is underwritten by a simple opposition between the universal and the particular, the latter being conceived as that which ruins the possibility of the former.[21]

In the terms of the present argument, criticism in cinema arises when the figural, in all its banal specificity, refuses to be subsumed under the discursive, with its drive to homogenization and 'comprehension'. It is here, in such a critical instance in cinema, that we can see the possibility of the postmodern mood arising; and those critical instances are proliferating not only in the re-emergence of *film noir* as a favoured form, but also in other contemporary cinema in which narrative space is not finally reduced to the merest level of a 'sign' or a signifier available to consciousness.

Cinema is one important example of a cultural practice which can offer the possibility of a critical postmodern mood. In the following chapter, I shall extend the range of this kind of argument into culture more generally.

[21] Ibid. 184. See also Pascal Bonitzer, 'The Silences of the Voice', in Philip Rosen (ed.), *Narrative, Apparatus, Ideology* (New York: Columbia University Press: 1986).

8. *Cultural Politics and Postmarxism*

The recuperation of history is fundamental to any criticism which would call itself Marxist. Jameson's injunction, 'Always historicize!', stands as a rallying cry even among those who would dispute Jameson's own relations to historicisms both old and new. It will be my contention here, however, that much of what passes for the most sophisticated Marxist theory, and much of what passes for the most vigorous in New Historical or Cultural Materialist research, has been unable to deal adequately with the relation of culture to history. In terms of the consideration of the relation between the aesthetic and the political, in terms of cultural critique, these criticisms have worked to reduce the historical to the status of the merely *traditional* (and sometimes to the anecdotal), with the consequence that in place of real and material histories criticism has produced a myth of history. My argument will be that the emancipation of history from the bounds of 'heritage' or 'tradition' depends upon a position that can only be called 'postmarxist'. Such a position is not, of course, simply a rejection of Marxism; it is, after all, post-*Marxist*, as Laclau and Mouffe have pointed out.[1]

Postmarxism might be thought here in an analogy with postmodernism, in which the 'post-', according to Lyotard, is better understood as 'un procès en "ana-" '; it attempts to locate the founding condition of the possibility of the formation of the modern (or of Marxism) which lies within the modern (or within Marxism) itself. In these terms, postmarxism will constitute the attempt to emancipate history from within a Marxist thinking which has become tainted with the very idealism—an

[1] The injunction 'Always historicize!' appears in Fredric Jameson, *The Political Unconscious* (London: Methuen, 1981), 9. See also Ernesto Laclau and Chantal Mouffe, *Hegemony and Socialist Strategy* (London: Verso, 1985), which prompted a debate in *New Left Review*. See Norman Geras, 'Post-Marxism?', *New Left Review*, 163 (1987), 40–82; Laclau and Mouffe, 'Post-Marxism without Apologies', *New Left Review*, 166 (1987), 79–106. For a good introduction to the ways in which the aesthetic has been treated by historical materialism, see Michael Sprinker, *Imaginary Relations* (London: Verso, 1987).

essentially non-historical idealism—which it sets out to oppose in the first place.[2]

The category of the aesthetic has always been a contentious one for criticism, both of a traditional or conservative kind and for a radical or Marxist mode. The problems become all the more pressing, as Benjamin indicated in 1936, with the advent of mechanical reproduction and cinematic form. It is crucial for any critical theory which would have contemporary radical and emancipatory credentials to acknowledge the political conditions of culture in the contemporary moment, a moment in which more sophisticated technological reproduction has complicated the issue of the relation between aesthetics and politics more than Benjamin or Adorno could imagine.[3] A rethinking of postmodern aesthetics is called for, and with it a reconsideration of the conditions of cultural politics. It is in relation to this that the present chapter, building on the questioning of the specific example of cinema previously, will engage the work of Paul Virilio and André Gorz. Through both of these, I shall attempt not only to address directly the issue of the materiality of time as a politico-cultural determinant of value, but also (and primarily) to resituate culture back in the frame of the idea of growth in a locality: *Bildung*.

1. POSTMODERN AESTHETICS

Near the beginning of *L'Horizon négatif*, Virilio proposes a problem of perception which dominates much of his thinking, and

[2] See Jean-François Lyotard, 'Note sur le sens de "post-" ', in *Le Postmoderne expliqué aux enfants* (Paris: Galilée, 1986), 26; Lyotard, 'Defining the Postmodern', in Lisa Appignanesi (ed.), *Postmodernism: ICA Documents* (London: Free Association Books, 1989), 7–10. Cf. also my arguments in Docherty, *After Theory* (London: Routledge, 1990; 2nd edn., Hemel Hempstead: Harvester-Wheatsheaf, forthcoming).

[3] Walter Benjamin, 'The Work of Art in the Age of Mechanical Reproduction', in *Illuminations*, ed. Hannah Arendt (trans. Harry Zohn; Glasgow: Fontana, 1973). See also, among Jean Baudrillard's writings, those which he produced since the mid-1970s: *L'Échange symbolique et la mort* (Paris: Gallimard, 1976); *De la séduction* (Paris: Denoël, 1979); *Simulacres et simulation* (Paris: Galilée, 1981); *Les Stratégies fatales* (Paris: Grasset, 1983); *La Gauche divine* (Paris: Grasset, 1985); *Amérique* (Paris: Grasset, 1986); *Cool Memories* (Paris: Grasset, 1987); *L'Autre par lui-même* (Paris: Galilée, 1987), *The Evil Demon of Images* (Sydney: Power Institute, 1988); *Figures de l'altérité*, with Marc Guillaume (Paris: Descartes & Cie, 1994).

which he himself acknowledges as a kind of foundational principle for what can only be called the post-phenomenological impetus of his work. The problem in question has implications for all aspects of his work: on the consideration of and theorization of war; on the relation of speed and technology to politics; on urbanization, de-urbanization and the demise of the geopolitical; on cinema as a martial logistics of perception; and so on.

Virilio tells of his beginnings as an artist, concerned with representation and figuration, and of his interest in the emergence of the *antiforme*, or what we might think of as 'interstitial deformation'. Drawing an object implies two more or less simultaneous operations. There is a movement of internal individuation which gives shape or form to the object represented; but this immediately articulates the external formation of a field against which the form is perceptible. The problem arises whenever a second drawn figure enters the same field to disturb this moment of representational figuring: 'En reproduisant sur la surface du papier deux objets bien réels, je ne pouvais éviter de faire surgir l'objet transparent de leur réciproque information.'[4] This, in fact, is an instantiation of cinematic dialectic, as proposed by Eisenstein in his descriptions of montage. The collision of two opposing or juxtaposed figures upon the same field proposes a *narrative* situation which transcends each of the single figures but which is generated from their mutual information or cross-shaping of each other. Virilio goes on:

> Ce qui me fascinait, c'était le tropisme du point où la forme et l'antiforme hésitaient encore, si je dépassais en poussant plus loin la mine de mon crayon, ce fameux point, la forme prenait le dessus. Si je restais en deçà, l'antiforme devenait le seul objet de l'apparence, l'objet à la fois du dessin et de mon dessein.[5]

This operation suggests to Virilio a particular operational dialectic relating to perception. As the analogy with the cinematic reveals, this dialectic is profoundly historical in that it is

[4] Paul Virilio, *L'Horizon négatif* (Paris: Galilée, 1984), 24.

[5] Ibid. 24. See also Sergei M. Eisenstein, *Film Form* (Cambridge, Mass.: Harcourt Brace Jovanovich, 1969); but cf. Gilles Deleuze, *Cinéma* (Paris: Minuit, 1983), ch. 3, for a set of fine discriminations about montage; and cf. V. F. Perkins, *Film as Film* (Harmondsworth: Penguin, 1972), 19–25, for a debunking of the 'mystique' of montage.

founded upon a paratatic narrative sequence (of form followed by antiform, followed in turn by new form, and so on). This is in contradistinction to most theories of representation currently available.

Most existing theories of representation, including Marxist theories, operate between the poles of the representation and its referent or, in the most banal of formulations, between appearance and reality.[6] This opposition is itself usually determined and organized under a *spatial* metaphor, in which the reality is thought to lie 'under' or 'behind' a surface appearance. This, clearly, is grounded in a latent phenomenological reduction, which proposes the availability of an essential reality determinable through specific appearances which are subject to critical demystification. It founds a whole strategy of criticism which depends upon (basically, hermeneutic) demystifications of one kind or another. In its most advanced form, such a critical strategy is a semiotic imbued with ideology-critique. Yet, in its phenomenological basis, it remains, to borrow Eagleton's words, 'an idealist, essentialist, anti-historical, formalist and organicist type of criticism'.[7]

Virilio subjects this problem of representation, with its inherent drive to an idealist phenomenology, to some speculative pressure, thereby opening up an entirely different problematic: the dialectic of appearance and disappearance constructed in historical sequence. In other words, he introduces an internal historicity to the issue of representation, announcing that there is a *temporality* to this rhetorical manœuvre. This move is akin to the strategy of de Man, for whom 'aesthetic ideology' was characterized by the prematurely organicist belief in the availability of a precise coincidence between consciousness and nature, and whose critique of such an ideology was postulated upon the temporality and contingency of language itself as the supposed transparent medium for this organicism.[8] The shift I wish to propose through this is like that between still photography and cinema, if we take these practices in a precise sense.

[6] See P. M. S. Hacker, *Appearance and Reality* (Oxford: Blackwell, 1987), for a more philosophical study of this question.

[7] Terry Eagleton, *Literary Theory* (Oxford: Blackwell, 1983), 60.

[8] For the analysis of this in de Man, see Christopher Norris, *Paul de Man* (London: Routledge, 1988), *passim*, but esp. pp. xii and xviii.

The photograph is, as it were, 'punctual', a punctuation or still point drawn from the flux of time and history. Cinema is not simply a kind of arithmetical building-brick series of such stills; rather, cinema takes place precisely in the *antiforme* of the photograph, in the dialectical relation or interstitial moment 'between' the still images, a location in which there is the perception not of the still at all but of that *movement* which is constitutive of cinema itself.[9]

Superficially, it might appear in the first instance that this Virilian problematic of representation is a recent phenomenon, a new departure from the previously paradigmatic 'spatial' opposition of appearance to reality. This would be misleading, for this is not simply a new development, a 'change' enabled by contemporary cultural conditions. It would be more accurate to suggest that this 'new' problematic was in fact always the case, that it was always the central theoretical question of representation, and that it actually informs and conditions the very possibility of the incidence and supervention of the 'appearance/reality' dialectic at specific previous historical conjunctures. In other words, what has 'changed' is that the basic theoretical issue, appearance/disappearance, is now more immediately visible. Prior theorizations have, for whatever reasons, occluded the basic problem under what Jameson might think as a 'strategy of containment' (the appearance/reality opposition as a strategic construct) in order to limit and circumscribe what can be thought about representation in a given cultural moment. Such a strategy of containment, in which appearance/disappearance is occluded under appearance/reality, obtains vigorously in the moment of a modernism deriving from eighteenth-century Enlightenment philosophies which claim access to the real by a certain rationality; a modernism persisting through to the demystifying strain in deconstruction. The conditions of that previous moment were

[9] This 'punctual' owes something (but not everything) to Roland Barthes's idea of the 'punctum' in *Camera Lucida* (trans. Richard Howard; London: Fontana, 1984). See also Gilles Deleuze, *Cinéma 1*, and *Cinéma 2* (Paris: Minuit, 1985) for fuller argumentation indicating the cinematic as precisely temporal movement, a 'movement-image' and a 'time-image'. Such ideas derive from the quasi-Bergsonism of Deleuze's work in general: see his *Le Bergsonisme* (Paris: PUF, 1966), and cf. also Deleuze, *Empirisme et subjectivité* (Paris: PUF, 1953), for another—Humean—source for such philosophy.

such that the appearance/disappearance relation had itself to 'disappear', enabled only to figure in its severely attenuated proto-phenomenological form as an opposition of ideological appearance to brute reality.[10] The present moment is simply more sympathetic to the reappearance of the fundamental theoretical opposition of appearance to disappearance, as Virilio's work testifies.

By extension, of course, semiotic ideology-critique would then be but the specific historical instantiation of something more fundamental, something whose *attenuated* form was semiotics or Marxism. A modernist phenomenological aesthetic, which is at one with the Marxist critique of ideology, is idealist through and through for the simple reason that it evades the element of historicity which is fundamental to the aesthetic as such. Marxism is complicit with such modernist idealism.

An example of such complicity is to be found in Eagleton's recent work on *The Ideology of the Aesthetic*. The aesthetic is a double-edged sword, according to Eagleton. On the one hand, it promises an unmediated relation between consciousness and history: the materiality of thought, so to speak. Yet, on the other hand, it thereby enables an aestheticization of the political, in its promise that the world is how it appears to consciousness 'immediately' or without the need for any critical consciousness, much less an autocritical consciousness. That is what Althusser would have considered as the 'obviousness' of ideology. But all is not yet lost. Marx saves us from this tendency to idealism, according to Eagleton, when he rethinks the category of the aesthetic not from the point of view of consciousness as such, nor of nature as such, but from the point of view of the labouring body which *mediates* the two. At this point, he can reveal the orientation of Marxist struggle and the aesthetic dimension of Marx's thought: 'The goal of Marxism is to restore

[10] For the way in which the real or the true has become marked in philosophy by pain, brutishness, or violence, see Hans Blumenberg, *The Legitimacy of the Modern Age* (trans. Robert M. Wallace; Cambridge, Mass.: MIT Press, 1983), 404: 'Lack of consideration for happiness became the stigma of truth itself, a homage to its absolutism'; and this effect is dated by Blumenberg to the age of Enlightenment. This continuing modernist impetus for a truth marked by absolutism persists to some extent in Christopher Norris's recent work, such as *The Truth about Postmodernism* (Oxford: Blackwell, 1993).

to the body its plundered powers; but only with the supersession of private property will the senses be able to come into their own. If communism is necessary, it is because we are unable to feel, taste, smell and touch as fully as we might.'[11]

This is a curiously ambivalent statement, from whose implications Eagleton occasionally shies away, especially when warning against the 'premature utopianism' which he detects in various strains of poststructuralism.[12] It may be true, of course, even if it is difficult to imagine how it might be tested or verified. The important point is that it clearly shares a modernist impetus towards the restoration of 'tradition', in the manner in which such tradition was thought by T. S. Eliot in his lamentations over the mythic 'dissociation of sensibility'. Eliot's reponse to this fabricated 'event' was to construct a 'tradition' which would help paper over the cracks of real, material, and discontinuous histories, leading eventually to those profoundly 'spatial' (indeed cartographic) poems 'The Waste Land' and the geographic *Four Quartets*, which enabled Eliot to locate himself not in history as such but in a tradition spatialized between Burnt Norton, East Coker, the Dry Salvages, and Little Gidding.[13] This profoundly Optimistic

[11] Terry Eagleton, *The Ideology of the Aesthetic* (Oxford: Blackwell, 1990), 201.

[12] Ibid. 226–30. On this question of the rehabilitation of 'experience', see, of course, the major source for attacks upon experience, Louis Althusser, 'Ideology and the Ideological State Apparatuses', in Althusser, *Essays on Ideology* (London: Verso, 1984). Althusser's importance for Marxist theory has followed an inconsistent pattern; but this aspect—the rigorous critiquing of any form of empiricism or 'experience' undergone by a 'subject'—has seemed to remain fairly central to a particular strain of contemporary British Marxism, persisting most vigorously in work such as that of Catherine Belsey and Antony Easthope. Eagleton's *Ideology of the Aesthetic* represents, among other things, a continuation of Eagleton's varied engagements with Althusser which dates at least from Eagleton's *Criticism and Ideology* (London: New Left Books, 1976); in the more recent work, there is the suggestion of a rehabilitation of the subject—though, of course, in a very different form from that which was available for it prior to Althusser. Eagleton asks right from the start of *Ideology of the Aesthetic*, for instance, 'how can any political order flourish which does not address itself to this most tangible area of the "lived" . . . How can "experience" be allowed to fall outside a society's ruling concepts?' (pp. 13–14). This question is posed neither in a *style indirect libre* which would assign it to the mouths of those who would control the human subject, nor in an entirely ironic fashion, as can be seen at later stages in the book (e.g. pp. 27–8, 197–8). The thinking re-establishes Eagleton's debt to his great precursor and teacher, Raymond Williams.

[13] For the 'dissociation of sensibility', see T. S. Eliot, 'The Metaphysical Poets', in *Selected Essays* (3rd edn.; London: Faber, 1951), 286–8. Eagleton, in *Ideology of the*

strategy offers a history seen from a hypothesized 'end' of history: the events described in *Four Quartets* may date from a distant past, but their importance is as a heuristic device explaining Eliot's present. The temporal difference is elided in the interests of establishing a 'consensual space' in which Eliot relates himself directly to his forebears and heritage. The same can be said for Eagleton when, for instance, Kant turns out to be Lacan and thereby helps Eagleton to write a 'history of the present'.[14] Such a history is oddly devoid of temporality when Eagleton *metaphorically* yokes together—in what is a somewhat metaphysical alignment—such diverse figures as Kant and Lacan.[15] It is necessary, in my own view, to find some way of evading the 'premature totalization' or the premature assumption of a consensual space which is immanent to such a strategy: it is important to acknowledge that temporality or *décalage* which is always involved in the aesthetic and which is consequent upon the fundamental opposition which structures the aesthetic, that between appearance and disappearance located in their dialectical, 'cinematic', or historical sequentiality.

Aesthetic, makes frequent tantalizing allusions to Eliot's thinking in this classically politically ambivalent 'modernist' essay, as when, for instance, he suggests the category of the aesthetic as that which makes available a materialization of thought which will be as recognizable as the smell of thyme, the taste of potatoes, the zest of a lemon, and so on, through an entire culinary vocabulary of 'tastes'. Eagleton, of course, is distancing himself from Eliotic thought throughout. Yet the burden of my present argument is that he fails to distance himself sufficiently; that, despite himself, there is what we might think of as a 'premature modernism' which equates with a 'premature Marxism' in his argument.

[14] Eagleton, *Ideology of the Aesthetic*, ch. 3, 'The Kantian Imaginary'. Cf. Eagleton, *Literary Theory*, 161–74.

[15] This is a substantiation of my claim in n. 13 above. The allusion is to Samuel Johnson, 'Cowley', in his *Lives of the Poets* (1781; Oxford: Oxford University Press, 1906), i. 14, discussing 'metaphysical' poets: 'Of Wit, thus defined, they have more than enough. The most heterogeneous ideas are yoked by violence together.' It is, of course, in this kind of 'wit' that Eagleton (and 'Theory') excel, finding homogeneities where others had perceived the greatest disparities, finding theoretical taxonomy where others had seen only the singularity of the event. But the effect of such wit is to provide the kind of premature totalization of a non-historical metaphoricity, which is 'metaphysical' in the sense of that word more available currently. In this metaphoric yoking of heterogeneity into homogeneity, there is a drive to erase that very aspect of heterogeneity which is given by the fact of historicity: the aspect of singularity, specificity. The postmodernist or postmarxist, in this instance at least, might be more carefully described as she or he who does not so much 'wage war on totality' as Lyotard puts it: she or he, rather, wages war on this tendency to premature totalization.

A postmodern aesthetic is an 'aesthetics of disappearance'. It is resolutely post-phenomenological in its introduction of the complication of the issue of an interior historicity to the aesthetic 'moment', a historicity which precludes precisely the kind of premature totalization which becomes available whenever history is collapsed into the more spatial or punctual categories of tradition or heritage, categories which are inescapably modernist and which remain caught up in a mythologization of history even at those moments when they proclaim their power to demystify and to reveal the historical in itself. Modernist aesthetics are inherently metaphysical and—what is worse for a radical criticism—idealist in their foundations in phenomenological thought.

Virilio's work helps to restore a historicity which figures within any specific aesthetic moment. His thinking vigilantly warns against the premature totalization under which consciousness proposes its materialization in history by acknowledging that the 'form' of that relation veers into its *antiforme*, and that this swerve is one which is dependent upon time and history itself, for the oscillation between the two refuses to become a fixed 'constellation', refuses to remain within the realm of the 'merely' geo-political and opens up a chrono-political aesthetics which struggles to retain a politics not contaminated by the very idealism which it sets out to challenge.

Consequently, the work of the New Historicists and of the Cultural Materialists finds itself in some difficulties. Both New Historicism and Cultural Materialism presuppose the availability of the 'form' of history. Both share to some extent the Foucauldian desire to be writing a 'history of the present' and they can succeed in this only to the extent that they can thereby explain the theoretical underpinning of their present procedures. Their 'present' in question is stabilized by the discovery of a set of criteria (theoretical procedures and explanations) which effectively justify their texts. The counter to this inherently idealist procedure is to bear witness instead to what Portoghesi in architecture called the 'presence of the past',[16] the

[16] See Paolo Portoghesi, *Postmodern* (trans. E. Shapiro; New York: Rizzoli, 1983). For some of the terms of the debates between Cultural Materialism and New Historicism, see Howard Felperin, *The Uses of the Canon* (Oxford: Oxford University Press, 1990).

effect of which is to destabilize the present, to accept the lack of a theoretical criterion upon which judgements and knowledge can be based, and thus, perhaps paradoxically, to open oneself to the alterity that is the past.

2. POLITICS IN THE UNSTABLE STATE

The 'aesthetics of disappearance' opens up a question of politics; indeed, politics is fundamental to such aesthetics. The dialectic of appearance and disappearance is founded upon a war mentality which Virilio derives largely from Clausewitz, who thought history as a dialectical process of struggles between attack and defence, leading to the realization of an eventual state of pure war.[17] This war is the foundation of the political for Virilio, because it is through war that there arises the need for and the maintenance of those geographical structures which delimit the space of city or state. But the formation of these boundaries is neither simply, nor even primarily, spatial: on the contrary, they are formed from a particular relation to time and are grounded in a specific internal historicity.

Virilio cites, for instance, the development of the elevated observation post in the history of war struggles. This elevated post gives a group of fighters or a community the time in which to decide among a number of possible military attitudes available to them in a given situation. It is in this time, in the *production* of time as such, that a war *mentality* becomes possible, in opposition to that *immediacy* which is integral to more 'primitive' conditions of struggle. It is in time as *mediation*, thus, that there is produced what Virilio calls 'une *liberté* nouvelle':

Lorsque l'éventualité de la fuite pastorale disparaît avec l'implémentation agricole et le changement de nature de la richesse (un bien non transportable), il ne suffira plus d'être rapidement informé sur son milieu, *il faudra aussi l'informer*, c'est-à-dire tenter de conserver *sur place* son *avance* sur l'ennemi, d'où la construction autour du tertre,

[17] Paul Virilio, *Défense populaire et luttes écologiques* (Paris: Galilée, 1978), 14–15; Virilio and Sylvère Lotringer, *Pure War* (trans. Mark Polizotti; New York: Semiotext(e), 1983); Carl von Clausewitz, *On War*, ed. Anatol Rapoport (Harmondsworth: Penguin, 1968), *passim*.

d'enclaves protégées, d'enceintes, de palissades, destinées à *ralentir* l'agresseur.[18]

From this derives the growth or development of the space called the city, built upon the rampart. This space is conditional upon a logically prior temporal dialectic between the speed of the settler in claiming her or his ground and the slowness which she or he can impose upon the new aggressor. This dialectic of speed followed by slowness is of the essence of war itself, and is also a necessary relation for the development of the *polis*: the city is temporal before it is spatial. The tension between speed and slowness is endemic to what we might call 'significant space', by which I mean any space to which we will give a name, an identity, a history, or a culture: a political entity, in short. Any attempt to politicize the aesthetic must take such an interior temporality into account. The aesthetic is not just a phenomenological relation between consciousness as subject and nature as object, but is rather a relation constructed—and deconstructed—in a temporal foundation.

This difference is like the difference proposed by Deleuze between Cartesian and Kantian philosophies of the subject. Deleuze points out that for Descartes, 'je pense' proves 'je suis'. But for Kant, 'je pense' is true; 'je suis' is true; but one cannot be determined or derived from the other:

La réponse de Kant est célèbre: la forme sous laquelle l'existence indéterminée est déterminée par le Je pense, c'est la forme du temps . . . mon existence indéterminée ne peut être déterminée que *dans le temps* . . . D'un bout à l'autre, le JE est comme traversé d'une fêlure; il est fêlé par la forme pure et vide du temps.[19]

We have here the foundation of that whole mode of thinking which fractures the wholeness of the subject, a mode of thinking which has helped shape cultural modernity. Thinking is displaced into a mode of alterity where, in the words of Rimbaud, 'je EST un autre', or where the 'I', in Lacanian fashion, constantly disappears from itself and reappears in the guise of alterity. Cultural modernity is, in some ways, a series of exercises which try to deal with this new temporal fracturing of the

[18] Virilio, *Défense*, 17.

[19] Gilles Deleuze, *Différence et répétition* (Paris: PUF, 1968; repr. 1985), 116–17.

subject, a series of 'strategies of containment' in which the problematic temporal nature of subjectivity (and hence of politics) is displaced onto a spatial representation of the problem (in questions of colonial space, relations of hierarchy, strategies of exclusion, or inclusion).[20]

War is at root founded upon this ability to control appearances and disappearances: one makes oneself invisible, and renders the enemy visible and thus available for wounding. Virilio considers the example of the *maquisard,* who had to avoid the roads, to melt into a topography and even into an amorphous atmosphere: 'Il occupe alors le couvert de l'herbe et de l'arbre, les perturbations atmosphériques, la nuit.'[21] This becomes paradigmatic of the aestheticization of everyday life and of the militarization of the social within the contemporary political sphere.

The logic of this aestheticization of the quotidian militarized society is sequential. First, war depends upon a mode of subterfuge in which, through making oneself less visible, one eventually becomes capable of making the enemy appear—only to disappear almost immediately in the kill. Secondly, according to Virilio, there is in war a fundamentally homosexual charge: the hunt for food (for animals) gives way to the hunt for woman whose domestication will enable the homosexual hunt which is war itself.[22] The homosexuality of the resulting duel is at the root of the beautiful, for it too is based upon visual representations. The beauty in question is one which, in its various forms of battle-dress or body-painting and generalized corporeal decorum, is but the first degree of bodily torture: 'le beau est peut-être le premier *uniforme*.'[23] Thirdly, this 'beauty', which is in the first instance visible, presentable, gives way to a

[20] This also relates, clearly, to Michel Foucault, *Discipline and Punish* (trans. Alan Sheridan; Harmondsworth: Penguin, 1977), in which the 'birth of the prison' is seen as being dependent upon the kind of surveillance, and consequent ordering, exclusions or inclusions, made possible by the Benthamite Panopticon. The implications are more far-reaching for a thinker such as Baudrillard in his *Simulations* (trans. Paul Foss, Paul Patton, and Philip Beitchman; New York: Semiotext(e), 1983), 25: 'prisons are there to conceal the fact that it is the social in its entirety, in its banal omnipresence, which is carceral.'

[21] Virilio, *L'Horizon négatif*, 100.

[22] Ibid. 36–8.

[23] Ibid. 101–2. Cf. Baudrillard, *De la séduction*, 123: 'Le corps est le premier grand support de cette gigantesque entreprise de séduction.'

strategic *invisibility*, a mode of subterfuge in which 'le guerrier moderne est devenu un *fantôme*'.[24]

In the consequent fourth stage we have a significant new development in which alterity as such becomes stigmatized precisely because it refuses the principle of identity. Virilio argues that, since the Second World War, there has been a further shift in the aestheticization and militarization of everyday life in which there arises the confusion of friend with foe. At this fourth stage there is a complete loss of the uniform, but no nakedness: simply, the uniform is no longer required, for the beautiful has enabled that contemporary political situation in which the enemy is always feared as 'the enemy within', either on ideological grounds or in a condition of civil war. The militarization of everyday life is thus established, and with it goes an internalization of surveillance: Orwellian 'household spies' fear a generalized 'infection' or contamination from outside agents, from foreigners, Communists, viruses. At this point, there arises also the fragmentation of the social as such, for the social is threatened by the isolation of the individual as a spy suspicious constantly of colleagues, peers, lovers, and so on. This is the 'ère du soupçon', the moment in which a 'skeptic disposition' prevails in criticism and theory; and it is from this stage that a politics of disappearance is formulated.[25]

Three stages of social development can thus be described. First, there are 'sociétés massacrantes', which are tyrannical in their use of direct force. Secondly, there is the attenuated form of this violence in the 'société enfermante', the modern or classical policed society charted, in different ways, by Foucault and Baudrillard. Thirdly—and this is the contemporary situation—there emerges the new form of the 'société de la disparition légale'. It is this, and not a mystifying ideology, which a radical criticism or political theory must address, for it is this which has fundamentally destabilized the political as such in our time.

[24] Virilio, *L'Horizon négatif*, 108.

[25] The phrase 'l'ère du soupçon' is borrowed from Nathalie Sarraute, in her collection of essays, *L'Ère du soupçon* (Paris: Gallimard, 1956); for the 'skeptic disposition', see Eugene Goodheart, *The Skeptic Disposition in Contemporary Criticism* (Princeton, NJ: Princeton University Press, 1984).

The 'imagined communities' on which, as Benedict Anderson shows, a modern politics was based are themselves subject to disintegration.[26] As Virilio has it, the 'lieu d'élection' in which the social was enabled precisely by the identification of an individual with place has become instead a 'lieu d'éjection', in which the individual is increasingly alienated from the possibility of such social relation through the lack of such spatial identification. Increasingly, it is the *history* of a community rather than its imagined or real *location* which organizes political relation.[27] This is tantamount to a political disenfranchisement. The ancient agora or forum constituted a veritable *scene* for the practice of a politics which involved (some) people quite radically. Virilio invites a comparison of this agora with the Plaza de Mayo in Buenos Aires, where the mothers of the politically disappeared stand regularly to bear witness to the absence of their relatives. A direct presentation thus gives way to an aesthetic representation, for the Argentinian square is nothing more than a *screen* on which are projected the ghostly figures or shadows of people who are not, and who cannot be, there. There has been a radical inversion here, in the movement from scene to screen: 'si l'État politique prescrivait un droit de cité ou une identité nationale, l'État transpolitique implique a contrario, une perte d'identification, le discrédit progressif de toute citoyenneté de droit.'[28] The disappeared of Argentina and other directly oppressive political regimes, vitally important in their own right, are also symptomatic of a more generalized 'legal disappearance' of the citizen in contemporary political life.

Modern bourgeois democracy depends crucially on the counting of numbers and the fabrication of statistics. Ian Hacking has indicated that between 1830 and 1848 there was an 'avalanche of numbers', as 'a passion for counting—both things and people—incited the Western nations'. Copjec, drawing on this observation and on the work of Claude Lefort, indicates

[26] See Benedict Anderson, *Imagined Communities* (rev. edn.; London: Verso, 1991).

[27] Homi K. Bhabha, *The Location of Culture* (London: Routledge, 1994), constantly returns to the ways in which the spatial locatedness of identifiable culture is complicated by a temporality. As with thinking about post-colonial cultures, so also, I argue here, with colonizing and other cultures, if in different ways and with different attitudes to history.

[28] Virilio, *L'Horizon négatif*, 244.

that there are clear political ramifications in this. Statistics 'served to individualize the mass of the citizens, to create more and more kinds of people'.[29] Increasingly, also, statistics, by ensuring that people could be counted, did ostensibly represent them: people who may not appear under one actuarial heading none the less appear under others. It is in this figuring of number, and the organization of individuals under specific actuarial headings, that we see the emergence of a bourgeois democracy. We also see the fragmentation of the social as the individual indicates her or his propensity to be organized under a number of possible allegiances and affiliations. This not only guarantees the individual's *appearance* (figuring under one taxonomy), it also, paradoxically, ensures the individual's *disappearance* (as she or he fails to appear under others). Modern democracy can exist only by a process of maximizing appearances; and hence it can exist only in a totalized form according to which every possible taxonomical grouping in a social formation has the appropriate heading and hence the appropriate constitution in which all individuals are guaranteed to appear. Yet the fact is that such statistical totalities are factually impossible. The famous taxonomy of Borges which Foucault claims as a source for *The Order of Things* reveals this. The passage is the one quoting 'a certain Chinese encyclopaedia' in which it is written that

> animals are divided into: (a) belonging to the Emperor, (b) embalmed, (c) tame, (d) sucking pigs, (e) sirens, (f) fabulous, (g) stray dogs, (h) included in the present classification, (i) frenzied, (j) innumerable, (k) drawn with a very fine camelhair brush, (l) *et cetera*, (m) having just broken the water pitcher, (n) that from a long way off look like flies.[30]

In Borges, a similar drive to encyclopaedism drives the author of 'Pierre Menard, Author of the *Quixote*' when he enumerates

[29] Joan Copjec, 'The Phenomenal Nonphenomenal', in Copjec (ed.), *Shades of Noir* (London: Verso, 1993), 169. I quote her citation from Ian Hacking, 'Biopower and the Avalanche of Printed Numbers', *Humanities in Society*, 5/3–4 (1982), 281. The other work on which Copjec draws is Claude Lefort, *Democracy and Political Theory* (Minneapolis: University of Minnesota Press, 1988).

[30] Jorge Luis Borges, 'The Analytical Language of John Wilkins', cited in Michel Foucault, *The Order of Things* (London: Tavistock Publications, 1970), p. xv.

Menard's 'visible' work. In such instances, the drive to encyclopaedize is actually a drive to totalize, as seen in 'The Library of Babel' in which the library is said to contain all books, actual or possible.[31] But this is also an impetus seen at the roots of modernity, in the great Encyclopaedia projects of thinkers such as Diderot and d'Alembert.

Modern democracy is somewhat compromised by the ordering of things and persons, by the drive to taxonomize which, while ensuring the appearance of an individual element of a totality under one specific heading, actually serves thereby to fragment the totality and to ensure the disappearance of the same individual under other headings. In practical terms, the effect of this in contemporary political life is pervasive. European governments in recent times have found it appropriate to change the taxonomical headings under which unemployed people figure, for instance, in order to reduce the number of such people for official purposes. The result is that the unemployed begin—statistically at least—to disappear, replaced by a discourse which enumerates the numbers of people 'in employment', 'actively seeking employment', or, in a more recent turn which eliminates the category of unemployment entirely in British political discourse of the mid-1990s, 'Job Seekers'. Similarly, some political situations are such that they enable resistance only by disappearance, as for example in the recent British 'Poll Tax' fiasco, during which many individuals internalized a strategy of disappearance by refusing to register for the tax. Such individuals, whether complicit with their disappearance or not, are testimony to the fact that a modern political system of democracy which is dependent upon the abstract mathematical forms of numeration is prone to fall into a political structure of disenfranchisement through the politics of disappearance. Contemporary bourgeois governments do not engage in debate with their critics; rather, they encourage the official disappearance of such critics.

The resulting 'discrédit de citoyenneté' is, increasingly, the general position. This is partly due to various 'legal' or statistical manœuvres as described above, but it is also structural. As

[31] These stories are in Jorge Luis Borges, *Labyrinths*, ed. Donald A. Yates and James E. Irby (various trans.; Harmondsworth, Penguin, 1978).

André Gorz has argued, the militarization of work has made it impossible for each individual worker to identify with the collectivity of her or his class: 'Both the unity of the proletariat and the nature of work as the source of its universal power now lie outside and beyond the consciousness of proletarians.'[32] The myth of the collective, as that of tradition and class, is a further example of premature totalization, in that it presupposes the availability of a determining *unity*; but, as with all notions of unity, the constitution and demarcation of the 'unit' as such become extremely indeterminate, undecidable, contradictory.[33] This is all the more so in a democracy based on taxonomy, in which individuals may in fact be classed under more than one taxonomic group. Unity is itself a prematurely totalizing myth which serves to cover the ineradicable fact of heterogeneity and the interior historicity which precludes the availability of the unity even of the subject. The 'je' is always 'fêlé', always traversed by a number of discourses, always to be categorized in mutually exclusive taxonomies.

Unity, like totality, serves the function of erasing the historicity which is integral to the aesthetic, in just the same way as it occludes the fact that any individual may occupy, in differing ways, differing categories (class, gender, race being the groupings most discussed recently). When Virilio indicates the aestheticization of the political in the shift from scene to screen, from agora to Plaza de Mayo, what is at stake is an issue of representation. But it would be an error to suggest that the 'mere' representation of the disappeared of Argentina is grounded solely in the fact that they are not 'present' in the *space* of the Plaza; rather, one must stress the equal importance of the fact that such representation has a temporal or historical dimension. By this I do not simply mean that the representation is regularly repeated; I also mean to suggest that it reveals that political disappearances are not simply an event of the past (i.e. it is not merely the case that the someone 'has' disappeared), but rather that such disappearances occur in a sequential and

[32] André Gorz, *Farewell to the Working Class* (trans. Michael Sonenscher; London: Pluto Press, 1982), 29.

[33] See my comments on this in my review-essay on H. M. Daleski, *Unities* (Athens, Ga.: University of Georgia Press, 1985), in *Review of English Studies*, NS 38 (1987), 422–3.

historical rhythm, in time and in the ongoing if evanescent present. One such early literary example of this structure of appearance and disappearance is, of course, that found in the political murder in *Hamlet*, in which the ghostly appearance and disappearance of Old Hamlet help structure the play's movement. That ghost is in some ways a precursor of the ghostly figure which haunts the more recent example of Heaney's *Seeing Things* discussed earlier. More importantly, it is a kind of paradigmatic figure which calls not only an entire epistemology of empiricism, but also a democratic politics into question. Hamlet holding the image of his dead father before Gertrude is replicated in Argentina: people disappear, the women appear bearing witness in the images and photographs they carry to the felt absence, more people disappear, women reappear, yet more disappear, and so on. The effect of this is to question the very status of appearance as such within the social or political arena: the aesthetic—a chrono-aesthetic—of the Plaza de Mayo serves the function of reminding the citizen that she or he is nothing more or less than appearance, formal abstract or numerical figuring, and that she or he can be made to disappear—can be killed or in less extreme circumstances politically, culturally, socially disenfranchised—at the mediating whim of a governmental power.

The *polis* has become a 'lieu d'éjection'. It is no longer the marker of a stable space, city, or nation with which a citizen or stable subject identifies. The metropolis is nothing more or less than a position 'in transit', to and from which people migrate, in and through which people appear and disappear.[34] Some figure there prominently or frequently in their commuting to and from work; others simply pass through on an itinerary without a governing narrative of any description. This incessant delocalization, this version of a certain 'nomadism', is not a matter for celebration, for the migratory aspect of contemporary political life is a marker of the rupture of the social, a rupture between the subject and culture or community. It is

[34] See Gorz, *Farewell to the Working Class, passim*; cf. Gilles Deleuze and Félix Guattari, 'Plateau 12: 1227: Treatise on Nomadology—The War Machine', in their *A Thousand Plateaus* (trans. Brian Massumi; Minneapolis: University of Minnesota Press, 1987).

like the rupture of which Gorz speaks when he considers the relation between the abstract theoretical proletariat and real material proletarians.

The stable city-state or nation-state of the modern historical moment is replaced in our time by the 'état d'urgence', in which the temporality or historicity which is at the root of the political has become extremely apparent. Space in this sense has gone not only critical, but also diacritical; and the inhabiting of time has replaced the inhabiting of space as an organizing determinant of social life. Technology is partly responsible for this, leading to a state of affairs described thus by Virilio: 'Au temps *qui passe* de la chronologie et de l'histoire, succède ainsi un temps *qui s'expose* instantanément. Sur l'écran du terminal, la durée devient "support-surface" d'inscription, littéralement ou plutôt cinématiquement: *le temps fait surface*.'[35] One consequence of this is that, among other things, the form of urban life is not determined by space but rather by an 'emploi du temps', such that, for example, 'work-time' replaces the older, modern, definition of the social or political civic 'centre' surrounded by a periphery of 'suburbs' or privatized space; and such 'work-time' is defined in relation to 'holidays' or 'quality-time' instead of in relation to the privatized sphere of domesticity. A politics which does not address this orientation towards temporality or the historicity at the base of the relation between the aesthetic and the political in our time is simply a politics which serves to efface the social in all its lived material temporality: in other words, it effaces *culture*. Such a politics moves too quickly and too prematurely to a totality which effaces heterogeneity, historical specificity, and the politics of time or indeed history itself. Such a politics aligns itself around a spatial determination in which consensus notions of the true and the good prevail; in so doing, the problematization of consensus which arises when we address the historicity of culture, *Bildung*, is simply not faced. The inherent idealism of this modern, phenomenological politics cannot be reformed; it should therefore simply be rejected by any criticism which pretends to be genuinely critical, genuinely radical, genuinely historical.

[35] Paul Virilio, *L'Espace critique* (Paris: Christian Bourgois, 1984), 15.

3. CULTURE ORDINARY AND EXTRAORDINARY

'Culture is ordinary' was one of Raymond Williams's telling pronouncements. But what might it mean to describe culture this way? Specifically what might it mean in terms of a critical philosophy whose aim is to discover the historicity integral to the aesthetic, a historicity consistently ignored due to a recalcitrant tendency to idealism which persists in modern (including Marxist) critique? My argument here will be that the counter-tendency—call it a postmodern tendency if you will—illustrated throughout this study enables the articulation of culture within a specifically *social* (and not yet necessarily political) sphere of activity. On the one hand, this would certainly make culture 'ordinary', in the sense that it is a description at the most basic of levels of how humans live and interact; but on the other hand, the release of historicity within the aesthetic (the acknowledgement that all our forms of perception, including interpersonal perception, occur and recur in and through time) will determine that the instance of culture is always characterized by the eruption of the extraordinary into material and historical life. In other words, culture certainly is ordinary: but we *live* culture as the irruption into the ordinary and quotidian of an experience that cannot be simply contained, explained, or accounted for by our quotidian regulations, concepts, or practices.

There is a clear sense in which what Williams had in mind was the desire to acknowledge the materiality of culture, such that culture might simply be regarded as 'how humans live and work'.[36] Culture would thus include certain aspects of material life which are not conventionally thought of as 'cultural', especially by that class of people who have been trained to subscribe to the notion that culture represents some kind of activity deemed to be 'higher' in value than discussing holidays, playing sport, experimenting with fashion, and so on.[37] For

[36] Wolfgang Fritz Haug, *Commodity Aesthetics, Ideology and Culture* (New York: International General, 1987), 26.

[37] On this discrepancy between 'High Culture' and 'mass art' precisely as an effect or product of Modernism, see Andreas Huyssen, *After the Great Divide* (London: Macmillan, 1986), and Peter Bürger, *Theory of the Avant-Garde* (Manchester: Manchester University Press, 1984).

some in the post-Arnoldian tradition, culture has become associated with 'the best that has been thought and said', and is deemed to be characteristic of activities which have some 'transcendent' capacities, activities whose historical importance extends beyond the moment of their production to the extent that they sever themselves from such material historical conditions. Thus we have culture as 'high culture' divorced from the daily experiences of many people. Williams's aphorism, however, is clearly a statement based more upon a desire than upon the empirical observation of fact. The fact is that a specific class—that identified by Bourdieu as the 'aristocracy of culture'—has identified itself as an aristocracy in a war whose strategies and tactics depend upon their claims to possess an inherent 'taste' or a particular aesthetic sensibility.[38] This class asserts a priority upon the terrain of certain modes of aesthetic practices: theatre, opera, museums, the discourses of the 'fine arts', literature, and so on. This ostensibly aesthetic area of culture is also, clearly, a political area. By this, I mean no greater claim than that the 'aristocracy of culture' has managed to find an identity and a set of affiliations located in a specific terrain or 'significant space', usually the institutional spaces identified with high culture (museums, universities, various kinds of 'critics' forum' in different media, and so on).

This politics—like any politics whose foundational claims are thought in non-historical terms—is idealist to the core. 'Locating' themselves within a stable aristocracy, such persons have pretended to a condition which is 'traditional' in that it is both outside of time or not historically determined, and also in the sense that it evades the historicity of the aesthetic and collapses such a temporal dimension in art or culture into a merely spatial category: the canvas is discussed in terms of its interior formal structure and not in terms of its persistence, its loss of Benjaminian 'aura', its historical relation to other canvasses, the variations it underwent in its own making and so on. The theatre of art has become a doubly significant space (charac-

[38] See Pierre Bourdieu, *Distinction* (trans. Richard Nice; London: Routledge & Kegan Paul, 1984); cf. Galvano della Volpe, *Critique of Taste* (trans. M. Carson; London: Verso, 1978). The Arnoldian construction derives mainly from Matthew Arnold, *Culture and Anarchy*, ed. J. Dover Wilson (Cambridge: Cambridge University Press, 1932).

terized at once by the signs within the theatre and also by the theatre itself as sign) as has that space marked out by the frame of any work of art, any museum, any music, any painting or sculpture which evades the acknowledgement of the interior historicity of the work, the play, the museum itself. It makes no strategic sense to counter such a tendency with a political and critical stance which is equally contaminated by idealism, and which makes a claim for the 'accessibility' of culture or for the relocation of culture in certain other activities which enable the straightforward identification of another class as the bearers of culture in a more populist fashion. Suffice it to note for the present that we require a rethinking of strategies to counter the idealist tendency within the discourse of cultural studies.

In forming the 'politicization of the aesthetic' in a particular way, the 'aristocracy of culture' has succeeded in appropriating the aesthetic and in formulating it in terms of 'sites' or particular ritualized spaces and places in which an aesthetic discourse is available and appropriate. This is an effect of that specific 'project of modernity' valorized by Habermas and others which has its theoretical and discursive roots in a certain 'Enlightenment':

> When, then, does the space of the aesthetic arise as such a special space? It may have formed itself through several approaches. As a constituted space, however, forming a continuity up to today, it arises only at that time when the feudal state power reconstructs itself on a basis in which the elements of bourgeois society have become increasingly stronger in the face of the feudalist exploitation of peasants based on serfdom. The so-called 'absolutist' state structures itself as an administrative rationalism from top to bottom and treats the individuals of the society as its subordinates, or constitutes them, with the concept of that time, as its *subjects*. This formation is simultaneously the historical place of the enlightenment in Europe.[39]

Yet, according to the logic of my argument so far, it is an error to think the cultural and the aesthetic merely as 'space' or simply in geo-political terms. As Virilio indicates, significant space is itself a product of temporal relations, of the dialectics of speed and slowness, appearance and disappearance. It follows that it would be an error to think of the museum, say,

[39] Haug, *Community Aesthetics*, 134.

as just an architectural and cultural space or repository which 'contains' objects themselves endowed with some inherent 'cultural', 'radical', or 'critical' value determined by some inward or essential content. The full historicity—an interior historicity—of the aesthetic must be released if a radical criticism is to do justice to the severe and austere necessities implied in contesting the tendency to idealism inherent in any such 'spatializing' of the aesthetic in its political determination.

How, then, to define 'culture' in the wake of this? It is clear that what is an instrument of culture for one class (the aristocracy of culture) can be and often is an instrument of oppression for another class (those denied access to the aristocracy, those denied 'taste'). Culture, it follows from this, cannot be *simply* 'located': like power, it is an effect of relations. In this sense, culture is rather like politics itself. Gramsci and Foucault both make it abundantly clear that power is not some homogeneous, monumental entity; rather, power is an effect of social and political relations, its production coterminous with the conditions for its dismantling. Gorz extends this case, suggesting that it is a banal strategic error to conflate politics with power or even with the exercise of power, and that it is, consequently, equally erroneous to equate the political with the ethical which is, properly speaking, more appropriate to the sphere of the social: 'Politics is the specific site at which society becomes conscious of its own production as a complex process and seeks both to master that process and to bring its constraints under control . . . Politics is the site at which moral exigencies confront external necessities.'[40] Culture, I will argue here, is properly considered in these 'relational' and dialectical terms. Various definitions of culture and the cultural have been advanced at different times. Culture has been thought as that which is humanly valued; as that which is 'non-instrumental'; as that which is concerned with 'pleasure', politicized or not; as that which is focused on an oddly non-quantifiable 'value'; as that which is produced according to the exigencies of 'free time' or leisure; as that which is valuable in work; as that which constitutes or enables the formulation of personality; as well as those more conventional descriptions of culture as the mark of

[40] Gorz, *Farewell to the Working Class*, 117, 119.

'high art' in opposition to 'mass art', and so on. It has become a site for a particular struggle on the political Left, which has often made the mistake of trying to appropriate a separate realm identified as 'popular culture' for validation. In that tactic, culture has been confused with and identified again with some kind of value which, it is supposed, inheres within the work or within the critical aesthetic sensibility itself.

The notion of 'access' (itself a spatial metaphor), while important in pragmatic terms, is not sufficient for a critical philosophy of the relation between the aesthetic and the political. The idea that 'culture is ordinary' finds its extension in, for instance, Lyotard's nonce revalorization of the 'local' over the global, the local pragmatic narrative over the global *meta-récit*; in ecological thinking which suggests a mode of 'critical regionalism' which is at once respectful of local conditions and yet aware of internationalist communications and references;[41] and it finds its almost parodic extension in some of the complex thinking of Gorz.

Gorz argues for a different relation to work, in which ultimately there will be a kind of 'social contract' under which everyone will have an obligation to work, but for a drastically reduced time; and people will be able to choose when to work their ratio of, say, 800 hours per annum, spread however one wishes over a lifetime. This, argues Gorz, makes social, political, and economic sense. It also serves the function of eradicating a particular class-distinction; and, most importantly, it produces a vast amount of 'free time'. It is important, according to Gorz, that such free time be made 'convivial', in Illich's terms;[42] for it is thus that we will disable the 'leisure merchants'

[41] See Kenneth Frampton, 'Toward a Critical Regionalism', in Thomas Docherty (ed.), *Postmodernism: A Reader* (Hemel Hempstead: Harvester-Wheatsheaf, 1993). For a development of the notion of critical regionalism in a much more precise political sphere, see the essays collected in Richard Kearney (ed.), *Across the Frontiers* (Dublin, Wolfhound Press, 1988), which consider and debate the effects of a policy of critical regionalism for contemporary Ireland within the political sphere of Europe. Cf. also, in another specific exploration of this issue, Christopher Harvie, *Cultural Weapons* (Edinburgh: Polygon, 1992), where the focus is on Scotland in Europe. For an attack on the negative and reactionary aspects of widening 'access' to 'culture', see my 'Theory and Difficulty', in Richard Bradford (ed.), *The State of Theory* (London: Routledge, 1993).

[42] 'Convivial tools' are those which 'can be easily used, by anybody, as often or as seldom as desired, for the accomplishment of a purpose chosen by the user. The

from marking this time as just one more period for exploitation via debased and debasing products of a supposed 'mass culture'. With convivial tools, there will be formulated a kind of revival of the local and the traditional, in Benjamin's sense of 'tradition', into what Gorz thinks will become an expanded sphere of autonomy. It will thus become possible for all to enjoy a lifetime of cultural bricolage:

> Repair and do-it-yourself workshops in blocks of flats, neighbourhood centres or rural communities should enable everyone to make or invent things as they wish. Similarly, libraries, places to make music or videos, 'free' radio and television stations, open spaces for communication, circulation and exchange, and so on, need to be accessible to everyone.[43]

This seems frankly utopian. But the goal towards which Gorz directs himself here is one which is at one level at least entirely valid; and, importantly, it proposes a different strategy for a critical philosophy which has affiliations with some other postmodern or postmarxist thinking: convivial time as described here would depend precisely upon the experience of social alterity within a community.

Yet it is true to say that Gorz has failed to realize the full potential and implications of his ideas for 'freeing time'. Freeing time as he advises would certainly lead to making culture ordinary, in an obvious sense. But this is not really the point, and it can lead to a drastically limited argument which has contaminated much Left thinking, at least since Williams. For the *interior* historicity of such 'ordinary' cultural activity must also be acknowledged. If not, then the Left, despite itself, enables the identification of a 'high' culture conceived in essentialist terms; and, in order to establish its credentials as oppositionalist and critical, Left thinking produces as a counter to such essentialist notions a reactive formation of 'popular culture', whose very foundation has already been colonized by the aristocracy of culture in order to defuse from the outset any serious critical potential it might have; or, alternatively, Leftist

use of such tools by one person does not restrain another from using them equally' (Ivan Illich, *Tools for Conviviality* (London: Calder & Boyars, 1973), 22, as quoted in Gorz, *Farewell to the Working Class*, 96).

[43] Gorz, *Farewell to the Working Class*, 87.

thought validates the productions of a 'counter-culture' which itself is a prey to a capitalism which has no difficulty in accommodating dissent and protest by converting it into style or fashion, as happened with the cases of so-called 'designer-drugs' in the 1980s; as frequently occurs with the heterosexual 'straightening' of gay and lesbian fashions and lifestyles; or with the tamed stylizations of the anarchism of punk, and before that of Dada, and so on.

The reintroduction into the aesthetic and into culture of the temporality which is articulated within Virilian conceptions of the political is vital for a critical philosophy of culture. Its effect, in a word, is to save the social. The formula 'cultural sphere = free time' is, as Haug argues, invalid.[44] But it might be worth considering a formula which proposes that 'culture = the emancipation of time into the social = value'. This would mean that culture would be defined in terms of its ability to release a temporality of existence into the social sphere; or, that culture might be thought quite simply as that which produces the social *in its historicity*, as that which produces history.[45] The social would thus become the site for the evasion of a premature totalization to which the political and the aesthetic have been utterly susceptible. The social, as a realm in which culture is produced and which is commutatively produced by cultural activities and practices, becomes the means for the production of heterogeneity, alterity, heteronomies, and a *différance* whose interior historicity, considered quite simply as the production of time, can thus also be equated with value, as in some of the thought of Lyotard. This is not what I can call 'enlightenment time', a time whose value is measured in exchangeable time, or money:

> it will not help [the post-industrial Left] to enlarge the sphere of individual autonomy if the resulting free time remains empty 'leisure time', filled for better or worse by the programmed distractions of the mass media and the oblivion merchants, and if everyone is thereby driven back into the solitude of their private sphere.[46]

[44] Haug, *Community Aesthetics*, 29.

[45] Such a formulation would necessitate an overhaul of, for instance, the arguments of Steven Connor, in *Theory and Cultural Value* (Oxford: Blackwell, 1992).

[46] Gorz, *Farewell to the Working Class*, 87.

Rather, the time thus emancipated should be regarded as part of a dialectic of speed and slowness which enables the possibility—as in Virilian war strategy—of decision, criticism, judgement.[47]

Culture as bricolage is both ordinary and extraordinary. It is ordinary in the sense that it is quotidian, and that it makes no claims upon any transcendent value over against its local and material, historical or pragmatic value. Yet it is also extraordinary in the sense that its emancipatory acknowledgement of historicity and its production of the social is the production of a set of relations which are not themselves determined or determinable according to any specific 'theoretical' or totalizing idea. In short, culture is not the production of a spatial community, a 'thing' or consensus; rather, it is the production of history into the field of social relations and the concomitant production of difference and heterogeneity. Culture lies not in shared values (and certainly not in shared commodities), but in a shared historicity. This is no mere pluralism; rather, it is a critical philosophy which acknowledges the interior historicity not only of the aesthetic effect but also of the political act.

47 Such criticism or judgement, of course, according to the logic of this argument, should be that which Lyotard identifies, after Kant, as a kind of 'reflective' judgement, a 'judging without criteria'—a criticism without theory, perhaps—in the precise sense that it will not be a judgement whose formulations are predetermined according to a *prematurely totalized* politics, aesthetics, or ethics.

9. *Love, Truth, Alterity*

Vivre dans l'intimité d'un être étranger, non pour le rendre plus proche ou le contraire, mais pour qu'il demeure étranger, lointain et même inapparent, au point que son nom le contient tout entier. Puis jour après jour, jusque dans le malaise, n'être rien d'autre que le lieu toujours ouvert, la lumière impérissable au sein de laquelle cet être unique, cette chose demeure à jamais exposée, emmurée.

(Giorgio Agamben, *L'Idée de la prose*)

1. THE TRUTH ABOUT POSTMODERNISM

There is a strong rumour abroad that postmodernism is inimical to truth. A journalistic representation of postmodernism as some kind of nihilistic and unprincipled neo-pragmatist relativism is partly responsible for this particular fallacy. It should by this point be clear that what is presented or mediated by such sloppy thinking as postmodernism's 'relativism' is, in fact, precisely that attention to a material historicity characteristic of the postmodern mood. In academic discourse, the rumour regarding postmodernism's hostility to truth stems, I believe, from two separate sources, only one of which is genuinely 'postmodern'. These sources are the Lyotardian differend, and Derridean deconstruction (the latter of which is not, in my view, postmodern at all). In this concluding chapter, I shall attend to these in turn in order to clear the way for my claim that, in the postmodern mood in philosophy, we see a rehabilitation of a specific inflection of *love* as a determinant of thinking.

Lyotard starts from the supposition that the postmodern is characterized not by chronology but by a specific 'mood'; and, further, that the postmodern is an exercise in the re-figuring of modernity.[1] The mood in question is generated by a specific

[1] See Jean-François Lyotard, 'Answering the Question: What is Postmodernism?', in *The Postmodern Condition* (trans. Geoffrey Bennington and Brian Massumi;

attitude to knowledge, one which suggests that our epistemological anxieties or demands are not necessarily predetermined by the pursuit of agreed truth but rather by a pursuit of paralogy. That is to say, the point of philosophy is not to look for a truth which can be legitimized or guaranteed through its conformity to an already agreed set of rules for thinking, but rather to push our thinking to the point where we are not prepared for its results, to the point of a kind of surprise or to the point where there is an irruption of that which could not already be accounted for in our prior forms and rules of thinking. At an early point, he suggests that the postmodern mood is evoked by the Cretan Liar paradox. Take the most basic form of this paradox: the sentence, 'I am lying'. If this is true, it must be false; and if false, it must be true; and so on, indefinitely and undecidably. Lyotard will later develop this observation and will elevate its status into that of a far-reaching problem: the 'differend', a problem which has not only a philosophical component but also a specifically political component in its search for justice.

Steven Connor sums up the problem of the differend very neatly when he describes it as 'a disagreement that cannot be brought to the bar of any higher argumentative authority'.[2] A differend occurs when two parties disagree, and when the case made by the first party is in terms which are not recognized as valid by the second, and/or vice versa. As Lyotard more precisely puts it: 'a differend would be a case of conflict between (at least) two parties, that cannot be equitably resolved for lack of a rule of judgement applicable to both arguments. One side's legitimacy does not imply the other's lack of legitimacy.'[3] In some work developed from Lyotard's argumentations, this has come to be slightly more loosely understood. In any disagreement, the terms or the 'genre of discourse' in which one side of the argument (call it case A) is made, may well be constitutively different from the terms in which the opposite case (case B) is made; and, if this happens, it is unjust to judge case A in terms strictly applicable only to case B; and a differend occurs when

Manchester: Manchester University Press, 1984), and 'Réécrire la modernité', in *L'Inhumain* (Paris: Galilée, 1988).

[2] Steven Connor, *Theory and Cultural Value* (Oxford: Blackwell, 1992), 1.

there is no third 'language-game' to which both parties can subscribe. The well-known examples of this kind of problem are those which surround the illegitimacy of the revisionist Nazi historians such as Irving or Faurisson, in which Lyotard feels that we must simply accept that Faurisson, say, does not regard our own modes of evidential truth-telling as legitimate; or, for another commonly discussed example, the controversy over Salman Rushdie's *Satanic Verses*, in which one side wishes to argue that the text contravenes one Islamic law, while the other side does not see that the text is to be judged by such law or only by such law. In both these examples (and perhaps especially in the latter) we appear to lack a terrain on which to reach a consensus whose foundations are regarded as equally legitimate by both sides in the case.

A differend occurs, then, when we lack an overarching rule of judgement which would permit an adjudication between two rival propositions made in heterogeneous languages, or made from heterogeneous value-systems. Thus a differend can (and usually does) occur when we lack such a rule of adjudication between heterogeneous cultures or, much more broadly, between *theories*. We would thus have a problem in reaching *consensus*, and a problem in establishing *epistemological truth*, in any dispute. The postmodern 'incredulity towards metanarratives' (a refusal, consequent upon respect for the differend, to subscribe to any totalizing grand theory) has been taken, by a banal or journalistic criticism, to imply an extreme relativism not only in matters of value, but also in matters of truth. *If* truth is a function of linguistic propositions; *if*, further, it is dependent upon the regime of discourse in which it is enunciated; and *if*, finally, the world is made of heterogeneous realms of discourse lacking an overarching or homogenizing meta-rule or metanarrative, then truth as a category becomes extremely problematic, constantly threatening to degenerate into pragmatic notions of 'what is better in the way of belief'.

A similar problem arises in some poststructuralist thinking, in which the notion of truth-as-reference (the correspondence theory of truth) has come under a great deal of speculative

[3] Jean-François Lyotard, *The Differend* (trans. Georges van den Abbeele; Manchester: Manchester University Press, 1988), p. xi.

pressure. Deconstruction, for example, has helped codify a situation in which the truth-value of a proposition is no longer easily or immediately guaranteed by realism or by reference to a world supposed to be 'real' (because deemed to be self-present and thereby self-evidential) which validates the truth-claim. Paul de Man famously argued that 'What we call ideology is precisely the confusion of linguistic with natural reality, of reference with phenomenalism.'[4] What deconstruction is getting at in this kind of formulation, of course, is not that the pursuit of truth is illusory, but rather that the truth-claims of specific propositions are *premature* and illegitimate if they rely simply on the guarantee of the referential function of language, or on the 'self-evident'. This mode of deconstruction does not sit comfortably alongside any forms of empirical verification regarding philosophy's truth-claims; rather, it appears to open the way either to a formalist notion of truth (the notion of truth-as-coherence according to which some proposition is true if and only if it is internally coherent and cogently fulfils the terms and conditions of its own formal constitution) or to what appears to be a relativist abandonment of the absoluteness of truth.

The best response to the resulting Rortean neo-pragmatist position (often confused with a postmodern position) is that advanced by Habermas, in whose 'theory of communicative action' there is a strong residual desire for what the early Habermas called the rational pursuit of the best argument through the progressive operations of a non-coercive *Diskurs*. This is also the typical position of some contemporary philosophers, such as Christopher Norris or Alex Callinicos, who are sceptical of postmodernism.

Here is a succinct formulation of what is at stake here. Habermas writes:

> Discourse can be understood as that form of communication that is removed from contexts of experience and action and whose structure assures us: that the bracketed validity claims of assertions, recommendations, or warnings are the exclusive object of discussion; that participants, themes and contributions are not restricted except with

[4] Paul de Man, *The Resistance to Theory* (Manchester: Manchester University Press, 1986), 11.

reference to the goal of testing the validity claims in questions; that no force except that of the better argument is exercised; and that, as a result, all motives except that of the cooperative search for truth are excluded. If under these conditions a consensus about the recommendation to accept a norm arises argumentatively, that is, on the basis of hypothetically proposed, alternative justifications, then the consensus expresses a 'rational will'.[5]

In discourse thus understood, the drive towards truth is conditioned partly by an *ethical* demand: that of non-coercion and disinterestedness. Such an ethical demand might be proposed as an initial form of a philosophy of alterity, to the extent that it is concerned to modify the subject's point of view, her or his notion of what is reasonable, in the light of the point of view of the subject's Others. Although there is the desire in Habermas's formulation to overcome in a reasonable and non-coercive fashion any consequent differend between parties, there is none the less at least an initial acknowledgement that there may be a differend in the first place. Yet, within this ethical demand, there arises a difficulty. Lyotard and others have noted the 'soft imperialism' at work in Habermasian discourse.[6] What is at issue, I suggest, is basically a phenomenological problem in which alterity is at once advanced as a guarantee of ethical validity of truth-claims, while being simultaneously elided in the interests of one participant in the discussion, or in the interests of one language-game or regime of discourse—in short, in the interests of a philosophy of Identity under the form of consensus.

2. POSTMODERN LOVE

Much contemporary theory, exercised by the problematical nature of the validation or legitimation of truth-claims, has turned to the work of Levinas, in whom this ethical demand for

[5] Jürgen Habermas, *Legitimation Crisis* (trans. Thomas McCarthy; London: Heinemann, 1976), 107–8. See also Christopher Norris, *What's Wrong with Postmodernism* (Hemel Hempstead: Harvester-Wheatsheaf, 1992), *The Truth about Postmodernism* (Oxford: Blackwell, 1993), and Alex Callinicos, *Against Postmodernism* (Cambridge: Polity Press, 1989).

[6] See Lyotard and Richard Rorty, 'Discussion', *Critique*, 41 (May 1985), 581–4.

a philosophy of alterity finds its most overt articulation. Yet I shall argue that the philosophy of alterity has never been properly adhered to; and the reason for this is the lack of a philosophy of love. There has been, in modernity, an embarrassment over the category of love within a rational philosophical discourse or practice. Blumenberg indicates that, while, for the ancient world, the pursuit of truth was eudemonic, in the post-eighteenth-century world the pursuit of truth becomes marked instead by a specific kind of pain or austerity: the absoluteness of truth is paid homage to by a philosophy which acknowledges the truth as 'harsh' or difficult to bear. Such a homage is, further, a marker of philosophy's rigour and masculinist seriousness. What I add to this is the realization that such a harsh austerity finds it difficult to accommodate the category of love, a category which was an integral part of an ancient philosophy. The result is that a philosophy which, with love as a constituent aspect, might figure itself in terms of alterity, is replaced by a philosophy which formulates itself instead upon identity, circumventing the relation of love which would necessitate the discovery of a truth characterized by its social articulation or formation.

Various ways have been found to deal with such an embarrassment occasioned by the pressure exerted by love upon philosophy. First, it is rerouted into a discourse of 'taste'; then it ghosts aesthetics in the form of a somatic 'sensibility'; then it is displaced further into 'sentimentality' as a counter to the harshness of political necessity in the Victorian epoch; then, especially after Freud, it is reconsidered in terms of the scientism of psychoanalytic desire.

While such love is diverted or displaced in these ways, the condition of alterity can never be fully realized. In short, the basic problem as I see it in all current philosophies which strive to accommodate alterity is precisely the fact that they do indeed 'accommodate' alterity within an expanded philosophy of Identity. One is rather like Jameson confronted with feminism, when he famously argues that:

> The affirmation of radical feminism, therefore, that to annul the patriarchal is the most *radical* political act—insofar as it includes and subsumes more partial demands, such as the liberation from the

commodity form—is thus perfectly consistent with an expanded Marxian framework . . .[7]

There is here the typical drive to accommodate alterity by *fusing* it (or confusing it) with Identity. This, I shall argue, is fundamentally a position approximating to one condition—a weak condition—of love. What I shall argue is for the necessity of a stronger conception of love in philosophy or criticism, one which avoids the fusional, the fusion of the Other with the Same.

The problem is to reconcile the notion of truth-as-fact with that of truth-as-transgression. Philosophers such as Norris wish to hold on to some notion of reference, even if in attenuated form; yet, typically, they characterize truth as *transgressive*, as critical or oppositional, as a form of unmasking. On the one hand, truth grounds itself in the self-evident; on the other, it is simultaneously marked by a specific 'insight' which has overcome a blindness in order to reveal a truth occluded precisely by the self-evident.

In reply to this, I wish to suggest that we should take a different tack on the question of truth. I shall argue against truth as epistemology, and for truth as the eruption of a specific event; and I shall characterize that event through a specific configuration of love. It should not be too shocking to see the importance of love for philosophy or criticism. Ever since Plato, there has been an intimate link between the two. In the *Banquet*, for example, Plato suggests that love, like philosophy, is concerned with the indeterminate, with the intermediate states between ignorance and wisdom. Much, indeed, has been made of love in some recent feminist theory, though too often the issue of love has been theorized in terms only of psychoanalytic desire.[8]

Alain Badiou has gone some way towards a rehabilitation of love in philosophy. In his recent collection of pieces, *Conditions*,

[7] Fredric Jameson, *The Political Unconscious* (London: Methuen, 1981), 100.

[8] The most recent method of avoiding the embarrassment about the metaphysical conception of love in recent criticism has been in the turn to somatics and ethics. The notion of love explored here is to be figured without any repression under the forms of scientistic 'rigour' or theory, even at the risk of reintroducing metaphysics into what is essentially a materialist argument. In what follows, I none the less think the term myself in a rather austere fashion.

he strongly opposes the fusional concept of love. In this regard, he is rather like Elisabeth Badinter. Badinter writes, for instance:

> Jadis, le couple constituait l'unité de base de la société. Formé de deux moitiés qui chacune avait à cœur de jouer sa 'partition', il représentait une entité transcendante à chacune des parties [like a third regime of discourse which could adjudicate their differends]. Socialement et même psychologiquement, il était entendu que l'Un était incomplet sans l'Autre . . . La tendance actuelle n'est plus à la notion transcendante du couple, mais à l'union de deux personnes qui se considèrent moins comme les moitiés d'une belle unité que comme deux ensembles autonomes.[9]

Badiou philosophizes this position in *Conditions*: 'L'amour n'est pas ce qui, d'un Deux supposé donné en structure, fait l'Un d'une extase . . . L'amour n'est pas la déposition du Même sur l'autel de l'Autre . . . l'amour n'est pas même l'expérience de l'autre.'[10] For Badiou, love is an experience of the world, and not of a significant or signifying Other subject; and, in so far as it is that which allows the possibility of such an experience of the world, love is the *production* (or at least a governing condition of the production) of truth. Further, the experience of the loving subject, which is the substance of love, constitutes no knowledge of love: 'L'amour, comme expérience de la pensée, s'impense'.[11]

The argument now will be recognizable in terms of a postmodern predicament. Badiou argues a complex thesis, as follows:

(1) that there are two positions of experience, which he names as 'woman' and 'man' (with, of course, no determinate biological overtones);
(2) that these two positions are totally and utterly disjunctive; further such disjunction cannot be the object of an experience or of direct knowledge, for such knowledge would imply a third position; and,
(3) that there is no third position.

[9] Elisabeth Badinter, *L'un est l'autre: Des relations entre hommes et femmes* (Paris: Éditions Odile Jacob, 1986), 306–7.

[10] Alain Badiou, *Conditions* (Paris: Seuil, 1992), 255–6.

[11] Ibid. 257.

How is it possible, given the lack of a third position, to 'know' theses 1 and 2? As implied above, the question of a knowledge of love gives way here to an experience of love: a move from love as epistemology to love as ontology. For Badiou, the only way of being aware of theses 1 and 2 is through 'un événement singulier. Cet événement est ce qui initie la procédure amouteuse, et on convient de l'appeler une rencontre.'[12]

Now, the problem is that truth, to be truth, must be transpositional: that is, it cannot be dependent upon only local conditions or upon only a specific subject position, the position of the subject of the enunciation. And how can truth be transpositional, given the absolute disjunction between the two positions, woman/man? The expected answer would be to claim that there is a feminine science and a masculine science; just as one used to think that there was a bourgeois science and a proletarian (or a revolutionary) science. But, instead, Badiou begins from the paradox that truth is transpositional, and yet that there remains this radical disjunction between positions. Love, he claims, is the site on which this paradox is treated; love does not rid us of the paradox, but treats of it, engages with it; more precisely (almost akin to the Keatsian notion of Shakespeare's alleged 'negative capability'), love is that which makes a truth of the paradox itself. So, rather than love being that which regulates the relation of sexes, love is that which establishes the truth of their un-linking, their *de-liaison*.

To hold to thesis 2, i.e. the thesis of the total and absolute disjunction between positions of experience, is to make a comment dependent upon a specific mathematical philosophy of number: it is to say that the two positions cannot be counted as two. For, from what position would one count (given that there is no third position)? And so, thesis 1 becomes subject to a modification, thus: '*Il y a une position* et *une autre position.*' As Badiou has it: 'Il y a "un" et "un", qui ne font pas deux, l'un de chaque "un" étant indiscernable, quoique totalement disjoint, de l'autre. En particulier, aucune position-une n'inclut une expérience de l'autre, ce qui serait une intériorisation du deux.'[13] And here we are at the crux of the matter. For it is in this interiorization of the two that the phenomenology of love

[12] Ibid. 258. [13] Ibid. 262.

reaches an impasse in which either (a) alterity as such is weakened (Habermasian *Diskurs*); or (b) identity is annulled (Sartrean existentialism). In order to get past the phenomenology of love—or, in other words, in order to make the break into a philosophy of alterity—one must begin not from what we can call the 'amorous conscience' (that is, love as epistemology, love as knowledge), but from love as a process which is always of the nature of the 'event' (love thus as eventual, ontological).

It is such love which is aligned with truth and its production. Instead of truth being a function of linguistic propositions guaranteed by reference, truth, in this philosophy, precisely *is* the referent, the referent as event, as history, as the *encounter*.

3. ETHICAL POLITICS

I shall close with a brief comment on the politics of this situation. Previous theories of truth-telling, that is, those philosophies caught in the phenomenological impasse, depend upon a notion of truth-telling as critique. For example, when a critic wishes to make a truth-telling proposition about a given text, she or he will typically ask the question: 'from what position is this spoken?', hoping thereby to reveal the hidden or unstated assumptions governing the possibility of the text's formulations. Alain Finkielkraut argues against this manœuvre:

> D'où parles-tu? est la question totalitaire par excellence. D'où parles-tu? c'est à dire, qui, quand tu crois t'exprimer, parle en toi? . . . C'est la société en toi qui est coupable, donc tu est innocent; ainsi pourrait-on résumer le credo de l'humanisme moderne; c'est la société en toi qui est coupable, donc tu dois disparaître; tel est le principe fondamental de la pensée totalitaire.[14]

Before we face the problem of the differend and its corollary problematization of truth, I contend that we must 'hear' alterity, that we must undergo alterity as an event.[15] There has to be the *encounter* with alterity; and it is such an encounter which

[14] Alain Finkielkraut, *La Sagesse de l'amour* (Paris: Gallimard, 1984), 104, 112–13.

[15] See my study *After Theory* (London: Routledge, 1990), §4, for a more detailed examination of what it means to 'hear' alterity in these ways.

is constitutive of a stronger—philosophical—version of love. This post-phenomenological exposition of truth, of truth-as-event, will allow us to circumvent the totalitarian thinking which lurks even in the mode of so-called radical critique. It is this that we can call a postmodern mood, specifically a postmodern love: postmodern for the reason that it attends to the material historicity of alterity; love for the reason that it is the founding condition of the possibility of the realization of the historical event, the founding condition of 'the possibility of our being historical'.[16]

[16] This is a riposte to de Man, who concerns himself in 'The Rhetoric of Temporality' with the predicament of the 'impossibility of our being historical'. See de Man, *Blindness and Insight* (2nd edn.; London: Methuen, 1983), 211; cf. my attack on the position in *After Theory*, 100–6 and *passim*.

Bibliography

(The place of publication is London unless otherwise stated.)

AGAMBEN, GIORGIO, *L'Idée de la prose* (trans. Gérard Mace; Paris: Christian Bourgois, 1988).

ALTHUSSER, LOUIS, *Essays on Ideology* (Verso, 1984).

ANDERSON, BENEDICT, *Imagined Communities* (rev. edn.; Verso, 1991).

ANDREWS, ELMER, *The Poetry of Seamus Heaney* (Macmillan, 1988).

APPIGNANESI, LISA (ed.), *Postmodernism: ICA Documents* (Free Association Books, 1989).

ARNOLD, MATTHEW, *Culture and Anarchy*, ed. J. Dover Wilson (Cambridge: Cambridge University Press, 1932).

ARTAUD, ANTONIN, *Le Théâtre et son double* (Paris: Gallimard, 1964).

AUGUSTINE, *City of God* (trans. Henry Bettenson; Penguin, 1972).

—— *Confessions* (trans. R. S. Pine-Coffin; Penguin, 1961).

BACHELARD, GASTON, *La Poétique de l'espace* (Paris: PUF, 1957).

BADINTER, ELISABETH, *L'un est l'autre: Des relations entre hommes et femmes* (Paris: Éditions Odile Jacob, 1986).

—— *L'Amour en plus* (Paris: Flammarion, 1988).

BADIOU, ALAIN, *Manifeste pour la philosophie* (Paris: Seuil, 1989).

—— *Conditions* (Paris: Seuil, 1992).

—— *L'Éthique* (Paris: Hatier, 1994).

BAKHTIN, MIKHAIL, and MEDVEDEV, P. N., *The Formal Method in Literary Scholarship* (trans. A. J. Wehrle; Cambridge, Mass.: Harvard University Press, 1985).

BARTH, JOHN, *Lost in the Funhouse* (New York: Doubleday, 1968).

BARTHES, ROLAND, *Image–Music–Text* (ed. and trans. Stephen Heath; Glasgow: Fontana, 1977).

—— *Fragments d'un discours amoureux* (Paris: Seuil, 1976).

—— *Camera Lucida* (trans. Richard Howard; Fontana, 1984).

—— *et al.*, *Poétique du recit* (Paris: Seuil, 1977).

BARZUN, JACQUES, *Classic, Romantic and Modern* (Secker & Warburg, 1962).

BATAILLE, GEORGES, *Eroticism* (1957; trans. Mary Dalwood; Marion Boyars, 1987).

BATE, WALTER JACKSON, *The Burden of the Past and the English Poet* (Chatto & Windus, 1971).

BAUDRILLARD, JEAN, *L'Échange symbolique et la mort* (Paris: Gallimard, 1976).

—— *De la séduction* (Paris: Denoël, 1979).
—— *Simulacres et simulation* (Paris: Galilée, 1981).
—— *In the Shadows of the Silent Majority* (trans. Paul Foss, Paul Patton, and John Johnson; New York: Semiotext(e), 1983).
—— *Simulations* (trans. Paul Foss, Paul Patton, and Phillip Beitchman; New York: Semiotext(e), 1983).
—— *Les Stratégies fatales* (Paris: Grasset, 1983).
—— *La Gauche divine* (Paris: Grasset, 1985).
—— *Amérique* (Paris: Grasset, 1986).
—— *L'Autre par lui-même* (Paris: Galilée, 1987).
—— *Cool Memories* (Paris: Grasset, 1987).
—— *The Evil Demon of Images* (Sydney: Power Institute, 1988).
BAUMAN, ZYGMUNT, *Modernity and the Holocaust* (Cambridge: Polity, 1989).
BAYLEY, JOHN, *The Characters of Love* (Constable, 1960).
BECKETT, SAMUEL, *Molloy; Malone Dies; The Unnamable* (John Calder, 1979).
BENJAMIN, WALTER, *Illuminations*, ed. Hannah Arendt (trans. Harry Zohn; Glasgow: Fontana, 1973).
BHABHA, HOMI K. *The Location of Culture* (Routledge, 1994).
BLEICH, DAVID, *Subjective Criticism* (Baltimore: Johns Hopkins University Press, 1978).
BLOOM, HAROLD, *The Anxiety of Influence* (New York: Oxford University Press, 1973).
—— *A Map of Misreading* (New York: Oxford University Press, 1975).
—— *Poetry and Repression* (New Haven: Yale University Press, 1976).
—— *Agon* (New York: Oxford University Press, 1982).
BLUMENBERG, HANS, *The Legitimacy of the Modern Age* (trans. Robert Wallace; Cambridge, Mass.: MIT Press, 1983).
BONITZER, PASCAL, 'The Silences of the Voice', in Philip Rosen (ed.), *Narrative, Apparatus, Ideology* (New York: Columbia University Press, 1986).
BOOTH, WAYNE C., *The Company We Keep* (Berkeley and Los Angeles: University of California Press, 1988).
BORDWELL, DAVID, *et al.*, *The Classical Hollywood Cinema* (Routledge, 1985).
BORGES, JORGE LUIS, *Labyrinths*, ed. Donald A. Yates and James E. Irby (various trans.; Penguin, 1978).
BOURDIEU, PIERRE, *Distinction* (trans. Richard Nice; Routledge & Kegan Paul, 1984).
BROOKE-ROSE, CHRISTINE, *A Rhetoric of the Unreal* (Cambridge: Cambridge University Press, 1981).
—— *Xorandor* (Paladin, 1986).

BUCI-GLUCKSMANN, CHRISTINE, *Tragique de l'ombre* (Paris: Galilée, 1990).
BÜRGER, PETER, *Theory of the Avant-Garde* (Manchester: Manchester University Press, 1984).
CALLINICOS, ALEX, *Against Postmodernism* (Cambridge: Polity Press, 1989).
CAMUS, ALBERT, *Le Mythe de Sisyphe* (Paris: Gallimard, 1942).
CLARK, T. J., *The Absolute Bourgeois: Artists and Politics in France 1848–1851* (2nd edn.; Thames & Hudson, 1982).
CLAUSEWITZ, CARL VON, *On War*, ed. Anatol Rapoport (Penguin, 1968).
CONNOR, STEVEN, *Theory and Cultural Value* (Oxford: Blackwell, 1992).
CONRAD, JOSEPH, *The Nigger of the 'Narcissus'* (1897; Penguin, 1979).
COPJEC, JOAN (ed.), *Shades of Noir* (Verso, 1993).
CORCORAN, NEIL, *Seamus Heaney* (Faber & Faber, 1986).
DALESKI, H. M., *Unities* (Athens, Ga.: University of Georgia Press, 1985).
DAVIS, LENNARD J., *Resisting Novels* (Methuen, 1987).
DEANE, SEAMUS, *History Lessons* (Dublin: Gallery Books, 1983).
—— *Celtic Revivals* (Faber & Faber, 1985; repr. 1987).
DEBORD, GUY, *La Société du spectacle* (Geneva: Champ Livre, 1967).
DE GANDILLAC, MAURICE, *Genèses de la modernité* (Paris: Les Éditions du Cerf, 1992).
DELEUZE, GILLES, *Empirisme et subjectivité* (Paris: PUF, 1953).
—— *Le Bergsonisme* (Paris: PUF, 1966).
—— *Différence et répétition* (Paris: PUF, 1968; repr. 1985).
—— *Nietzsche and Philosophy* (Athlone Press, 1983).
—— *Kant's Critical Philosophy* (Minneapolis: University of Minnesota Press, 1984).
—— *Cinéma 1: L'Image-mouvement* (Paris: Minuit, 1983).
—— *Cinéma 2: L'Image-temps* (Paris: Minuit, 1985).
—— *Cinema 2* (trans. Hugh Tomlinson and Barbara Habberjam; Athlone Press, 1988).
—— and GUATTARI, FÉLIX, *Anti-Oedipus* (trans. Robert Hurley, Mark Seem, and Helen R. Lane; Athlone Press, 1984).
—— —— *A Thousand Plateaus* (trans. Brian Massumi; Minneapolis: University of Minnesota Press, 1987).
DELLA VOLPE, GALVANO, *Critique of Taste* (trans. M. Carson; Verso, 1978).
DE MAN, PAUL, *Blindness and Insight* (2nd edn.; Methuen, 1983).
—— *Allegories of Reading* (New Haven: Yale University Press, 1979).

—— *The Resistance to Theory* (Manchester: Manchester University Press, 1986).

DERRIDA, JACQUES, *L'Écriture et la différence* (Paris: Seuil, 1967).

—— *Limited Inc. a b c* (Baltimore: Johns Hopkins University Press, 1977).

—— *La Carte Postale* (Paris: Flammarion, 1980).

—— *Margins: of Philosophy* (trans. Alan Bass; Brighton: Harvester, 1982).

—— *Given Time 1: Counterfeit Money* (trans. Peggy Kamuf; Chicago: University of Chicago Press, 1992).

DOCHERTY, THOMAS, *Reading (Absent) Character* (Oxford: Oxford University Press, 1983).

—— *John Donne, Undone* (Methuen, 1986).

—— *On Modern Authority* (Brighton: Harvester, 1987).

—— review of H. M. Daleski, *Unities*; in *Review of English Studies*, NS 38 (1987), 422–3.

—— *After Theory* (Routledge, 1990; 2nd edn., Hemel Hempstead: Harvester-Wheatsheaf, forthcoming).

—— (ed.), *Postmodernism: A Reader* (Hemel Hempstead: Harvester-Wheatsheaf, 1993).

—— 'Theory and Difficulty', in Richard Bradford (ed.), *The State of Theory* (Routledge, 1993).

—— review of Christopher Norris, *The Truth about Postmodernism*, in *Textual Practice*, 8/3 (1994), 503–7.

DONNE, JOHN, *The Complete English Poems*, ed. A. J. Smith (Penguin, 1973).

EAGLETON, TERRY, *Criticism and Ideology* (New Left Books, 1976).

—— *Literary Theory* (Oxford: Blackwell, 1983).

—— *The Ideology of the Aesthetic* (Oxford: Blackwell, 1990).

EASTHOPE, ANTONY, 'Why Most Contemporary Poetry is So Bad', *PN Review*, 48 (1985), 36–8.

EISENSTEIN, SERGEI M., *Film Form* (Cambridge, Mass.: Harcourt Brace Jovanovich, 1969).

—— *The Film Sense* (trans. and ed. Jay Leyda; Faber, 1986).

ELIADE, MIRCEA, *Le Mythe de l'éternel retour* (Paris: Gallimard, 1949).

ELIOT, T. S., *Selected Essays* (3rd edn.; Faber, 1951).

ERASMUS, DESIDERIUS, *Praise of Folly*, in John P. Dolan (ed.), *Essential Erasmus* (New York: Mentor Books, 1964).

FEDERMAN, RAYMOND (ed.), *Surfiction: Fiction Now . . . and Tomorrow* (Chicago: Swallow Press, 1975).

FELMAN, SHOSHANA (ed.), *Literature and Psychoanalysis* (Baltimore: Johns Hopkins University Press, 1982).

FELPERIN, HOWARD, *The Uses of the Canon* (Oxford: Oxford University Press, 1990).

FERRY, LUC, *Homo Aestheticus* (Paris: Grasset, 1990).

FINKIELKRAUT, ALAIN, *La Sagesse de l'amour* (Paris: Gallimard, 1984).

FISH, STANLEY, *Self-Consuming Artifacts* (Berkeley and Los Angeles: University of California Press, 1972).

—— *Is There a Text in this Class?* (Cambridge, Mass.: Harvard University Press, 1980).

—— *Doing What Comes Naturally* (New York: Oxford University Press, 1992).

—— *There's No Such Thing as Free Speech* (New York: Oxford University Press, 1994).

FOSTER, HAL (ed.), *Postmodern Culture* (Pluto Press, 1983).

FOUCAULT, MICHEL, *The Order of Things* (Tavistock Publications, 1970).

—— *Discipline and Punish* (trans. Alan Sheridan; Penguin, 1977).

GAY, PETER, *The Enlightenment* (Oxford: Oxford University Press, 1966).

GEIST, KATHE, *The Cinema of Wim Wenders* (Ann Arbor: UMI Press, 1988).

GERAS, NORMAN, 'Post-Marxism?', *New Left Review*, 163 (1987), 40–82.

GOFFMAN, ERVING, *The Presentation of Self in Everyday Life* (Edinburgh: Edinburgh University Press, 1956).

GOODHEART, EUGENE, *The Skeptic Disposition in Contemporary Criticism* (Princeton, NJ: Princeton University Press, 1984).

GORZ, ANDRÉ, *Farewell to the Working Class* (trans. Mike Sonenscher; Pluto Press, 1982).

GUILLAUME, MARC, and BAUDRILLARD, JEAN, *Figures de l'altérité* (Paris: Descartes & Cie, 1994).

HABERMAS, JÜRGEN, *Legitimation Crisis* (trans. Thomas McCarthy; Heinemann, 1976).

—— *The Philosophical Discourse of Modernity* (trans. Frederick Lawrence; Cambridge: Polity, 1987).

HACKER, P. M. S., *Appearance and Reality* (Oxford: Blackwell, 1987).

HAMON, PHILIPPE, 'Pour un statut sémiologique du personnage', *Littérature*, 4 (1972), repr. in Roland Barthes *et al.*, *Poétique du récit* (Paris: Seuil, 1977).

HAND, SÉAN (ed.), *The Levinas Reader* (Oxford: Blackwell, 1989).

HARTMAN, GEOFFREY, *The Fate of Reading* (Chicago: University of Chicago Press, 1975).

HARVEY, DAVID, *The Condition of Postmodernity* (Oxford: Blackwell, 1989).

HARVEY, W. J., *Character and the Novel* (Chatto & Windus, 1965).
HARVIE, CHRISTOPHER, *Cultural Weapons* (Edinburgh: Polygon, 1992).
HAUG, WOLFGANG FRITZ, *Commodity Aesthetics, Ideology and Culture* (New York: International General, 1987).
HEANEY, SEAMUS, *Wintering Out* (Faber & Faber, 1972).
—— *North* (Faber & Faber, 1975).
—— *Preoccupations* (Faber & Faber, 1980).
—— *Seeing Things* (Faber, 1992).
HEGEL, G. W. F., *The Phenomenology of Spirit* (trans. A. V. Miller; Oxford: Oxford University Press, 1977).
HEIDEGGER, MARTIN, *Poetry, Language, Thought* (trans. Albert Hofstadter; New York: Harper & Row, 1975).
HIRSCH, E. D., *Validity in Interpretation* (New Haven: Yale University Press, 1967).
HUTCHEON, LINDA, *Narcissistic Narrative* (Waterloo: Wilfrid Laurier University Press, 1980).
HUYSSEN, ANDREAS, *After the Great Divide* (Macmillan, 1986).
ILLICH, IVAN, *Tools for Conviviality* (Calder & Boyars, 1973).
IRIGARAY, LUCE, *Speculum* (Paris: Minuit, 1974).
—— *Ce sexe qui n'en est pas un* (Paris: Minuit, 1977).
ISER, WOLFGANG, *The Implied Reader* (Baltimore: Johns Hopkins University Press, 1974).
JAMESON, FREDRIC, *The Political Unconscious* (Methuen, 1981).
—— 'Postmodernism and Consumer Society', in Hal Foster (ed.), *Postmodern Culture* (Pluto Press, 1983).
—— 'Postmodernism: or, the Cultural Logic of Late Capitalism', *New Left Review*, 146 (1984), 53–92, reprinted in Thomas Docherty (ed.), *Postmodernism: A Reader* (Hemel Hempstead: Harvester-Wheatsheaf, 1993).
—— *The Ideologies of Theory*, 2 vols. (Routledge, 1988).
—— *Postmodernism: or, the Cultural Logic of Late Capitalism* (Verso, 1991).
—— 'The Synoptic Chandler', in Joan Copjec (ed.), *Shades of Noir* (Verso, 1993).
JAUSS, HANS ROBERT, *Toward an Aesthetics of Reception* (trans. Timothy Bahti; Brighton: Harvester, 1982).
JOHNSON, BARBARA, *The Critical Difference* (Baltimore: Johns Hopkins University Press, 1985).
JOHNSON, SAMUEL, *The Lives of the Poets* (1781; Oxford: Oxford University Press, 1906).
JOSIPOVICI, GABRIEL, *The World and the Book* (Macmillan, 1971).
JUDOWITZ, DALIA, *Subjectivity and Representation in Descartes* (Cambridge: Cambridge University Press, 1988).

KEARNEY, RICHARD (ed.), *Across the Frontiers* (Dublin: Wolfhound Press, 1988).
KENNER, HUGH, *Samuel Beckett* (London: John Calder, 1962).
KERMODE, FRANK, *The Sense of an Ending* (New York: Oxford University Press, 1967).
—— *Forms of Attention* (New York: Oxford University Press, 1985).
KOLKER, ROBERT PHILLIP, and BEICHEN, PETER, *The Films of Wim Wenders* (Cambridge: Cambridge University Press, 1993).
KRISTEVA, JULIA, *Histoires d'amour* (Paris: Denoël, 1983).
—— *The Kristeva Reader*, ed. Toril Moi (Oxford: Blackwell, 1986).
—— *Étrangers à nous-mêmes* (Paris: Gallimard, 1988).
KROKER, ARTHUR, and COOK, DAVID, *The Postmodern Scene* (Macmillan, 1988).
LACLAU, ERNESTO, and MOUFFE, CHANTAL, *Hegemony and Socialist Strategy* (Verso, 1985).
—— 'Post-Marxism without Apologies', *New Left Review*, 166 (1987), 79–106.
LAING, R. D., *Knots* (Penguin, 1969).
LECERCLE, JEAN-JACQUES, *Philosophy through the Looking-Glass* (Hutchinson, 1985).
—— *The Violence of Language* (Routledge, 1990).
—— *The Philosophy of Nonsense* (Routledge, 1994).
LENTRICCHIA, FRANK, *After the New Criticism* (1980; repr. Methuen, 1983).
LEVENSON, MICHAEL H., *A Genealogy of Modernism* (Cambridge: Cambridge University Press, 1984; repr. 1986).
LEVIN, DAVID MICHAEL, *The Opening of Vision* (Routledge, 1988).
LEVINAS, EMMANUEL, *The Levinas Reader*, ed. Sean Hand (Oxford: Blackwell, 1989).
LOWELL, ROBERT, *For the Union Dead* (Faber & Faber, 1965).
LYOTARD, JEAN-FRANÇOIS, *Discours, figure* (Paris: Klincksieck, 1971).
—— *Rudiments païens* (Paris: Union Générale d'Éditions, 1977).
—— *Instructions païennes* (Paris: Galilée, 1977).
—— *Tombeau de l'intellectuel* (Paris: Galilée, 1984).
—— *The Postmodern Condition* (trans. Geoffrey Bennington and Brian Massumi; Manchester: Manchester University Press, 1984).
—— *Le Postmoderne expliqué aux enfants* (Paris: Galilée, 1986).
—— *L'Inhumain* (Paris: Galilée, 1988).
—— *The Differend* (trans. Georges van den Abbeele; Manchester: Manchester University Press, 1988).
—— *The Lyotard Reader*, ed. Andrew Benjamin (Oxford: Blackwell, 1989).

—— *The Inhuman* (trans. Geoffrey Bennington and Rachel Bowlby; Cambridge: Polity Press, 1991).
—— and THÉBAUD, JEAN-LOUP, *Just Gaming* (trans. Wlad Godzich; Manchester: Manchester University Press, 1985).
—— and RORTY, RICHARD, 'Discussion', *Critique*, 41 (May 1985), 581–4.
MACCABE, COLIN, *Godard: Images, Sounds, Politics* (bfi publications, 1980).
MCGUCKIAN, MEDBH, *Venus and the Rain* (Oxford: Oxford University Press, 1984).
—— *The Flower Master* (Oxford: Oxford University Press, 1982).
—— *On Ballycastle Beach* (Oxford: Oxford University Press, 1988).
MACHALE, BRIAN, *Postmodernist Fiction* (Methuen, 1987).
MACINTYRE, ALISTAIR, *A Short History of Ethics* (Duckworth, 1967).
—— *After Virtue* (2nd edn.; Duckworth, 1985).
MADDOX, JAMES H., Jr., *Joyce's 'Ulysses' and the Assault upon Character* (New Brunswick: Rutgers University Press, 1978).
MARX, KARL, *The Eighteenth Brumaire of Louis Bonaparte* (Peking: Foreign Languages Press, 1978).
MAST, GERALD, and COHEN, MARSHALL (eds.), *Film Theory and Criticism* (2nd edn.: New York: Oxford University Press, 1979).
MEHLMAN, JEFFREY, *Revolution and Repetition* (Berkeley and Los Angeles: University of California Press, 1977).
MILLER, J. HILLIS, *Fiction and Repetition* (Oxford: Blackwell, 1982).
MITCHELL, W. J. T., *Iconology* (Chicago: University of Chicago Press, 1986).
MONTAIGNE, MICHEL DE, *Essais*, 3 vols. (Paris: Garnier-Flammarion, 1969).
MORETTI, FRANCO, *The Way of the World* (trans. Albert Sbragia; Verso, 1987).
MORRISON, BLAKE, and MOTION, ANDREW (eds.), *The Penguin Book of Contemporary British Poetry* (Penguin, 1982).
MORRISSETTE, BRUCE, *Les Romans de Robbe-Grillet* (Paris: Minuit, 1963).
—— *The Novels of Robbe-Grillet* (Ithaca, NY: Cornell University Press, 1975).
NORRIS, CHRISTOPHER, *Paul de Man* (Routledge, 1988).
—— *What's Wrong with Postmodernism* (Hemel Hempstead: Harvester-Wheatsheaf, 1992).
—— *The Truth about Postmodernism* (Oxford: Blackwell, 1993).
—— *Truth and the Ethics of Criticism* (Manchester: Manchester University Press, 1994).

ONG, WALTER J., *Ramus: Method and the Decay of Dialogue* (Cambridge, Mass.: Harvard University Press, 1958).

ORR, JOHN, *Cinema and Modernity* (Cambridge: Polity, 1993).

ORWELL, GEORGE, *Inside the Whale* (Penguin, 1962).

PASCAL, BLAISE, *Œuvres complètes* (Paris: Seuil, 1963).

PERKINS, V. F., *Film as Film* (Penguin, 1972).

POPE, ALEXANDER, *Poems*, ed. John Butt (Methuen, 1975).

PORTOGHESI, PAOLO, *Postmodern* (trans. E. Shapiro; New York: Rizzoli, 1983).

POULET, GEORGES, *Proustian Space* (Baltimore: Johns Hopkins University Press, 1977).

RABELAIS, FRANÇOIS, *Œuvres complètes*, i, ed. P. Jourda (Paris: Garnier Frères, 1962).

RICHARDS, I. A., *Science and Poetry* (Kegan Paul, Trench, Trubner & Co., 1935).

ROBBE-GRILLET, ALAIN, 'Notes sur la localisation et les déplacements du point de vue dans la description romanesque', *La Revue des lettres modernes*, 5/36–8 (summer 1958), 128–30 (or 256–8; double pagination).

—— *Dans le labyrinthe* (Paris: Minuit, 1959).

—— *Pour un nouveau roman* (Paris: Minuit, 1963).

RORTY, RICHARD, *Contingency, Solidarity, Irony* (Cambridge: Cambridge University Press, 1990).

ROSEN, STANLEY, *The Ancients and the Moderns* (New Haven: Yale University Press, 1989).

ROSSET, CLÉMENT, *La Philosophie tragique* (Paris: Quadrige/PUF, 1960; repr. 1991).

—— *L'Objet singulier* (new expanded edn.; Paris: Minuit, 1979).

SAID, EDWARD, *Beginnings* (New York: Basic Books, 1975).

—— *Orientalism* (Routledge & Kegan Paul, 1978).

—— *The World, the Text, the Critic* (Faber & Faber, 1984).

—— *Covering Islam* (Routledge & Kegan Paul, 1985).

SARRAUTE, NATHALIE, *L'Ère du soupçon* (Paris: Gallimard, 1956).

SARTRE, JEAN-PAUL, *La Nausée* (1938; repr. Paris: Folio, 1977).

SCHICKEL, RICHARD, *Double Indemnity* (bfi publications, 1992).

SEARLE, JOHN, *Speech Acts* (Cambridge: Cambridge University Press, 1970).

SERRES, MICHEL, *Éclaircissements: Entretiens avec Bruno Latour* (1992; Paris: Flammarion, 1994).

SPRINKER, MICHAEL, *Imaginary Relations* (Verso, 1987).

STEINER, GEORGE, *The Death of Tragedy* (Faber & Faber, 1961).

STOEHR, TAYLOR, 'Pornography, Masturbation and the Novel', *Salmagundi*, 2 (1967–8), 28–56.

SWINDEN, PATRICK, *Unofficial Selves* (Macmillan, 1973).
SWINGEWOOD, ALAN, *The Novel and Revolution* (Macmillan, 1975).
TAINE, HIPPOLYTE, *History of English Literature*, 4 vols. (Edinburgh: Edinburgh University Press, 1873–1908).
TODOROV, TZVETAN, *Poétique de la prose* (Paris: Seuil, 1971).
VATTIMO, GIANNI, and ROVATTI, PIER ALDO (eds.), *Il Pensiero debole* (Milan: Feltrinelli, 1983).
VIRILIO, PAUL, *Vitesse et politique* (Paris: Galilée, 1977).
—— *Défense populaire et luttes écologiques* (Paris: Galilée, 1978).
—— *L'Horizon négatif* (Paris: Galilée, 1984).
—— *L'Espace critique* (Paris: Christian Bourgois, 1984).
—— *Esthétique de la disparition* (Paris: Galilée, 1989).
—— *War and Cinema* (trans. Patrick Camiller; Verso, 1989).
—— *L'Inertie polaire* (Paris: Christian Bourgois, 1990).
—— and LOTRINGER, SYLVÈRE, *Pure War* (trans. Mark Polizotti; New York: Semiotext(e), 1983).
WATT, IAN, *The Rise of the Novel* (Penguin, 1957).
WILLIAMS, RAYMOND, *The English Novel from Dickens to Lawrence* (Chatto & Windus, 1973).
WITTGENSTEIN, LUDWIG, *Tractatus Logico-Philosophicus* (trans. D. F. Pears and B. F. M'Guinness; Routledge, 1961).
WOLEDGE, BRIAN (ed.), *Penguin Book of French Verse I* (Penguin, 1961).
WOOLF, VIRGINIA, *The Common Reader* (2nd ser.; Hogarth Press, 1929).
ZERAFFA, MICHEL, *Personne et personnage* (Paris: Klincksieck, 1969).

Index